T0323780

EVERY DOCTOR

The second edition of this well-received text advocates for a transformational change in the way doctors protect their mental health, look out for their colleagues, co-create a kinder, more humane work culture and lead health system reform. Offering practical strategies and real solutions, based both on medical literature and the wisdom of experienced doctors, the new edition reimagines healthcare, where every doctor is encouraged and supported to:

- Prioritise psychological wellbeing and physical protection
- Promote healthy workplace cultures, fairness and safety
- Build strong relationships by sharing challenges
- Save lives through medical co-leadership
- Rediscover the joy in medicine

Brimming with poignant and hopeful stories and quotes from a diverse array of doctors from many different specialities and at all career stages, the book is a celebration of the growing global interconnectedness and the changing face of the medical profession. An invaluable support and companion for those in the early years of medicine, *Every Doctor* is a must-read for all doctors across all specialities and wherever they practise in the world, because exemplary care of patients, peers, profession and self is a lifelong journey.

EVERY DOCTOR
HEALTHIER DOCTORS =
HEALTHIER PATIENTS

Second Edition

Leanne Rowe
General Practitioner, Past Deputy Chancellor
Monash University, Australia

Vihangi Abeygunawardana
Intensive Care Registrar
Northern Health, Australia

Michael Kidd
General Practitioner, Past President
World Organization of Family Doctors (WONCA)

CRC Press
Taylor & Francis Group
Boca Raton   London   New York

CRC Press is an imprint of the
Taylor & Francis Group, an **informa** business

Second edition published 2023
by CRC Press
6000 Broken Sound Parkway NW, Suite 300, Boca Raton, FL 33487–2742

and by CRC Press
4 Park Square, Milton Park, Abingdon, Oxon, OX14 4RN

CRC Press is an imprint of Taylor & Francis Group, LLC

© 2023 Leanne Rowe, Vihangi Abeygunawardana, and Michael Kidd

First edition published by CRC Press 2018

ISBN: 978-1-032-28434-7
ISBN: 978-1-032-28432-3
ISBN: 978-1-003-29682-9

DOI: 10.1201/9781003296829

Typeset in Minion
by Apex CoVantage, LLC

Every Doctor *is dedicated to every doctor who risked their lives during the COVID-19 pandemic and to all the colleagues and friends we lost.*

Contents

Acknowledgements

Firstly, thank you to our patients, who allow us the privilege of walking alongside them during their most vulnerable moments. In writing this book, we were constantly humbled by the lessons they teach.

As authors, we wish to thank Jo Koster (Senior Publisher – Medicine & Life Science, CRC Press/Taylor & Francis), and the team at Taylor & Francis, including Neha Bhatt, for their tremendous assistance and support. We also wish to thank Dr Peter Jasek and Dr Gifar Hassan, our medical editors, for their input and feedback.

The new edition *Every Doctor* has been extensively re-written after our interviews with hundreds of our colleagues in 2021 and 2022. We are deeply grateful to each and every one of them for their precious input.

We also wish to specifically acknowledge the influence and mentoring of many colleagues, who provide us with shining examples of medical co-leadership. We very much appreciate our many wonderful friends from Australian and international Medical Colleges (including the Royal Australian College of General Practitioners[1] and the World Organisation of Family Doctors[2]), as well as those from the Department of General Practice, Monash University[3] (Professor John Murtagh, Professor Danielle Mazza, Dr Craig Hassed and many more). Dr Mark O'Brien, an Australian medical practitioner and Programme Director of the Oxford University Healthcare Leadership Programme, helped us identify our theme in Part 4, including encouraging every doctor to recognise their leadership role as an agent of change[4].

In the United Kingdom, Dame Clare Gerada[5], Lord Nigel Crisp[6] and Dr Olivia Smith[7] provided inspiration and encouragement through their publications and interviews. In Europe, we were reminded about the power of doctors' stories after meeting Professor Bohumil Seifert, Dr Ludmila Bezdíčková and Dr David Halata at The Society of General Practice (under the J. E. Purkyně Czech Medical Association[8]) who told us about many examples of great medical co-leadership by community general practitioners during the COVID-19 pandemic and the poignant ground swell of support for Ukrainian doctors.

The revised edition of *Every Doctor* would not have been possible without the contributions by many other esteemed colleagues, who are acknowledged throughout the book.

We wish to pay special tribute to Dr Erin Philpott, an internal medicine doctor New Mexico, USA, who begins our book with a powerful story of hope despite working under extreme adversity, providing much needed validation for other colleagues: 'The whole experience of writing down my vulnerabilities and sharing them in a hope of making a difference for someone else has been rewarding'. The example of her dedication, selflessness and humility personifies not only the contributors to our book, but every doctor who continues to care across the globe.

The following esteemed colleagues contributed stories, articles and quotes with outstanding generosity:

Alexie Puran (p. 39)
Amy Derrick (p. 157)
Bruce Tonge (p. 73)
Catherine Crock (p. 247)
Christopher Dowling (p. 156)
Clare Gerada (p. 219)
Claire Weekes (p. 22)
Craig Hassed (p. 32)
Cynthia Haq (p. 110, 232)
Danielle Martin (p. 44)
David Bennett (p. 73, 115)
Dharmaraj Karthikesan (p. 131)
Dinesh Palipana (p. 249)
Dhruv Khullar (p. 229)
Erin Philpott (p. 10)
Evelyn Daniel (p. 155)
Faith Fitzgerald (p. 97)
Geoffrey Toogood (p. 185)
Giselle Withers (p. 61)
Grant Blashki (p. 161)
Helen Milroy (p. 211, 254)
Jane Wilson-Howarth (p. 205)
Jocelyn Lowinger (p. 56)
Justin Coleman (p. 151)
Kim Arlington (p. 195)
Leon Piterman (p. 231)
Louise Stone (p. 19)
Margaret Kay (p. 81)
Mukesh Haikerwal (p. 90)

Neil Offord (p. 15)
Peter Goldsworthy (p. 207)
Philip Hébert (p. 98, 153)
Ranjana Srivastava (p. 177)
Richard 'Harry' Harris (p. 252)
Ronald Epstein (p. 102)
Steve Robson (p. 171)
Tim Baker (p. 99)
Vicki Kotsirilos (p. 157)
Vikram Patel (p. 186)

Your stories and experiences matter more than ever.

The ongoing love, support and inspiration from our families continues to sustain our work including our co-authorship of *Every Doctor*. There are no words that could adequately express our gratitude to Peter Jasek, Louie Jasek, Alastair McEwin, along with Jill Kidd, Champa and Haresh Abeygunawardana, Chris Jasek, and Zareena Khodabux – as well as Myshka, Oscar and Mia.

Finally, thank you to our readers. We continue to seek and welcome suggestions from every doctor about what works and what does not, in practice. Your clinical observations and feedback matter. Please contact us with your comments via www.everydoctor.org

We are listening.

Drs Leanne Rowe, Vihangi Abeygunawardana
and Michael Kidd

Notes

1. Royal Australian College of General Practitioners, Australia: www.racgp.org.au/
2. Global Family Doctor: www.globalfamilydoctor.com/
3. Department of General Practice, Monash University, Australia: www.monash.edu/medicine/sphpm/general-practice
4. Dr Mark O'Brien: www.sbs.ox.ac.uk/about-us/people/mark-obrien
5. Dame Clare Gerada, *Beneath the White Coat Doctors, Their Minds and Mental Health*, Routledge.

6. Lord Nigel Crisp, *Turning the World Upside Down Again: Global Health in a Time of Pandemics, Climate Change and Political Turmoil*, Routledge.
7. Dr Olivia Smith, *Mind Maps for Medical Students*, Routledge.
8. www.svl.cz/en/czech-society-of-general-practice/

A note from the authors

This is not an academic textbook. It is based on the clinical observations and wisdom of many experienced medical and health practitioners (p x–xiii Acknowledgements). However, there are prominent sections on mental health throughout the book, which have drawn on the **ICD-11** International Classification of Diseases 11th Revision,[1] as well as reference to Beyond Blue: The National Depression Initiative[2] and the Black Dog Institute[3] in Australia.

---

[1] International Classification of Diseases, *11th Revision, the Global Standard for Diagnostic Health Information ICD-11*: https://icd.who.int

[2] The National Depression Initiative, Australia, Beyond Blue: www.beyondblue.org.au/

[3] The Black Dog Institute: www.blackdoginstitute.org.au/

Authors

Leanne Rowe is a rural doctor and clinical professor at the Department of General Practice, Monash University, Australia, who has cared for other doctors as patients for many years. In the past, she has served as the Chairman of the Royal Australian College of General Practitioners, Deputy Chancellor of Monash University and non-Executive Director of a number of foundations including Beyond Blue: the national depression initiative in Australia. She has also served as a non-executive director on a range of public and private health-related boards, across many specialities, including hospitals, and aged care, mental health, telehealth, radiology, pathology and medicolegal providers.

Vihangi Abeygunawardana is our new co-author. She has worked in public hospitals across Brisbane and Melbourne in Australia over the last 4 years, and, in particular, has gained a deep insight into the challenges doctors in training have faced during the global pandemic. She has worked extensively in the medical, surgical and frontline COVID-19 wards at Melbourne's Austin Hospital, and as of 2022, she has been an ICU registrar in metropolitan and regional Victoria.

Michael Kidd is a general practitioner and currently the Deputy Chief Medical Officer of Australia and Professor of Primary Care Reform at the Australian National University, based in Canberra. In the past, he has served as President of the World Organisation of Family Doctors and President of the Royal Australian College of General Practitioners; Professor and Chair of the Department of Family and Community Medicine University of Toronto, Canada and Professor of Global Primary Care with the Southgate Institute for Health, Equity and Society at Flinders University in Australia. He consults with the World Health Organisation and a number of other international organisations on global health.

Website: www.everydoctor.org

Introduction

Why we re-wrote *Every Doctor*

Medicine can be a fantastic career.

It can be a privilege to witness the courage of our patients and gain extraordinary insight into ordinary life. How lucky we are to continuously learn about cutting-edge healthcare advancements and develop bonds with colleagues who become lifelong friends across international borders. In our own communities, it can be deeply rewarding to provide the highest standard of healthcare to our patients and to be recognised as respected local, national and international leaders.

However, in order to stay mentally strong, continue to provide the best care to our patients, do our job effectively and find satisfaction in the work, we must confront the fact that medicine also has a dark side. In the original edition published in 2019, *Every Doctor* put forward solutions for the common challenges doctors face, such as chronic exposure to patient misery, trauma and death; mental illness and suicidality in the medical profession; toxic medical workplace cultures due to bullying, discrimination, racism and harassment; medical workplace violence; and medicolegal issues.

This new edition has been extensively re-written to also confront the recent impact of international public health crises such as the COVID-19 pandemic, natural disasters, global conflict and wars on the care of our patients. Since early 2020, such events have disrupted our work and claimed well over six million lives.

As our health services are continuing to face new challenges and threats, it is more important than ever to recognise the mental and physical health impacts on every community – and every doctor. The revised edition of *Every Doctor* is therefore relevant to all doctors across all specialities at every career stage from medical students to retired doctors. Across the world, doctors are a diverse group of professionals, but our shared traits have come to the fore in the last few years; we are hard-working, dedicated, courageous and deeply concerned.

DOI: 10.1201/9781003296829-1

How can *Every Doctor* help every doctor?

Every Doctor is advocating for a transformational change in the way doctors protect their mental health, look out for their colleagues, co-create a kinder, more humane work culture and lead health system reform. As doctors, we have more influence than we often realise to effect real change and to become agents of change – together. Our book offers practical strategies and real solutions, based both on medical literature and the wisdom of experienced doctors.

The new book reimagines healthcare, where every doctor is encouraged and supported to:

1. Prioritise psychological and physical protection first
2. Promote healthy workplace cultures, fairness and safety
3. Build strong relationships by sharing challenges
4. Save lives through medical co-leadership

Prioritise psychological and physical protection first

Part 1 focuses on advanced self-protection. Information about self-help, including healthy nutrition, exercise, meditation and mindfulness is every-where, but how do doctors realistically find the time to prioritise self-care when simply getting through each day can be a challenge in itself? Our book acknowledges the extreme demands of our work; long hours with infrequent breaks, a continuous responsibility to provide the highest standard of patient care, difficult clinical decision-making in high-stress environments, and the need to provide ongoing support for our colleagues. For many doctors, rou-tine psychological protection is as critical as wearing properly fitted personal protective equipment (PPE) – and the consequences of failing to do this can be dire.

The first section includes stories of hope and inspiration from our col-leagues on staying mentally strong. We discuss a diverse array of topics includ-ing ways to re-assess balanced goals in all dimensions of our lives; make time for what we care deeply about and what matters most to us; nurture loving relationships with our partners, children, family and friends; stay optimistic through adversity; re-write our inner narratives about negative or traumatic experiences; sleep well naturally; prevent burnout and mental illness; and enlist regular support and comprehensive preventive healthcare from our own doctors.

Promote healthy workplace cultures, fairness and safety

Part 2 confronts the common lack of resourcing of contemporary human resources practices in healthcare, which are the root cause of negative or toxic workplace cultures. As individuals, we can feel powerless to address problems such as workplace bullying, harassment, bias and discrimination, racism and patient violence. But together, we can effectively advocate in our workplaces for human resources, fairness, equity and safety, as well as co-creating harmonious clinical teams and positive workplace cultures.

This second section includes chapters on addressing common sources of peer conflict; responding to challenging interactions with patients; managing patient anger and violence effectively; learning from mistakes, patient complaints and clinical incidents; and eliminating sexual harassment, discrimination, racism and bullying.

Build strong relationships by sharing challenges

Part 3 discusses the importance of building stronger relationships with colleagues to sustain us throughout our challenging careers, recognising that a harsh medical workplace culture is often at the root of continuing high levels of mental illness and suicide in the medical profession. In this section, we emphasise every doctor's role in supporting colleagues to seek mental health care early. As a profession, we have not only failed to prevent, recognise or manage work-related mental injury in doctors, we attach a damaging stigma to mental illness rather than accepting it as a common condition that requires evidence-based treatment.

In this section, there is a clarion call for senior doctors to look out for earlier career colleagues, especially in the current environment. During the COVID-19 pandemic, new doctors have commenced their medical careers under perilous circumstances at the front line, often feeling disconnected and traumatised while working long hours with suboptimal supervision and training. In their 20s and 30s, they have been isolated from their families and missed out on the medical collegiate and social connections that usually provide essential personal support. Their early years have been marred by loss, loneliness, and fear. As many of them have not been fully acknowledged for their outstanding courage and dedication, the old adage 'it was much worse in my day' is like pouring salt into a new wound.

Save lives through medical co-leadership

Part 4 answers the question: 'Why would we take on a leadership role when being a doctor is an overwhelming responsibility in itself?' Whether we recognise it or not, every doctor is already a leader. If clinical work feels chronically overwhelming and health system bureaucracy is degrading the quality of our patient care, we can tap into our leadership capacity and connect with colleagues to advocate for systems change. Although this can feel unachievable as individuals, there are many positive examples where groups of doctors have united against brick wall health bureaucracies to improve the quality, access and safety of patient care, as well as our own working conditions.

If we have limited time beyond the demands of our clinical work, we can indirectly support other doctors in leadership roles to advocate for critical public health and health equity issues at global, national and local levels. Our membership in our medical associations including our colleges matters more than ever. We have recently seen the vital work of world health and medical organisations responding to the pandemic; international medical aid organisations, united in providing medical supplies to war-torn countries; and national and local medical groups giving practical support to doctors at the front line of natural disasters. These initiatives demonstrate how many tens of thousands of doctors can come together to support other colleagues and save lives.

We have re-written *Every Doctor* as a tool kit for every doctor, and we recommend drawing on different sections when relevant to our careers rather than the impossible task of trying to implement everything at once. For example, younger doctors in training programs and studying for exams may benefit from Part 1 on psychological protection and Part 3 on building stronger relationships with senior colleagues. Those who are in later stages of their careers may have more time to advocate for fairer workplaces or take on additional leadership roles without sustaining any 'career damage'. The chapters are written as food for thought and discussion, rather than as prescriptive guidelines on continual self-improvement.

Each section of the book is brimming with poignant and hopeful stories and quotes from a diverse array of doctors from many different specialities and at all career stages. Their words are a celebration of the growing global interconnectedness and the changing face of the medical profession.

Overwhelmingly, the new edition of *Every Doctor* sends a deeply authentic message of love, hope and acknowledgement for all doctors, who are continuing to serve communities across the world with courage and dedication – you are not alone.

Every doctor prioritising psychological and physical protection first

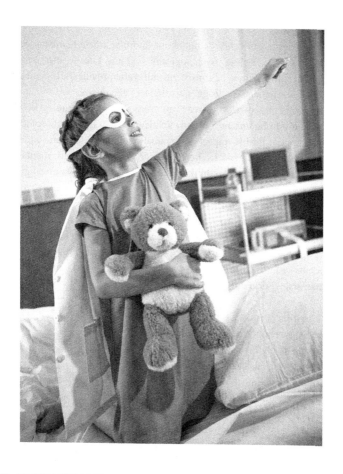

DOI: 10.1201/9781003296829-2

Intellectually, we know that we provide better patient care when we feel alert and healthy, but few of us find time to actually prioritise our wellbeing. There is a disconnect between what we say and do. How many of us are filled with joy and optimism when we enter our workplaces? How can we rediscover the enthusiasm we experienced as we entered medicine or commenced our internship?

Physical self-protection in any workplace is regarded as essential. Many doctors routinely wear personal protective equipment (PPE) to protect themselves in everyday encounters with patients. It is now widely accepted that doctors should avoid working when physically unwell to protect patients and colleagues – and ourselves. However, psychological protection to protect our emotional wellbeing and prevent common mental health problems continues to be neglected.

Psychological protection is not about donning a dehumanising emotional armour. It's about feeling psychologically well and safe, so that we have the energy and enthusiasm to be consistently kind and provide the highest standard of care for our patients, colleagues, workplaces and ourselves.

We would not carelessly wear our masks below our noses because we understand it to be unsafe. Similarly, inadequate psychological protection can compromise our health, impact on the quality of our patient care and result in other adverse consequences. There are high rates of burnout, mental illness, self-medication and suicidal thinking among doctors, mostly unrecognised and untreated.

Part 1 outlines some practical self-care strategies to help us thrive at work. We do however recognise the limitations of individual self-care. Recommending resilience training to a doctor stuck in an unrelenting workplace can be as ineffective and harmful as trying to manage a compound fracture with a Band-Aid. But before we tackle some of the systemic issues in our workplaces in Parts 2–4, it is essential we don our psychological protection in Part 1.

1. Re-writing personal stories of hope
2. Staying mentally strong under pressure
3. Making time for what matters most
4. Reassessing goals in all dimensions of life
5. Rethinking optimism with self-compassion
6. Preventing and managing burnout
7. Sleeping well naturally night or day
8. Nurturing loving relationships at home
9. Trusting our own treating doctor

Re-writing personal stories of hope

In our many interviews which formed part of our research for this new edition of *Every Doctor*, our colleagues commonly told us they did not wish to revisit the COVID-19 pandemic – or read about it. We fully understand this sentiment, but we need to confront what we have learnt from it upfront in Chapter 1. This allows us to fully acknowledge the distressing impact of the pandemic on all our lives, and only then can we move on from this context constructively without the cloud of the coronavirus dominating other chapters.

'*Everyone just wants to move on – don't dwell on the pandemic in your book*' may be a common response, but is it a healthy one? We acknowledge that for many clinicians, particularly early career doctors, the pandemic is defined by loss. Loss of career progression, exam preparedness and training opportunities. Loss of certainty about the future, growth in friendships and relationships, and formative social and emotional experiences. Loss of patients, colleagues, and resources in unprecedented volumes. Many of us are grieving for the loss of family members, friends and colleagues across the globe and facing a long uncertain future of hardship. Thinking about the COVID-19 pandemic – and grieving these losses – is not straightforward.

Chapter 1 may therefore trigger painful memories, particularly in doctors continuing to serve patients and communities where the consequences of the pandemic are omnipresent. When there is a lack of support for recurrent trauma, avoidance can be a survival tactic. However, while avoidance of thinking about negative or traumatic events through overwork or superficial distractions outside work can provide temporary relief from unpleasant memories, it does not stop recurrent intrusive thoughts and rumination when we are vulnerable or triggered. Superficially, we may be surviving from day to day or presenting a stiff upper lip, but we are far from feeling content in life and work. If this is the case, it is entirely understandable if our readers prefer to defer reading Chapter 1 until after they fully work through their losses, grief and trauma with family, friends, colleagues or treating professionals. This can take time.

Before we face the realities of the pandemic in Chapter 1, we wish to acknowledge the enormous contribution of doctors in treating patients with COVID-19 and non-COVID-19 conditions. Doctors showed up under

DOI: 10.1201/9781003296829-3

impossible circumstances in acute hospitals, aged care facilities, general/family practice and other specialist consulting rooms, and community and mental health settings in metropolitan, regional and remote centres. Those who were unable to continue direct patient care contributed in other significant ways. These selfless efforts continue to be inadequately recognised by our communities, our profession and ourselves.

Although doctors, nurses and other health workers were heralded as heroes by the media during the pandemic, many clinicians bore the brunt of patient angst and anger, felt oppressed and frustrated by the inertia of health bureaucracies, were isolated from the support of family, friends and colleagues, and were frequently attacked by the anti-vaccination movement. As a consequence, many colleagues are now feeling despondent, exhausted or considering leaving the medical profession. This is a cruel injustice for health professionals, which will worsen dire health workforce shortages, and in turn, negatively impact our communities.

This ongoing travesty and the challenges described above are what motivated us to rewrite *Every Doctor*.

To fully confront and understand the many devastating realities of the COVID-19 pandemic, we begin our book with two powerful stories from intensive care consultants, who also provide us with a message of hope about what they observed and learnt.

Inside these walls

Hope has long left these halls. Inside the swinging doors of the intensive care unit, death and devastation consume us. Outside, the sun continues to rise and fall, the rhythm and routine of life plod onward. Lines of cars pass the jumbotron at the city's edge announcing 'COVID Cases Up' and 'Hospital Resource Strained.'

I wonder if people notice the pixelated words on the sign, their meaning, if it impacts their day-to-day life? Is it a reminder to wear a mask at the grocery store? Do they think about what may happen if they get into a car accident or have a heart attack? Does it offer motivation to get vaccinated? Do they hesitate to visit us when they really need to come?

As a physician in the intensive care unit, the sign conjures an incessant, unfolding tragedy for me. Strained, I think, lacks illustrative poignancy.

There has been an exodus of healthcare workers from our hospital. Like everywhere, we are sad, exhausted, disenchanted, angry, and burned out. Many are seeking new professions, retiring, or are lured by travel wages and crisis pay. The healthcare sector has lost nearly half a million workers since 2020 and as many as 66% of critical care nurses have considered leaving the profession entirely. Paradoxically, the number of patients has grown significantly and they are sicker than ever.

For those of us who remain, our arms and legs shake under the heavy weight of a healthcare system in duress. More patients pile in as both a direct and indirect impact of the pandemic. Still, we don our yellow gowns, blue gloves, and now hazy face shields and sit with fear, sadness, courage, memories, and devastation. People, so many unvaccinated COVID-19 positive people – slip away, eerily lucid and aware of their demise to the last minute.

Many patients still linger in my mind, their families' faces as tiles on a screen or voices on the phone. My list of intended condolence cards I have yet to write is long and overwhelming, scribbled handwriting – mine – of names I cannot forget.

I remember one patient in particular, his brown eyes wide-open, the blacks of his pupils like discs, his lungs failing. We joined hands at his request; my blue rubber gloves separated us by imperceptible microns. The air between us was swollen with hope and fear. He requested a prayer and made me promise he would not die. I heaved my words to the sky and begged his god, mine, whoever would listen and promised. Then I reached for more tangible tools and earthly fixes: medication and intubation. The flat line stretched across the monitor – much like the long ocean horizon – posing the question of what is beyond. I still hear my voice reluctantly instructing CPR to stop minutes later. He was my age. I still feel his hands in mine. His mom was unreachable as she was getting her vaccine.

In the beginning, we wondered if we too would fall ill, and take COVID-19 home to our families. Some of us did. A paramedic texted his friend 'I think it is time for me to be intubated,' aware of his declining status. We remember each of those who are no longer here.

We are now struggling to care for easily treatable diseases due to the sheer volume of COVID-19 positive individuals requiring care. Surgeons now operate on more advanced cancers due to missed routine screenings. Elective procedures were put on hold. Breast and cervical cancer screenings dropped by 87% and 84% respectively when compared to the previous five-year average. Colon cancer screenings have dropped by 28% to 100% at different points in the pandemic across the world. Delayed cancer diagnosis will play out with an increase in advanced, preventable cancers over upcoming years. The projections are grave.

Depression and suicide are rampant and addiction pervasive. People are succumbing to the wasteland of numbing intoxication after jobs lost *secondary to the pandemic and so much death with so few mental health resources in the four-corners region.*

In contrast to last fall, when no visitors were allowed in the hospital, we now allow one visitor per patient. One woman sat with her dying mother last Friday and asked me, 'How many people are in the same situation as me today?'

'Too many to count,' I answered.

I spend hours trying to help some families understand the nuances of medicine that have taken me years to master. But I can say one thing simply: We have no miracles to offer here. If you arrive in the hospital unvaccinated with COVID-19, regardless of your age, the effectiveness of the available medications for treatment pale in comparison to the highly efficacious vaccine.

Within these walls, we have said so many prayers, made countless phone calls, and have spent nearly two years shouldering the heavy burden of sorrow. Even when no visitors were allowed, no one died alone, because we were with them.

*Regardless of what you choose, we will be here for you as we always have been. But we beg you now to choose you, your family, your friends, your community, and us. And when you are driving by that message on the jumbotron, take a deep breath and think of me, of each of us, your health-care workers. **We are still here looking for those glimmers of light at the end of this tunnel. I will focus on them. I hope you will too.***

Dr Erin Philpott[1]

What can we learn from our stories?

Whether we have worked at the front line of the COVID-19 pandemic or in other areas of the health system, we can resonate with Dr Erin Philpott's observations when her hospital was in crisis, and the situation in the US seemed grim at the end of 2021. After her workload had settled somewhat, she was able to reflect on the positive response to publishing her article in her local paper:

What I found most interesting were the messages from other physicians and the validation it seemed to provide to them by helping them identifying their feelings

---

[1] Dr Erin Philpott is an internal medicine doctor working as a hospitalist at San Juan Regional Medical Center which is a community-owned hospital bordering the Navajo Nation in Farmington, New Mexico. She is the assistant medical director of the hospitalist group and the chairperson of the intensive care unit. Her training, research and interests are centered around global health, health equity and respiratory viruses.

in words. Additionally, it seemed to provide physicians of specialities outside the ICU and hospitalist realm a perspective that they had not fully considered, which seemed to offer me/us validation that what we were doing and living through was/is hard. We as physicians are able to feel sad and be bothered by all of this. The whole experience of writing down my vulnerabilities and sharing them in a hope of making a difference for someone else has been rewarding.

Stories like this speak volumes about who we are as a profession, and the extreme challenges we continue to face, which is why we have included the voices of our colleagues throughout this book. These stories remind us we can be immensely proud to be part of our medical community.

Telling our stories can be therapeutic, but we are often prevented from doing so because of patient confidentiality considerations – or because we simply cannot find the words. But by fully confronting our stressors in this way, we can find a way through them. For example, when we stop to acknowledge the impossible demands of our work, we can give ourselves permission to prioritise proactive self-care and psychological protection (Part 1). We can also heal after trauma by proactively seeking strong relationships with like-minded colleagues (Part 3).

The hero's journey[2]

Retelling our stories can also help us make peace with our inner narratives about negative or traumatic experiences. Whether we are challenged by a pandemic or any traumatic event, what can help is to try to accept all our human emotions – our justified emptiness, sadness, anger, fear, or despair. We can rewrite our inner narratives about loss, grief and burnout to create balanced stories about personal change, courage and hope under extreme adversity. This is not about a 'false positive' approach to re-thinking – it's about authentically and fully recognising what we learnt and achieved by sharing our stories. Only then can we heal and move on.

But this is not easy to do alone.

One way to re-examine our internal stories through a new lens is to consider the common themes underpinning the 'hero's journey'. Although

---

[2] *The Hero with a Thousand Faces* (first published in 1949) is a work of comparative mythology by Joseph Campbell. A third edition, compiled by the Joseph Campbell Foundation and published by New World Library, was released as the 12th title in the Collected Works of Joseph Campbell series in July 2008.

many clinicians dismissed the 'health worker hero' label during the pandemic, it is worth remembering Joseph Campbell's timeless messages about true heroism in his book *The Hero with a Thousand Faces*, first published in 1949.

To summarise, Campbell's reluctant hero is presented with a call to action, which they initially refuse because they consider themselves incapable of the task or fear going outside their comfort zone. When a mentor encourages or inspires the unassuming protagonist to step up and face a risk or threat, major obstacles stall any progress. The potential hero initially fails a few tests and is forced to confront the real reason for their journey, which is to overcome inner doubts or human flaws. The hero's tumultuous journey builds character and provides insight into a unique purpose or skill in preparation for an even greater future challenge. By persevering, the hero is personally transformed, thereby achieving their big goal. However, this only occurs after a period of inner turmoil, after which the hero finds inner peace by recognising the value of choosing a difficult path to not only make a difference to others, but to grow personally. They reluctantly return to their ordinary world and eventually successfully achieve a balance between who they were before their journey and who they are now.

Regrettably, many healthcare heroes' journeys are yet untold. While there may be poor external acknowledgement of what doctors and other health practitioners have contributed in recent public health crises, we can re-write our personal stories of hope and heroism to find inner peace and internal validation.

Here are some questions to help you challenge your inner narrative after facing adversity, negative experiences or trauma:

- How did you get through your darkest hour?
- Were there times you failed or felt afraid?
- Who supported you? Who did you support?
- How has your life changed? How have you changed?
- What new technical and communication skills did you learn?
- What did you learn about being human and your emotions?
- How did you work with others to make a difference?
- Have you acknowledged your own courage when you persevered despite adversity?
- What steps can you take to find peace with yourself?

Here is another example of a hero's journey, written by Dr Neil Offord, at the Australian and New Zealand Intensive Care Research Centre at Monash University, and the Department of Critical Care, at the University of Melbourne.

We need silence in the noise of a pandemic

There is so much noise in this pandemic – a constant barrage of words and numbers, daily updates of infections, hospital and vaccine rates, dollars spent, and number of deaths. We talk at each other in small groups about what we could have done better. We yell at each other on social media and in the streets about what we should do next. With so much noise, there is no space to listen.

At the centre of this pandemic, we listen – in the silence behind the glass walls of our COVID-19 intensive care units (ICUs), with the sigh of mechanical ventilation replacing laboured breathing, behind our plastic face shields, where the noise is gone.

This silence is needed. It creates space to learn, to understand the patients we care for as people, not just the disease that brought them to us. As our society enters the third year of this pandemic, is it time to be silent, to listen to each other?

As an intensive care specialist, I have learnt that silence is the first crucial step in delivering person-centred care. If we ask, then stay silent and listen, patients will tell us what they value, their goals, what they are prepared to lose, and what is not negotiable.

When the patients cannot speak, we ask their families to provide this voice. We ask them to send us photos that we laminate and stick to the walls of their loved one's room. Photos that show patients as people, upright, in their clothes, surrounded by those they love, in the places they cherish, doing what they enjoy. These stories and images build a picture of patients as people, and allow us to provide care aligned with what matters to them. This picture starts with a blank canvas of silence.

It is not easy for families or healthcare workers to do this. Silence is not naturally comfortable for most of us, particularly when it seems heavy with emotion. As clinicians, we tend to fill the long pauses, while patients and families gather their thoughts, with a barrage of numbers, facts, prognostic percentages, and opinions. When we do this, we stop listening, families stop talking, and we replace patient voices with our noise. We risk losing sight of the person, reducing them to a disease or physiology, at worst a numerical response to treatment. We risk creating an outcome they do not want or cannot tolerate.

Over the past two years of COVID-19, when I have stopped and listened, I have heard a lot in this silence.

I have heard what patients value, what they are afraid of losing, and what they have lost. I have met patients in COVID-19-restricted hospitals who are separated from their loved ones and alone. I have witnessed the sadness of elderly men and women entering hospital with a new diagnosis of cancer or sudden deterioration in a long-standing disease. In a world with no hospital visitors, they were lonely. When leaving home meant their partner had to enter care, they were overcome with guilt. If their admission was for weeks or months, they were devastated by the knowledge they may never see their partner again, may die apart after a lifetime together.

I have seen the shock and grief of young mothers and fathers after emerging from unconsciousness and mechanical ventilation, required while their lungs recovered from severe COVID-19 pneumonia, to realise they had not seen their children for months.

It is clear what we value, what we do not want to lose.

I have heard what my colleagues are giving up for each other, and for our community, and I am worried. There is more of everything that is hard, less of what is joyful. More hours, sicker patients, more personal protective equipment, more distress, and more anger from isolated families.

Our ICU doctors and nurses are anxious about what they are losing or have lost – time with families, friends, sleep, exercise, holidays, or just being alone. They feel guilty they have abandoned personal responsibilities, parenting children, the needs of elderly parents, supporting family and friends. They feel a sense of duty to each other and to our community. They are grateful for colleagues who have asked how they can help, listened to the answers, then turned up to care for patients, cut back to reduce the demand on our system, or talked to distressed families for us. They are grateful to community groups who have fed or entertained us. They are daunted by the reality that this is not over and fearful they cannot continue this relentless pace.

I have heard and seen what my community has lost and what may be intolerable.

In 2021, two of my friends died. One died in the lull between lockdowns. His family were at his bedside, and we were able to come together at his funeral as friends and family, to celebrate his life, and to mourn our loss. My other friend died interstate, during widespread lockdowns, and many of us sat alone in rooms around the country, watching a funeral on a screen, before re-entering our normal day. We did not gather, share stories, take time together to ease each other's loss.

In years to come, I wonder if we will recognise how much we have lost from these lonely funerals, cancelled weddings and skipped major milestones.

I have listened to health leaders from our ICUs, hospitals, emergency services, and governments come together for two years to endlessly model and relentlessly plan; to try and build capacity to protect us against the worst of the overwhelmed systems witnessed globally; to wrestle with the logistics and enormity of this seemingly impossible balance of preventing death, while leaving life bearable; to do this year after year. I have, like all of us, watched this spill into our public debate.

It is loud out there, with all of us, in all this noise and numbers. There is less silence, less listening, and a lot to understand. As we start another year with COVID-19, have we stopped and asked each other what we value as a community? What we have lost and may still lose? Have we listened to each other to understand the mental health, economic, and multigenerational impact of isolation and pandemic disease? Have we understood the risks of an exhausted hospital workforce?

In the silence of our patient interactions, we learn what matters. Perhaps we should do this next as a society. Damp the noise and listen.

Associate Professor Neil Orford[3]

As tempting as it is to avoid the pain of the COVID-19 pandemic, we felt that we could not accurately reflect on the experiences and incredible selflessness of every doctor without fully acknowledging it in detail upfront in *Every Doctor*. While it can be triggering and deeply unsettling to relive, this detailed context in Chapter 1 allows us to move onto all other sections without the dark cloud of the coronavirus hovering over each chapter. Instead of focusing on the pandemic in the rest of this book, we have highlighted the lessons learnt that transcend the virus and will continue to apply in future practice. For these reasons, there is only cursory reference to the pandemic in other parts of *Every Doctor*.

Summary

Our stories matter more than ever before.

The stories from two intensive care specialists, Associate Professor Neil Orford in Australia and Dr Erin Philpott in the United States, summarise

---

[3] Associate Professor Neil Orford is part of the Australian and New Zealand Intensive Care Research Centre at Monash University, as well as the Department of Critical Care, at the University of Melbourne. He is a Board Member of the College of Intensive Care Medicine of Australia and New Zealand.

many of the immense challenges that doctors endured during the COVID-19 pandemic – but also leave us with a message of hope about what we have learnt about the power of listening during a crisis. '*In the silence of our patient interactions, we learn what matters. Perhaps we should do this next as a society. Damp the noise and listen*'.

During the pandemic, doctors have displayed extraordinary courage in the face of overwhelming grief, trauma and death – whilst in isolation. Many have bravely admitted their vulnerabilities while continuing to selflessly serve their patients and reaching out to support other colleagues. Others have justifiably retreated to career respite and retirement after being subjected to impossible challenges.

Whether we work in intensive care or in other clinical settings, we can re-write our experiences of loss, grief and burnout to create constructive narratives about personal change, courage and hope under extreme adversity. Trying to shut out the damage wreaked by pandemic or any other trauma is not only futile, it's damaging. Together, we can do much more to recognise what we learnt and achieved by sharing our stories. Only then can we heal and move on.

Staying mentally strong through intense stress

Unfortunately, the one thing we know in our profession is that bleeding hearts eventually cease to beat. Doctors are burning out. This causes one of two outcomes; they become cold and sometimes unintentionally cruel foot soldiers in a dysfunctional system, or they become unwell themselves.

Moral distress is a predictable response to situations where we feel we have an ethical responsibility to do something about a problem but we cannot act in a way that preserves our integrity. As the pandemic continues, there are things we know will continue to be critical for the wellbeing of our patients: safe housing, a secure income, and, particularly for our critically unwell mental health patients, including access to tertiary care when needed. We pour our resources into patients needing this care but we are often unable to acquire appropriate services and our care is an insufficient substitute. Sprinkling a little bit of light cognitive behavioural therapy on the surface of the problem gives an illusion of care, but little real support.

Dr Louise Stone[1]

As Dr Louise Stone points out, attempts to offer superficial wellbeing strategies at times of intense moral distress are futile and offensive. Often the best we can do in this environment is to acknowledge and validate our anxiety as we would do for our patients.

Common sources of intense stress

After a busy and stressful week spent longing for a break and crawling to the finish line, how do you feel? Do you find yourself feeling a little lost, inexplicably restless but vaguely irritated and too exhausted to do anything on your time off? Are you reaching for a few glasses of wine while scrolling social media in front of the TV news, and wondering why you are not enjoying your time off or why your brain cannot stop ruminating when you are trying to sleep?

---

[1] Dr Louise Stone, is a General Practitioner and Associate Professor, Social Foundations of Medicine, Australian National University Medical School, ACT, Australia.

DOI: 10.1201/9781003296829-4

Think about the way you have trained your brain to respond to your work. You make hundreds of important decisions a day in a multitude of human interactions. You are trained to fix things, but you are constantly exposed to patient grief, anger and trauma, often associated with treatment-resistant chronic physical and mental illness. You are a detail-orientated perfectionist, but work is far from perfect, and details are missed amongst the immense workload. You are constantly on high alert as the next crisis may be just around the corner. The opportunities for tension and conflict with colleagues and management are endless. It is entirely predictable that your brain continues to 'fight' and your body continues to 'fly or freeze' when you have a moment of stillness and try to relax.

Our communities continue to have very high expectations of doctors as care providers and community leaders. Doctors are expected to be always competent, caring, concerned, responsible and dedicated. The external and internalised pressure to constantly maintain these qualities can be exhausting, particularly while dealing with inevitable trauma, grief, conflict and physical exhaustion at work.

It is only human for doctors to experience symptoms of acute and chronic stress when caring for communities overwhelmed by economic pressures and public health challenges. But it is also important to remember that at a personal level, intense stress can occur with the accumulation and combination of everyday life events. Never underestimate the stress associated with career transitions, marriage and relationships, parenting, illness or death of a loved one, separation and divorce, retirement, change in business or financial status, taking on a mortgage or loan, conflict with children or extended family, moving house or clinic or even the long-awaited holiday season.

Signs of acute and chronic stress

Sympathetic nervous system stress responses are of course normal. These reactions can be helpful in keeping us alert, motivated to meet deadlines or pass exams and aware of danger. These stress responses become pathological when there is continued and unrelenting activation of the autonomic nervous system.

The signs of acute stress are easy to identify: dry mouth, muscle tension, sweating, palpitations and breathlessness. Low-grade repetitive chronic stress can be more difficult to pinpoint and may include:

- Feelings of quiet desperation and being unable to cope
- Feelings of helplessness or hopelessness

- Worrying excessively and unreasonably about things outside our control or things that have not happened yet
- Frustration, irritability and pent-up anger
- Intolerance of minor setbacks or transgressions by others
- Excessive mood swings
- Withdrawing into daydreams
- Compassion fatigue or inability to feel empathy for others
- Tearfulness and sadness
- Indecisiveness and being prone to mistakes
- Inefficiency, doing many things at once and always being rushed
- Inflexibility and resistance to change
- Lack of interest in recreational pursuits or self-appearance

Unpleasant physical symptoms of acute or chronic stress include:

- Chest pain, tachycardia and hypertension
- Apathy or exhaustion but trouble sleeping
- Headaches, dizziness or shaking
- Musculoskeletal problems including tension, aches and pains and jaw clenching
- Gastrointestinal problems
- Weakened immune system

Pre-empting and responding to stress

As periods of low-grade and intense stress are inevitable in a medical career, it can help to pre-empt and prepare for this. Here we discuss the 'the pressure cooker', 'the anxiety code', and 'the advanced mental health resuscitation kit' as examples of strategies to help us identify our own individual manifestations of stress early and manage acute and chronic negative stress.

Keeping the lid on our pressure cooker

Think about yourself as a pressure cooker. It can help to list all the stresses that fill your internal pressure cooker and how to reduce the pressure well before your cooker lid explodes.

- What are the signs of an overfull pressure cooker (your symptoms of stress)?
- What are the things that fill your pressure cooker (your sources of stress)?
- How do you release the pressure well before your pressure cooker is compromised (your solutions to stress)?

If you would like to explore this in more detail, on the left side of a page, list all the times and situations when you felt stressed over the past few days, and on the right side, try to answer these questions:

- What did you think, do or try when you felt stressed?
- Did it help?
- What could you have done differently?
- What may help next time?
- What were the circumstances beyond and within your control?
- What can you do about them?
- Where can you seek support?
- Imagine your problem has been solved, how would you feel?
- How would you know this had happened?

Cracking the anxiety code

Dr Claire Weekes, an Australian general practitioner, was nominated for the 1989 Nobel Prize for her international best-selling books on effective management of anxiety. Her extraordinary life has been recently documented by Judith Hoare in her book, *The Woman Who Cracked the Anxiety Code*.

Here are some ways to respond to intense stress, which we have adapted from the four principles of managing anxiety by Dr Weekes:

1. **Fully confront all your concerns**. Try to find a few minutes of peace with a blank sheet of paper. Write down all your major and minor stressors – all those upfront concerns and the worries in the back of your mind. Rather than avoiding your issues, confront them full on. Embrace your emotions, including the unpleasant ones. Reassure yourself that you have every reason to feel stressed when you review your long list.
2. **Accept that life is challenging** – There will always be issues you cannot fix. There will always be too many things on your list. You are human – not superhuman. Try to accept what you cannot change. Try to identify the issues you have influence over. Try to schedule a future time to remind yourself to identify

and implement some solutions with like-minded colleagues – not while you are stressed and in need of rest.

3. **Float above your thoughts**. Try to observe your thoughts from afar to give your brain a break. Your time off work is a precious opportunity to nurture and rejuvenate yourself. Doing nothing and feeling bored on your time off may initially feel unpleasant, but try to accept these temporary feelings as positive – they mean your mind is slowing down. You are not your thoughts – try to float above your thoughts.

4. **Let time heal**. As there is a complex biological basis for your anxiety and fears, you may not feel better immediately with relaxation. Be patient with yourself. While you are waiting for your stress hormones to settle, bask in love and reconnect with people who provide mutual support and energise you. Protect yourself emotionally, set boundaries with those who deplete you and practice self-compassion. It is normal to feel how you do. You will feel better in time when you *let it be or let it go*.

Preparing an advanced psychological resuscitation kit

A personal medical bag is a well-accepted part of a doctor's advanced resuscitation toolkit to respond to physical emergencies away from the workplace. As doctors, we are of course expected to provide more than basic first aid. In the same way, it is worth preparing a personalised advanced psychological resuscitation kit for inevitable times of acute stress. Basic mental health first aid is unlikely to be adequate for emotional trauma in doctors.

If you find it difficult to stop thinking about work problems, patients or people, this is completely understandable. It may be helpful to pre-empt the mental steps you will take after experiencing psychological shocks at work. We can't overestimate how important it is to seek informal debriefing with a trusted colleague, family member or friend to help you feel validated. Simple actions such as talking with people who love you, physical activity in the fresh air and/ or mindfulness (Chapters 3 and 7) and relaxation techniques (Chapters 5 and 6) can help enormously.

What doesn't help is allowing negative thinking to fester on your precious time off work. Your unhelpful inner voice may ask: 'What's wrong with me? Why can't I cope? Am I not cut out for this?' It can be overwhelming worrying about issues you cannot influence or potential future problems which may never manifest. Try instead to reassure yourself that it takes time to unwind, relax physically and enjoy slowing down.

It may help to remind yourself of some pre-prepared words for self-support to draw on in times of intense stress:

- When you write down all the major and minor, real and imagined sources of your stress, anxiety or fears, you will realise that your mental fatigue or exhaustion is completely justified. This is obviously not a good time to make life changing decisions about ending your career and your relationships or worrying about local, national or world events over which you have no control.
- As mentioned in *Cracking the Anxiety Code*, try to prioritise the issues over which you have some influence and diarise a future time to consider solutions – hopefully by enlisting the support of like-minded colleagues and friends. Remind yourself that your hypervigilant introspection, perfectionism and risk-averse nature make you a great doctor, but are rarely helpful on your time off. You don't have to fix everything.
- If you can reduce your time spent worrying, you will have found time for the things that help you heal. For example, being fully present to nurture healthy, mutually supportive and loving relationships, or connecting with others to share a meal, exercise and sport, fresh air, relaxation and hobbies. You can also immerse yourself in the beauty of nature, music or entertainment to counter negative or traumatic images in your mind.
- Try to use positive psychology techniques (Chapter 5) to remind yourself what is going well in your life and do things you usually enjoy, even when you don't feel like it. Give yourself permission to thoroughly recharge your emotional batteries to about 80–100% on your time off. Practising medicine while running on an empty battery is remarkably difficult; you will 'run out' quickly if you only recharge to partial capacity. Every doctor experiences temporary times when demands are excessive and respite is unattainable such as when sitting exams, covering additional shifts in workforce shortages or living in a locked-down city. If it is simply not possible to recharge your batteries, reassure yourself that this too shall pass; the stressful period is temporary. Try to schedule a future break or holiday to look forward to.
- It is usually an unhelpful use of time to brood or ruminate on the same dysfunctional thoughts without questioning 'is this thought useful or helping me?' or 'how are these thoughts making me feel?'
- In the following chapters in Part 1, you will identify common negative beliefs and thinking patterns that make you susceptible to intense stress.

The stress we create for ourselves

At times, our reaction to symptoms of stress may be to withdraw from other people. It is common to feel as though we have nothing left to give after a challenging day, week or month at work. While time for solitude is often helpful, especially for those of us who are introverted, prolonged isolation will fail to rejuvenate us. Distancing ourselves from other people, especially our main supports, may create a spiral of increasing problems including loneliness, depression and excessive alcohol and drug use.

Sometimes we may ruminate about our sense of martyrdom. Putting in 100% effort, 100% of the time, is exhausting, and the self-expectation *to be everything to everyone all of the time* can lead to an exaggerated sense of responsibility. Many high achievers never feel perfect enough. It is easy to become emotionally detached when there is no outlet for painful emotions. It is worth thinking about how we may create unnecessary distress by failing to meet our own impossible expectations and failing to seek personal support.

Emotional intelligence is about self-control, self-mastery and the ability to get on with oneself and others. It is about feeling, understanding and using emotions positively. If we are going to be effective clinicians, we need to develop a high level of emotional intelligence, recognise the warning signs of stress, and make changes in our lives to restore a sense of balance. Most of the time we know the right things to do, but there is a gap between knowing and doing. Sometimes, the greatest challenge is just putting into place what we already know we should be doing to reduce stressors.

Dealing with excessive demands is a normal part of being a doctor. For this reason, it is important to be honest with ourselves, to actively seek support, to identify our strengths and weaknesses and to proactively look after our minds and bodies.

Why reducing stress is important

There is a complex biological basis for normal and abnormal stress responses; this is the subject of ongoing research and a hotly debated topic in academic medical literature.

An example of breakthrough research in our understanding of the human stress response is the Nobel prize-winning work of Australian-American molecular biologist Professor Elizabeth Blackburn, on telomeres. Telomeres are repeating segments of non-coding DNA at the end of our chromosomes responsible for our cellular health. In her book, *The Telomere Effect, Living Younger, Healthier, Longer*, Professor Blackburn describes how 'stress gets into our cells', and results in shorter telomeres, premature ageing and chronic disease. Reassuringly, she also documents research on ways to rejuvenate our telomeres including healthy nutrition, a positive response to emotional challenges, regular exercise, mindfulness (Chapters 3 and 7), meditation and 'restorative activities'.

There is a complex interplay between our neurological, metabolic, cardiovascular, musculoskeletal and other systems, which is beyond the scope of this book. Instead, our simple message is this: intense stress is inevitable in a medical career, but we can become more aware of our physical and psychological stress responses. We can minimise our 'flight and fight' reactions by consciously trying to reduce our pulse, blood pressure and respiratory rate through mental exercises and relaxation techniques. As it can take time for our biological responses to settle after acute stress or psychological trauma and injury, we need to be patient with ourselves if we find it difficult to relax at work or after work.

Ignoring chronic stress can lead directly to mental illnesses such as depression, anxiety and panic disorder, and physical illnesses such as cardiovascular disease, metabolic and immune disorders and chronic fatigue. Chronic stress may also indirectly predispose to us to chronic disease through unhealthy behaviours such as excessive alcohol use, smoking or gambling. Stress can therefore either trigger or aggravate many diseases and pathological conditions.

On the other hand, if we pre-empt and prepare for intense stress, we can control our responses to emotional shock, trauma and psychological injuries with mentally healthy habits and mental exercises.

What if an advanced psychological resuscitation kit doesn't work?

In the next chapters, we discuss mentally healthy habits in more detail, including how to meticulously manage time, build mindfulness into each day and prevent and manage burnout. However, please do not continue to self-manage your stress if these techniques are not working. Please seek early professional help from a trusted general practitioner/family physician, psychologist or psychiatrist to help you prevent or identify any mental health problems.

Unfortunately, many doctors accept burnout like a badge of honour and regard seeking help for mental illness as a sign of weakness or incompetence. This is one reason mental illness is significantly under-recognised and undertreated in doctors. Many inaccurately self-diagnose and inadequately self-manage their condition, often while continuing to function at work at great expense to themselves. Not surprisingly, many doctors tend to battle on alone and seek help late during a crisis when they are more burnt out, ineffectively self-medicated, resistant to treatment, prone to relapse and at risk of suicide. In Part 3, we discuss how we can change this.

Summary

Negative stress can be destructive to our lives and medical careers. Our sources of stress are many – time pressures, unrealistic expectations, lack of workplace support, juggling work and family responsibilities, patient care issues, professional competency issues, and the impacts of global and local health challenges. The list is endless. There is always something to worry about.

In order to respond to extreme stress, we can try to unpack the symptoms and sources of stress and seek solutions for dealing with the inevitable stress that we face across many facets of our lives. We can try to focus on solutions for issues within our control.

'Keeping the lid on our pressure cooker', 'cracking the anxiety code' and 'personalising an advanced mental health resuscitation kit' can be useful tools in times of intense stress. However, if these strategies are not working, please seek early help from a trusted general practitioner, psychologist or psychiatrist. Please do not battle on alone.

Making time for what matters most

A doctor must work eighteen hours a day and seven days a week. If you cannot console yourself to this, get out of the profession.

Dr Martin Henry Fischer

Feeling 'in control' is an illusion

During the 20th century, these famous words from American physician, Dr Martin Henry Fischer (1879–1962), were often quoted to students on their first day of medical school with the message: 'Medicine will consume your life – get used to it or leave'.

While most people in the 21st century would dismiss this quote as a wildly unrealistic expectation, many doctors continue to experience chronic occupational stress. Excessive clinical caseloads, long hours, constant interruptions and impossible demands are all too common. Time off work is often eroded with study and continuing professional development, overtime and on call (often at short notice), red tape and other onerous administrative tasks (usually all unpaid and therefore not counted). In high-speed medical life, never-ending to do lists never get finished, and any sense of time management or control over our lives is an illusion.

These realities are difficult to reconcile with what doctors know about occupational stress as a predisposing factor to burnout, depression, anxiety and physical conditions such as cardiovascular disease. It is also a paradox that some parts of the medical profession continue to subscribe to the out-dated view that doctors must be workaholics, and in contrast, others recognise compulsive overworking and work addiction as a psychiatric condition. According to the ICD-11, obsessive-compulsive personality disorder can be characterised by an abnormal preoccupation with work productivity and overthinking or obsessing about work to the exclusion of interpersonal relationships and enjoyable activities on time off.

The underlying problems of excessive work demands and expectations described previously, do not lie with individual doctors, nor is the onus on us

DOI: 10.1201/9781003296829-5

to conjure non-existent time for what matters in a day already stretched paper thin. Nevertheless, while it may be difficult to regain a sense of control over our lives, we can step back from the chaos of work for a few moments, and make choices about our priorities.

The following sections on meticulous time prioritisation and mindfulness challenge us to consider what matters most at work and outside of work, including time for recovery and rejuvenation of our health – to in turn allow us to care effectively for our families, our patients and our communities. Later, Part 2 of *Every Doctor* discusses ways that doctors can work together to effectively advocate for healthy workplace cultures that promote fairness and safe work hours and conditions. First, let's try to identify what we can do as individuals to make best use of our limited precious time, protect our health and reduce our inevitable occupational stress.

Meticulous time prioritisation

There are 168 hours in each week. Many of us spend an average of about 56 hours per week sleeping, leaving us with over 100 hours of waking time. Taking into consideration some variability in working hours and other fixed commitments from week to week, this may leave a surprisingly flexible 20–60 hours a week, which we may be able to carve out to replenish and restore ourselves.

We can be proactive in allocating our flexible hours to our priorities and outsourcing what can be delegated to others. For example, we can prioritise eating healthy food and exercising with family, helping out a friend or spending time on pleasant pastimes like planning a much-needed holiday, reading a great book or listening to music. We can allocate time for much needed slowing down, idleness, solitude, deep relaxation and sleep. We can save a lot of time and frustration by delegating our financial, legal and business matters to competent, qualified professionals.

There will be times when the demands on our lives are excessive – we may be working over 80 hours a week, doing night shifts or struggling with nights on call, whilst sitting for exams and covering a sick colleague. We may be preoccupied with preschool children or a sick wakeful child, relationship problems, elderly parents, a chronic illness or home renovations. Some administrative tasks cannot be delegated.

A medical career is fraught with excessive challenges. Patients die unexpectedly, people become angry, peer scrutiny can be harsh, the threat of medicolegal action is real, medical workforce shortages create pressures, and disturbed sleep is common. It's a lot to mentally process after we finish work, and while debriefing can help us work through this, rumination can impede our much-needed recovery before our next commitment.

In these times of immense pressure, when there are very few flexible hours available to us in a week, meticulous time prioritisation is even more important. It is simply not possible to offer consistent high-quality patient care unless we allow adequate time outside work hours to rest, rejuvenate and replenish ourselves. Time off doing nothing outside work hours is never wasted.

It can be worth filling out a diary to monitor how we are spending our flexible time outside of work to identify ways to free up time. This may involve getting up earlier, declining energy-depleting meetings or unnecessary social events, reducing time spent ruminating or complaining, doing shopping and banking online to avoid queues, outsourcing cleaning and non-essential administrative duties, and spending less time mindlessly scanning TV channels or streaming services, social media, emails and smartphones.

Most doctors by nature are people pleasers and find it hard to say 'no' or disappoint when others ask them for favours. We have a strong, sometimes debilitating sense of duty to others. However, when we stop to remind ourselves what really matters most in our lives and in medicine, we can be tougher with delegating and deferring things that matter very little in the long run. Saying 'no' to protect our precious time off can actually make us better doctors/partners/friends/parents by protecting against burnout, fatigue and resentment. It takes time and courage to push back and say 'no', but sometimes, we need to be somewhat ruthless in allocating time to what is important to us at work and at home.

It is also important to consider ways to improve our effectiveness at work to try and reduce excessive work hours. Of course, it is unrealistic to expect doctors to create efficiencies when we are already multiskilling, processing complex information and making hundreds of clinical decisions in time limited consultations, whilst delaying breaks. Nevertheless, are there ways to improve administrative systems and practice management by reducing red tape, paperwork, duplication of tasks or interruptions? On the other hand, are there times when it is possible to consciously slow down during work hours? Can we try to slow our breathing and relax our muscles while enjoying being in the moment with patients and colleagues, in order to feel calmer at work and to preserve our energy throughout the whole day?

As mentioned in the previous chapter, stressed doctors often maintain a hypervigilant mode of thinking outside of work by ruminating about the day or pre-empting tomorrow's challenges, while juggling non-work responsibilities. Even our leisure time may feel unpleasant because we experience discomfort if we are not being productive. Consequently, we may suffer from mental fatigue and inertia on our time off work but also find it difficult to sleep. This common cycle of overstimulation, mental exhaustion and sleeplessness impedes our ability to enjoy our time off work.

Another common trap is to continually strive to be more efficient by rushing, only to fill new found free time with additional to do lists and more and more tasks. It is counterproductive if we continually defer gratification and self-care, forgetting to pause and to enjoy being in the present moment with our families, our colleagues, our patients – and ourselves.

To counter all these pressures, it can help to build the practice of regular mindfulness into each day at work and when recovering outside work. Mindfulness can help us consciously slow down and take time to enjoy living and working every day.

Making time to live consciously and think clearly through mindfulness

Being mindful is about being fully aware of the present, and observing thoughts and sensations without judging them as good or bad, right or wrong. Unfortunately, many doctors dismiss mindfulness because they can't stop thinking or they assume they do not have time. Others complain it is boring!

Of course, mindfulness is not a magic bullet for all our problems, but it can help to us to live more consciously, think clearly, restore our daytime energy and sleep better at night. Dr Craig Hassed describes how we can build mindfulness into each day. In Chapter 7, psychologist Dr Giselle Withers also describes her approach to mindfulness for sleeping well naturally.

Building regular mindfulness into every day

Mindfulness, in its simplest and most universal sense, is a mental discipline that involves training attention – it also implies cultivating an attitude of openness, interest and acceptance. It teaches us how to use the mind in a different way and focus on the things that are most useful and helpful in our lives.

When our mind is wandering, we are not paying attention to what we are doing. This results in more mistakes, less efficiency and less enjoyment. Secondly, what is the mind doing when we are not paying attention? Well, we might be wishing to experience happiness resulting from the imagination, but this only gives us a very superficial experience of the life we are actually leading and never leads to a stable and deeply satisfying level of wellbeing. In fact, the constant desire to be somewhere else (some other place or time) can produce a slowly growing sense of dissatisfaction with where we are here and now. Furthermore, when we are not paying attention is the time when the mind gets up to 'mischief' in the form of worry and rumination which are at the very heart of anxiety and depression.

One cannot 'stop the mind from thinking' and any attempt to do so generally leads to heightened tension and frustration. We can, however, learn not to be so reactive to it. This takes the emotive force out of it. Analogously, many trains of thought come into our minds but we can learn not to be moved by them – not by trying to stop them or fight with them, but by learning that we don't need to get on board any old train of thought that comes into our minds. That takes a lot of awareness.

What we give our attention to is important because we give the power to whatever the attention is directed to. In giving attention to fearful, anxious, angry or depressing thoughts, we almost 'meditate' upon them, progressively making them more 'real' and compelling. When we take such imaginings and mental projections to be real, they govern our lives, behaviour and responses to events and, over time, they can change the brain's chemistry, set up a cascade of events throughout the body and accelerate illness. Obviously, one cannot 'meditate our problems away'.

Mindfulness is therefore not a method of tuning out but rather tuning in. It is not a method of distraction but rather a method of engagement. It is the stressed, anxious, angry and depressed state of mind that is the distracted state – mindfulness is the remedy.

A day is just like a book. If it isn't punctuated, it becomes a blur and makes little sense. These 'punctuation marks' are times of consciously coming to rest so that we can remind ourselves to be present and pay attention. For this reason, the two following practices are suggested. The 'full stop' could be practiced for anything from 5 to 30 minutes twice a day depending on motivation and opportunity, and the 'comma' for 15 seconds to 2 minutes as often as you remember throughout the day. The comma is particularly useful between having completed one activity and beginning another.

The full stop

Sit the body in a chair so that the spine is upright and balanced but relaxed. Have the body symmetrical and allow the eyes to gently close. Now, move the attention gently through each step. Be conscious of the body and its connection with the chair. Feel the feet on the floor. Notice if the feet are tense. If so, allow them to relax if they want to. Similarly, be aware of the legs and allow them to relax if they wish, and so gently move up through each part of the body: the stomach, hands, arms, shoulders, neck and face. If tension or discomfort remains, just notice the presence of tension or discomfort without judgment. Now take in a deep breath and slowly and gently let the breath out. Repeat this twice more, then just allow the breathing to settle into its own natural rhythm without having to control it in any way. If you observe a tendency to try and control the breath, just impartially notice that. Simply be conscious of the breath as the air flows in and out of the nose. If thoughts come to your awareness, allow them to come and go without judgment and let the attention return to the breathing. There is no need to struggle with the activity of the mind, nor even wish that it wasn't there. Like 'trains of thought', just let them come and go. After a time, let the attention move to the listening. Hear whatever sounds there are to hear without having to analyse the sounds. Once again, if thoughts come, let them pass. If the mind becomes distracted, for example by listening to some mental commentary or chatter, simply notice and return to the sounds as a gentle way of returning to the present moment. At the end of this exercise, simply be aware of the body again and then slowly allow the eyes to open. After a few moments, quietly move into whatever activities await you.

The comma

This exercise can take anywhere from a few seconds to a couple of minutes. It is a short punctuation in a busy day between finishing one activity and starting another, for example before starting the car, beginning a meal, before an interview, or between patients. It helps to 'clean the slate', making us fresher for the next activity. The steps and principles are the same as above but just much shorter. Be aware of the body and allow the posture to be balanced and relaxed but upright. Let the body relax generally by taking one or two deep breaths and breathing the tension out. Then let the breath settle and allow the attention to rest with it. Then be aware of the environment and the sounds in it as they come and go. Do not prolong the comma past what is appropriate for that moment, then move quietly into whatever awaits you. If you are in a busy office and it would be conspicuous to close your eyes, just keep them open but rest them on a point as you practice.

Mindfulness improves how effectively we function, has direct benefits by changing the body physiologically and metabolically, has indirect benefits by improving our lifestyle, enhances relationships and compassion, improves the way we cope with life challenges and enriches our enjoyment of life.

Professor Craig Hassed[1]

Summary

No matter what challenges we are facing, we have more choice about how we prioritise or free up our time at and outside work than we may realise. With meticulous time prioritisation, we can gain greater influence over how we spend our precious time, particularly how we enjoy our time off work. By identifying flexible hours outside of our work, we can proactively plan how to spend time off and to allocate time to rest, wind down and relax. We can delegate tedious administrative and household tasks where possible. In those weeks burdened with heavy workloads and additional family pressures, it is especially vital to prioritise time out.

If we are struggling to cope and enduring each day to the next, it is important to reconsider what really matters most to us, carefully allocating time for mindfulness, rejuvenation, nurturing relationships, solitude and taking well-deserved time off by having the courage to say 'no' to unnecessary work and social commitments.

---

[1] Professor Craig Hassed is the coordinator of mindfulness programs across Monash University and the founding Director of Education at the Monash Centre for Consciousness and Contemplative Studies. Professor Hassed developed and integrated the world-first mindfulness-based healthy lifestyle course called the Health Enhancement Program into the Monash University medical curriculum and other Australian and international universities. www.monash.edu/__data/assets/pdf_file/0004/694192/The-health-benefits-of-meditation-and-being-mindful.pdf

Reassessing goals in all dimensions of life

When you know your why, you can endure any how.

> *Professor Viktor E. Frankl, Austrian neurologist, psychiatrist,*
> *philosopher, writer and Holocaust survivor*

An unwavering belief in the value of our work

Whatever our speciality and wherever we practice in the world, and whether we work as a solo doctor in a remote Indigenous community, as a member of a team of clinicians in a city clinic or hospital or lead a global medical organisation with tens of thousands of members, our work can make a profound difference to people's lives. An unwavering belief in the value of our work over time can help us transcend daily challenges and can remain a source of our stability as we travel through different stages of our lives and careers.

Goals and priorities

We may recognise that although our achievements are admirable, our medical career goals do not sustain us through the inevitable everyday setbacks or major crises of our lives. A medical career is highly competitive and uncertain. The sooner we accept this, the easier it will feel.

Of course, to progress our careers, we must be committed and dedicated to our goals. But if we believe we will only be happy when we are successful in achieving a particular subspecialist training position (although there are hundreds of applicants), passing all exams (the first time) or securing a highly desired hospital or practice appointment, we can forget to enjoy our lives and appreciate our journeys. Paradoxically, if we put everything into our work at the expense of everything else, we are less likely to achieve our career goals because our unhealthy obsession is likely to impede our performance at interviews, assessments and work.

DOI: 10.1201/9781003296829-6

For these reasons, it can help to try to think about goal setting and priorities across different dimensions of our lives beyond our medical careers.

It may also help to consider the famous question posed by the late poet Mary Oliver:

Tell me, what is it you plan to do with your one wild and precious life?

Try this exercise

Your spiritual life. What is most important in your life? What do you find uplifting and are you pursuing this? What are your values and are you living them? How are you caring for your soul? Who inspires you and why?

Your relationships with other people. Which relationships are most important to you? What qualities do you seek in your relationships? Are you spending enough time with people you love and who provide you with support?

Your mental health. Are you experiencing joy in your life? How are you being proactive in protecting your own mental health?

Your physical health. Are you taking care of your physical health as well as you advise your own patients to do the same? How can you fit more exercise into your everyday schedule? When did you last see your own doctor for a comprehensive preventive health check-up?

Your social and personal life. What leisure activities energise you and give you the greatest pleasure? Are you doing them? Have you planned regular periods of leave from your work?

Your security. Financial security is an important goal, but has money become too prominent in your life? How much money is enough? Have you taken the time to seek competent financial and legal advice?

Your legacy. At the end of your career, what will you be most proud of? What legacy will you leave in your eventual retirement and why is this important to you? How do you define a successful life?

What are your specific realistic goals in the next few months? At times, your main goal will be just to get through each day. At other times, you will find you can transcend major challenges by focusing on the overarching purpose of your life, or in contrast, by being present in the moment, remembering to enjoy the journey rather than always striving for a distant goal.

A brief private diary

Consider keeping a journal or diary to help you maintain your focus on your goals. It may include your own observations, your insights into humanity, letters from your patients and your reflections on your mentors, your teachers and your work. Over time, it will become a precious record of your life.

The following story by Dr Alexie Puran, a Pediatric Emergency Medicine Physician from New York, exemplifies the benefits of finding purpose by documenting our journeys and making sense of our stories.

Storytelling to empower

There is no greater power on this earth than story.

Libba Bray

Storytelling is a powerful way to connect with ourselves, our patients, and our fellow healthcare professionals. In recent years, the six-word story, a six-word sentence that is written to tell a story, has become increasingly popular. The most famous example of a six-word story is by novelist Ernest Hemingway, who according to legend, wrote: 'For sale: baby shoes. Never worn.' In just six words, a heartbreaking narrative is told, which evokes emotion and leaves us yearning to learn more.

In November 2006, Larry Smith, founder of SMITH Magazine, created the Six-Word Memoir Project[1] by asking its readers to describe their lives in exactly six words. Since then, the six-word concept has become a global phenomenon with over a million stories shared on sixwordmemoirs.com.

My six-word story: Power to reconnect and connect

As a physician working in a Pediatric Emergency Department in New York City, I saw first-hand the emotional toll the pandemic had on my fellow nurses and physicians. In an effort to support my team's resiliency and well-being and also knowing the power of the six-word prompts, I designed a fun, meaningful activity, My Six-Word Story. Staff members were invited to submit six-word stories on their inspiration in choosing a career in medicine.

There was great support and enthusiasm from the staff as the activity did not require a significant amount of time, allowed staff to be creative with using only six words, and provided a shift in focus away from the pandemic towards positive thoughts. The six-word stories submitted were inspirational and the staff was surprised with what I did with their stories.

Each story was amplified visually with illustrations I added to them. These poster stories were placed on a bulletin board (now known as the Story Board by the staff) and compiled into a book for all to enjoy. Additionally,

---

[1] www.sixwordmemoirs.com

I made prints of each story for the staff to hang up on their refrigerator, desk, or wall so they can always remember their 'why.'

Reading everyone's six-word stories sparked conversation amongst our team and interest in learning the back-stories behind them. Hearing the personal stories of our fellow colleagues revealed our common interests, mutual beliefs, and shared values.

Staff six-word stories

Child of system, now system leader.
Making it better: little by little.
Ordinary people can do extraordinary things.
The change I want to see.
Following giant footsteps, making my own.
Be strong, be beautiful, be you.
Being humane makes you a hero.
It is a privilege to serve.
Be the voice, for those without!

Staff Comments on My Six-Word Story Project included:
'Being able to put decades of hard work and dedication into the simplest 6 words was a freeing experience.'
'Reminded me why I chose nursing as a profession.'
'I feel like seeing everyone's story was a window into their lives.'
'Inspired by their stories.'
'We have all felt a lot of emotions during this time and I think sadness was an overarching theme, however this piece signified a feeling of conquering/overcoming together.'
'It provides us constant motivation visually and verbally.'

Six words. One story. What's yours?

Perhaps everyone needs a six-word story. I invite you to write your own six-word story on your 'why', or adapt My Six-Word Story to help support the well-being of your fellow colleagues. Reconnect with your 'why' at the start of each day by reciting your six-word story. Connect with your colleagues in the human experience by sharing your six-word stories with each other. Your story matters.

Dr Alexie Puran[2]

[2] Dr Alexie Puran is a Pediatric Emergency Medicine Physician in New York City and is an Assistant Professor of Clinical Pediatrics at Columbia University's Vagelos College of Physicians and Surgeons. Dr Puran currently serves as Co-Chair for the Physician Council at the Beryl Institute.

Summary

A shared belief in the big impact of our work can be a unifying goal when navigating the challenges of medicine with our colleagues.

A new look at our goals and priorities in all of the dimensions of our individual lives can provide a sense of resolve where daily setbacks are common, and may become a source of inspiration in times of disappointment, extreme stress and trauma. Paradoxically, if we put everything into our work at the expense of everything else, our unhealthy obsession is likely to impede our performance and prevent us from achieving our career goals.

For these reasons, it can help to try to think about goal setting and priorities across different dimensions of our lives beyond our medical careers, including our spiritual lives, relationships, physical and mental health, social lives, security and legacies.

5

Rethinking optimism with self-compassion

If you want others to be happy, practise compassion. If you want to be happy, practise compassion.

The Dalai Lama

What are you optimistic about?

Here are some of the answers to this question which we recently posed to doctors:

'The power of public health measures.'
'The funding of telehealth.'
'Reduced air pollution.'
And from a general practitioner in remote Australia: 'I always live like this in isolation and I love it. We even have enough toilet paper.'
There was also valid pushback to this question with comments like: 'Don't talk to me about false or forced optimism.'

Many felt overwhelmed by:

- *'Information overload, the rapid adjustment to telehealth and the disruption of referral pathways.'*
- *'Many patients are presenting with severe mental health issues due to isolation, unemployment, substance misuse and family violence.'*
- *'Increased bureaucracy and human resources issues such as termination of staff, employees taking sick leave, and many other practice management issues, which are distressing as we have previously been a happy family.'*

Some brave colleagues also admitted to experiencing raw fear during recent public health crises. In these situations, we are reminded of the fragility of our own lives and of those we love. How can we protect our mental health and

DOI: 10.1201/9781003296829-7

maintain our optimism for the sake of our families, our patients, our communities, our colleagues and ourselves when the world is in turmoil?

Here are some inspirational reflections from colleagues, who challenge us to rethink optimism in the face of adversity:

- *'Observing my community with fresh eyes and the resurgence of local communities with soul.'*
- *'Watching the world slow down and people focusing on what is essential, especially family.'*
- *'The changing winds everywhere.'*
- *'The unbelievable sense of community and collegiality in many parts of healthcare.'*
- *'Finally talking openly about mental health in doctors and their feelings.'*
- *'The community openly valuing healthcare workers and the outpouring of love and support towards us.'*
- *'A window to a potentially different way of working.'*
- *'The stories of love and belonging and kindness I have seen around my own community and the world.'*

What are you optimistic about?

Here is an optimistic story from Dr Danielle Martin, a family physician from Canada about the joys of being a doctor.

Be of use

The first baby you deliver on your own, the first X-ray you read correctly, the first time you break bad news, will be amazing moments, and many of them will stay with you for decades – but you should know that the rewards only get deeper. That's because the first time you do something as a doctor, in your heart of hearts, it will be mostly about you.

But each subsequent time, it will become more and more about the person you are helping. Observe yourself as you evolve in this way. The less you worry about whether you are doing it right, the more clearly you will see the human in front of you. As your bravado fades, your compassion will grow. It is one of the many gifts this career will give you.

Not infrequently people – even your patients – will ask you, 'how do you do it?' referring to the 24-hour shift or the difficult procedure in the middle of the night. I predict that mostly you will respond with humility, but at times secretly you will be tempted to wear your fatigue and your belea-guerment like a badge of honour.

Huge numbers of physicians report signs of burnout these days – and there is a movement for work-life balance and personal wellness that is growing in response. We all have an interest in helping to build a resilient medical community, but the answer isn't pizza parties or yoga classes.

As the Institute for Health Care Improvement in the United States puts it – and I quote – 'The most joyful, productive, engaged staff . . . appreciate the meaning and purpose of their work'.

There is now considerable evidence that when people know their work helps others, they feel less emotionally exhausted and their mental health is better. Physical health, too, improves when we help others. In other words, knowing that you are of use is an energizing force that promotes personal resilience.

Of course, we all need to sleep enough, eat well, get outdoors, spend time with our families and recharge. Of course, there is more to life than work.

But the act of bringing your skills to help another person or spend-ing time on a project that is meaningful is also good for you. It is not the alternative to your life. It is life. You will be able to say, through your entire career, that in your work, you meet extraordinary people, you learn, you are humbled and moved, and you contribute. You are of use to others. This is what will inoculate you against burnout and cynicism.

Take heart in how useful you can be. Be of use as much as you can, as often as you can. That will fill you up.

Dr Danielle Martin[1]

Psychological techniques

There are a number of psychological techniques to help us maintain our opti-mism throughout challenges. Importantly, before we try to 'rethink' optimism, we need to understand why doctors can be prone to pessimism.

In medicine, we are trained to be hypervigilant for anything that may go wrong. We are always preparing for the worst case scenario, and unconsciously scanning the world for threats. Additionally, we are often exposed to the deeply painful dimensions of medicine: misery, trauma, injustice, anger, bullying,

---

[1] Dr Danielle Martin is a Family Physician and Chair of the Department of Family and Community Medicine at the University of Toronto. Her bestselling book *Better Now: Six Big Ideas to Improve Health Care for All Canadians* was published in January 2017.

violence and death. We are also frequently confronted with the reality of poverty, child abuse, violence, and drug and alcohol abuse that our patients and their families experience.

As our medical careers progress, it is not surprising that we can develop a negative cognitive bias that at times transcends reality. Conditioned to be overly risk averse, we sometimes assume the worst without evidence and when it is no longer helpful. As it can feel like there is always something to worry about, it can be difficult to remain optimistic and courageous.

To counter these common thinking traps, it can help to draw on some psychological techniques, with self-compassion. Here are a number of recommended approaches to help us manage our negative biases and thinking:

- Cognitive behavioural techniques can help us challenge our unhelpful beliefs and common faulty thinking patterns, which predispose us to feeling negative or sad.
- Positive psychology strategies shift the attention away from challenging or accepting the negative to focus on the positive by practising gratitude, kindness and forgiveness. It can help us recognise and develop our inner strengths and gain a sense of accomplishment, pride and optimism by shifting attention to nurturing positive relationships and simple pleasures.
- Mindfulness and relaxation exercises work well if we do them regularly as we condition our brains to 'let go' and transcend unwanted thoughts (Chapters 3, 6, 7).

Cognitive behavioural techniques

Unless we are seeking solutions, it is usually an unhelpful use of our time to allow our minds to brood or get stuck on the same dysfunctional thoughts over and over again, without questioning 'is this thought useful or helping me?' or 'how are these thoughts making me feel?'

Here are some examples of common negative thinking patterns:

- Catastrophising situations. Today was awful, terrible, horrible. If you repeat this in your mind, how do you feel? 'Awful, terrible, horrible'? 'I can't stand it anymore'? Although these thoughts may feel entirely justified, what impact will they have on your short and long-term mental health? Are catastrophic thoughts useful to you in any way? Is it possible to find a calmer inner voice? How does it feel if you try to repeat the following statements? 'Yes, it is difficult, but I have gotten through problems before and I will try to do my best'.

'This is the most challenging period in my life, but I can connect with others to find a way through it'.

- Black-and-white thinking supposes that situations or events are either good or bad, which is rarely the case. On a daily basis, we may perceive a day as very good or very bad based on whether we received any negative patient feedback. But when we stop and consider everything that happened, why do we allow one patient complaint to blur the many positive interactions we had with other patients? It can be more helpful to think about the shades of grey in our lives. Try to become aware of the more rational feelings and thoughts in between the extremes of black and white in our everyday lives.

- Common negative over-generalisations are thoughts such as 'Things always go wrong', 'Everyone at work is against me' and 'No-one understands how I feel'. These reactions are rarely helpful. Automatic generalisations may be challenged with constructive self-talk like 'Work has been stressful for everyone recently, but I'll try not to take things personally', or 'Talking to like-minded colleagues or friends will help me feel better'.

- Mind reading involves making assumptions about what someone else thinks of us or believes about us. The evidence for such assumptions needs to be questioned, for example 'How do I know this?' 'How can I be sure?' and 'Could my colleague have something else on their mind?'

Positive psychology

Positive psychology does not detract from the issues inherent in our hospitals and workforces that make 'remaining positive' feel impossible and at times, laughable. It does not negate the notion that we are burnt out and working dangerous hours in suffocating bureaucracies with little regard for real life. It simply offers another tool, that, if we are in the headspace to utilise it, can emphasise our small wins, our good days and the refreshing parts of our job.

American psychologist and author Professor Martin Seligman has written extensively on positive psychology in his book, *Flourish*, and he has described three common belief patterns that may predispose people to negative thinking. Here are some considerations adapting the three principles to the context of doctors' health:

- *Personalisation* – We may inappropriately assume responsibility for a clinical incident we did not cause and experience self-doubt. We need to remind ourselves that it is usually the system of healthcare, funding shortfalls and workforce shortages which directly result in many adverse events rather than individual error.

- *Permanence* – This is an error in thinking that the impact of an event (for example, a dispute with a colleague, a complaint from a patient or a clinical error) will be lifelong. With experience, we recognise and reassure ourselves that negative experiences fade and we will feel better in time.
- *Pervasiveness* – We may form an unhelpful belief that a period of career turmoil affects all areas of our lives and is insoluble. This is rarely the case, and we can try to cultivate positives in other dimensions of our lives to counteract challenges. Our medical careers do not define us – we can find solace in our relationships with family and friends, who love us for who we are not what we do.

We can try to incorporate positive psychology into our lives in small ways and find beauty in medicine by recognising what we often take for granted. For example, we may gain immense satisfaction by practising kindness and influencing early career doctors and medical students by modelling positive behaviours. Our lives can be enriched by learning from inspirational stories of our patients' courage through adversity. Taking a few minutes to feel gratitude for our own health, our family and our ability to enjoy simple pleasures in life can make a difference to our mood state. And we can try to reach out to each other in challenging times, developing deep connections with others.

Try this exercise

Outside of work, try to seek simple pleasures. Identify enjoyable things in your day which bring you joy and do them every day – reading to your child, walking the dog, breathing clean air, feeling the sun on your skin, hugging your partner, laughing with a friend, talking to your parents, singing, listening to music, taking a bath, gardening, swimming, cooking healthy food, riding a bike, learning another language, dancing, smelling fragrant flowers, taking photos, writing, reading poetry, watching a sunset, tasting fresh fruit and growing something from seed or fresh herbs on your windowsill. What are the simple things you enjoy? Write them down and try to do more of them every day.

Summary

While deeply satisfying and full of diverse opportunities, a career in medicine can also present many complex challenges. In our daily work, we witness or vicariously experience a great deal of physical and emotional suffering and trauma. These repeated harrowing experiences can predispose us to negative cognitive biases and unconscious hypervigilant responses. In these circumstances, self-compassion is required to maintain our optimism.

To counter our negative thoughts, we can try to understand common faulty thinking patterns and habits, and use simple cognitive behavioural and positive psychology techniques. We can remember that we are often witness to inspirational displays of courage in our patients, their families and our colleagues. We can also gain a sense of accomplishment, pride and optimism through our deep connections with people.

6

Preventing and managing burnout

It's your reaction to adversity, not adversity itself that determines how your life's story will develop.

Dieter F. Uchtdorf

Burnout is common. According to the ICD 11, it encompasses the three domains of exhaustion, cynicism and reduced professional efficacy. In everyday life, we see it manifest as uncharacteristic irritability, fatalism, loss of professional identity, reduced productivity and efficiency, and increased sick leave. While recovery from burnout is very much possible, if not addressed it can progress to mental ill health and suicide.

Back in 2013, as reported in the internationally known Australian Beyond Blue National Mental Health Survey of 14,000 doctors and medical students, 47.5% of younger doctors (<51 years) reported emotional exhaustion, 17.6% reported low professional efficacy and 45.8% reported high cynicism, well surpassing measures of burnout in non-medical professionals. Work-life imbalance was the most common source of stress (26.8%). Approximately one quarter (24.8%) of doctors reported having thoughts of suicide – a rate significantly higher than the general population.

In the ten years since the Beyond Blue study was published, public health crises have exposed our flawed and stretched healthcare systems, which predispose high levels of burnout in all health workers, including doctors. There is no doubt these systems need an overhaul. But what can we do to protect ourselves?

Sometimes, we only need a good rest and a debrief, rather than overthinking it. Simple strategies can help such as reaching out and developing connections with others. In Chapters 3 and 7, the benefits of mindfulness are described in detail. In this chapter, we explore a number of practical strategies that may assist us in recovering after difficult days at work, including challenging negative thinking patterns and unrealistic inner belief systems as well as the vital importance of debriefing to prevent and manage burnout.

DOI: 10.1201/9781003296829-8

Challenging negative thinking patterns

Switching off after work is easier said than done. It can be difficult to slow the brain after a long intense day. Our overstimulated brain can go into overdrive as we process the day's events, often thinking about what we forgot to do, what we must do tomorrow, and how we interacted with others.

Sometimes it is difficult to stop intrusive thoughts and rumination about problems at work. We are trained to operate with a risk-averse filter that notices the negative.

Try this exercise

Think about what you pay attention to when you are not working. Try to consider a recurrent problem that comes to your mind frequently in your free time. Here are some helpful questions to try to understand and reduce unhelpful thoughts:

What is the evidence for this way of thinking about the problem?
Is there another explanation for what I am feeling or what is happening?
What is the worst that could happen in this situation?
What is the best that could happen out of this?
What is the most realistic way things could work out?
What would I advise a colleague if he or she were facing the same situation?

Recognising unrealistic belief systems

Challenging negative thinking can be more difficult if you have unconscious unrealistic belief systems. Are any of these inner beliefs underpinning your negative thinking patterns?

I need other people's approval to make me happy.
I should always have complete control over my feelings.
It is weak to feel anxious or sad.
I should never make mistakes, and I should always be right.
I must anticipate all risks.
I must know everything and fix every problem.

Try some more reassuring forms of 'self-talk' such as:

I am human. I have feelings, and it is sometimes helpful to express them.
I do not need approval, but I would like support.
I am dealing with many complex challenges, and it is not possible to mitigate all clinical risks.
All doctors make errors and mistakes, which we can try to prevent and learn from together.
It is not possible to know everything, but I know where and how to access relevant information.

Try to practise prefacing your self-talk with words like 'I would prefer' or 'I will try', rather than 'I shouldn't be thinking or feeling like this', 'I am always negative' or 'I must not feel like this'.

The power of debriefing

Human beings only have a finite capacity for witnessing and vicariously experiencing suffering, and yet, we experience highly stressful incidents and deep suffering on a regular basis in medicine. Empathy, sympathy and compassion – the characteristics that make us good doctors – also make us human and hence vulnerable.

There is no doubt of the shared comfort and reassurance provided by debriefing after a stressful day or unexpected incident. Debriefing, a collective group reflection with the goal of individually and collectively processing a profound experience, is known to reduce acute and chronic stress responses amongst staff and increase staff satisfaction and group morale. It can also help to informally debrief individually with peers, mentors or other like-minded colleagues on a regular basis.

Despite the importance of debriefing, many health services do not have formal debriefing policies in place. Health workplaces must establish guidelines and realistic opportunities for formal and informal debriefing sessions for doctors at all stages of their careers, particularly for doctors in training.

Reframing burnout can help us manage it better

It is well known that burnout is endemic in the medical profession. I have found that one-size-fits-all approaches such as mindfulness, meditation, relaxation exercises or other self-care activities have a role, but they don't address the complexity of moving parts contributing to burnout or necessarily deal with its impacts on an individual.

The problem: What does burnout look like and how does it arise?

Burnout is a complex issue and can be a bit of a masquerader. Although some people come to me and explicitly say they are burnt out, many don't recognise this at all. Rather they present with wanting help with issues such as:

- Career decisions – whether they should change roles or specialties or leave healthcare altogether;
- Feeling like an impostor or lacking confidence in times of transition;
- Procrastination and motivation – particularly in terms of exam or interview preparation.

It's only once we start talking that burnout reveals itself as an underlying issue. Other clues that signal burnout may include a tendency towards frustration, irritation and anger in the face of relatively small issues that would (in normal times) pass by unnoticed.

It's useful to think about these emotional and behavioural responses in terms of the classic Yerkes-Dodson inverted U stress curves which are a theoretical approach to describing the relationship between stress (physiological arousal) and performance:

Stress is good for us when it enhances our performance. If we had no stress, we wouldn't get anything done. We often feel at our best when our skill set is well matched to a particular challenge and enter into flow. However, many of us are pushed out of this optimal performance zone on a chronic basis into a stretch zone, meaning we are spending too much time in heightened physiological arousal driven by cortisol and other stress hormones. This is entirely functional for short-term events, such as exams, interviews or performing a cardiopulmonary resuscitation. However, if we hang out there too long, then we lose cognitive capacity and ability for emotional regulation and can easily tip over the edge into overwhelm and burnout.

Given the sheer amount of recent disruption in work and life, it is not surprising that any of us are spending too much time in the stretch zone. The consequences can be catastrophic. At a personal level, burnout can have *a negative impact on relationships and trigger depression or anxiety, substance misuse, addictions or even suicide. At a professional level, burnout is associated with a risk of increased errors, complaints, reduced productivity, increased sick days, and leaving the job altogether, which can have an impact on patients and the system as a whole.*

Predisposing factors

It seems that certain personality styles may increase an individual's vulnerability to burnout. Perfectionism and other personality traits such as conscientiousness (meaning you are highly organised, reliable and self-disciplined) and neuroticism (a tendency for anxiety, tension, moodiness) are weak predictors of burnout. Of course, these types of behaviour are highly valued in health, so maybe there's some baseline vulnerability for us all. Similarly, it seems theoretically likely that a past history of related conditions such as depression, anxiety and trauma would increase the risk of burnout.

Precipitating factors

Precipitating factors are the external triggers and situations that can spark burnout. There is so much about the health system that is complex, unstable and stress-inducing. Much of this is a recipe for overwhelm and burnout. We can try to modify our response to triggers, but at an individual level, their existence cannot be changed.

Perpetuating factors

I think of perpetuating factors as those that broadly involve the way we react to external situations. These, unlike precipitating factors, we do have control over and include factors such as maladaptive coping styles including unhealthy eating, substance misuse (alcohol or other drugs) or isolating ourselves from friends and family and other sources of support.

Perpetuating factors also include a having a pessimistic explanatory style with regard to external circumstances or events. This means having a habitual way of explaining external events as personal (my fault), permanent (it will always be like this, nothing will ever change) and pervasive (this affects everything, nothing is good).

It's easy to see how these very common responses serve to keep adding fuel and oxygen to the fire. While optimistic explanatory styles can be learned, it does take effort and practice.

Even more powerful than having a pessimistic explanatory style are the hidden beliefs, assumptions and 'shoulds' that control us without us knowing, like the way strings control puppets. These reflect the hidden curriculum and unstated cultural expectations and serve to keep us frozen in particular patterns of behaviour such as the inability to say no (even when it is possible to do so), turning up to work when we are sick, and feeling like we can never let anybody down (except ourselves, our families and friends). Unless these assumptions are addressed, it is very difficult to take time for a self-care routine.

Protective factors

Using asthma as analogy is a really useful way to think about protective factors. In asthma, the broad principles of management are:

- *Ensure the patient understands the condition and how it is managed;*
- *Identify triggers and reduce or avoid exposure to them if possible;*
- *Reduce reactivity to triggers with preventers;*
- *Manage symptoms with relievers that arise despite preventive steps;*
- *Ongoing monitoring.*

These principles can be applied to burnout.

Self-help is fantastic and, like asthma, the more a person is engaged and empowered in their own health, the better overall control there will be. But even with excellent self-management, there comes a time where professional support is necessary. Burnout is no different, and there should be no shame in seeking support for managing this.

Like keeping an eye on peak flow, monitoring ourselves for our personal signals of burnout is important. Despite the best asthma management plans, asthma attacks can still happen. So too with burnout. Given the ongoing nature of external triggers and precipitating factors, it may be that burnout is not 100% avoidable. No matter how good we are at stress management, or how resilient we are, there are some circumstances and situations in which recognising, preventing and responding to burnout becomes a lifestyle choice that we must take as seriously as managing asthma or other chronic diseases.

Dr Jocelyn Lowinger[1]

---

[1] Dr Jocelyn Lowinger's Reframing Burnout Can Help Us Manage It Better was first published in *MJA Insight Plus*, 31 August 2020: https://insightplus.mja.com.au/2020/34/reframing-burnout-can-help-us-manage-it-better/. Dr Jocelyn Lowinger has an Honours degree in Medicine (1994) and a Master of Science in Coaching Psychology.

Summary

Burnout is common amongst doctors; prevents us from enjoying our lives and puts us at risk of developing mental illness. By recognising the predisposing, precipitating, perpetuating and protective factors for burnout, we can prevent and manage this serious condition.

Sometimes we only need a good rest and a debrief rather than overthinking it, but at other times, it's difficult to slow our minds on our time off and we can feel overwhelmed and mentally exhausted. In these situations, we can challenge our common negative thinking patterns and unhelpful inner belief systems. Switching off after work is easier said than done if we are driven doctors, but we can understand more about our personality traits which deter us from rejuvenating ourselves on our time off.

Sleeping well naturally day or night

Sleeping well naturally is fundamental to being able to function well. For doctors, insomnia can significantly interfere with the quality and safety of our interactions with patients and colleagues and predispose us to mental illness.

When routine sleep hygiene strategies do not work, we can make the mistake of managing our sleep poorly. Self-prescription for insomnia occurs frequently amongst doctors, and dependence is more common than doctors may recognise. It is certainly not easy to achieve adequate and quality sleep when managing shift work, on-call rosters, exam preparation, young children and other family commitments. However, there are effective non-drug solutions which not only help us manage inevitable acute and chronic insomnia, but can relieve daytime stress, fatigue and sleepiness – naturally.

Why is insomnia common in doctors?

First, let us fully confront why we as doctors can develop intractable problems with sleep. As in all areas of medicine, it's important to identify and manage the root cause.

From early in our training, we work after hours, night shifts, and on call, often woken from a deep sleep with emergencies. We may have to take phone calls at all hours, and often need to attend to our administrative work late in the day on a brightly lit computer. We seldom have time to relax, meditate or exercise during the day due to our heavy workloads, including exam preparation after working long and challenging shifts. Given we rarely have time to process experiences during working hours, it is common to lay in bed ruminating about our interactions with patients and colleagues, clinical decisions and exposure to trauma, suffering and conflict.

Periods of acute insomnia are common and normal under these circumstances. However, if we respond to acute insomnia in unsustainable ways, chronic insomnia can become an unhealthy habit, which is harder to break as our careers progress. Disturbances in our body clocks do not respond to quick fixes.

DOI: 10.1201/9781003296829-9

The ICD 11 classification of chronic insomnia is defined as *'a frequent and persistent difficulty initiating or maintaining sleep that occurs despite adequate opportunity and circumstances for sleep and that results in general sleep dissatisfaction and some form of daytime impairment. Daytime symptoms typically include fatigue, depressed mood or irritability, general malaise, and cognitive impairment. The sleep disturbance and associated daytime symptoms occur at least several times per week for at least 3 months'.*

Compared to many of the complex illness and health conditions doctors treat each day, acute or chronic insomnia can be underestimated and its seriousness discounted. Often it is not until the conditions are personally experienced that the complexity of this biopsychosocial disorder is recognised and fully appreciated.

Why don't generic sleep strategies work in doctors?

While it's worth trying generic sleep hygiene interventions, do not be discouraged if these strategies do not work. Medicine is not a generic job.

It can be difficult or impossible for doctors to adhere to the well-known advice to avoid:

- Daytime or evening naps.
- Lying in bed ruminating or worrying.
- Work or stressful phone calls or emails immediately before bedtime.
- Rethinking about today or tomorrow's stressful events.
- Drinks containing caffeine or alcohol.
- Exercise near sleep time.
- Doing anything in bed except for sleeping and sex, such as reading.

It may not be easy to break the sleep/wake/insomnia cycle with the usual advice to only go to bed when sleepy, set a routine time for getting up in the morning, or schedule relaxation and physical exercise throughout the day (not just before sleep).

If these routine sleep hygiene strategies do not work, it's easy to slip further into the anxious cycle of fearing inadequate sleep and hence not coping or making errors at work. Doctors, who have easy access to prescription and over-the-counter medicines, are then at risk of making the mistake of reaching for a quick temporary fix drug treatment.

Short-term use of medications such as 'melatonin and sedating antihistamines can have a place, particularly when our body clocks are disturbed by night shifts. Any long-term use of sleeping tablets (particularly benzodiazepines) or alcohol will create dependence, addiction and tolerance. This is harmful and counterproductive – and against the advice of our medical regulators.

Self-medication is also unsafe when sleep disturbance is a symptom of mental or physical health problems, as these conditions require evidence-based treatment. For example, sleep apnoea may require investigation and treatment with continuous positive airway pressure (CPAP), and can have dangerous sequelae if managed with self-treatments such as sedating antihistamines or alcohol. Post-traumatic stress disorder and nightmares require an independent psychiatric assessment and comprehensive management, not self-prescribing of psychotropic medication.

When we manage insomnia poorly, we can predispose ourselves to major life and career problems – which can understandably create a downward spiral of further stress and anxiety. Chronic insomnia can then become a 24-hour problem.

The following section has been written for *Every Doctor* by psychologist Dr Giselle Withers, who has developed a specialised online sleep course, A Mindful Way to Healthy Sleep Program[2] (www.amindfulway.com.au). The program provides structured video-based modules teaching the five components of cognitive behavioural therapy for insomnia (CBTi), and includes formal training in mindfulness meditation. The program, which is summarised below, has been evaluated in an independent study by Monash University, Australia.[1]

How can we overcome these special challenges with insomnia?

Acute and chronic insomnia are highly distressing conditions that can leave people feeling helpless, powerless, and out of control. Not only can doctors feel ill-equipped to manage insomnia in their patients, particularly when dependency and tolerance issues with medication are evident, but their own experience of insomnia can feel even more alarming.

It can be helpful to remember that insomnia affects many doctors and is not a reflection on you or your ability to cope with stress. Nonetheless,

---

[1] www.amindfulway.com.au

sleep problems are often the first indicator that something is out of kilter in your life, and therefore it is worth taking the time to understand and examine the underlying causes.

Mindfulness and CBTi provide a holistic and biopsychosocial treatment to address the predisposing, precipitating and perpetuating factors of insomnia, with long lasting benefits and protection from potential future relapses. This is not a quick fix.

It takes time, patience and a willingness to support, trust and protect your body's natural sleep processes. This may require some changes to your sleep routine, including examining your relationship to sleep, as well as exploring new ways in which you can reduce mental, emotional and physical hyperarousal throughout the day, such that your mind and body can settle into an optimal state of calm and relaxation in the evening and during the night.

Mindfulness training for insomnia

Regular mindfulness practice improves sleep, but how and why does it help?

Mindfulness is an awareness that is cultivated by attending to the present moment in a particular way, which includes being openminded, flexible and non-judgmental. Mindfulness is often misunderstood as simply a tool for relaxation, or it is used to focus the mind to prevent rumination and worry. While it does have these benefits, cultivating mindfulness offers you much more than this. When you practice mindfulness regularly, you are actually developing a set of personal or attitudinal qualities that increase resilience, emotional intelligence and self-awareness. These qualities, often called 'mindfulness principles', include patience, trust, acceptance, non-judging, letting go, non-striving and beginner's mind, and it turns out that each of these qualities plays an important role in overcoming insomnia and coping with the daytime effects of poor sleep.

One of the key drivers of the insomnia cycle is an attachment to sleep and increased effort placed on getting to sleep. The process of 'trying' to sleep adds pressure to the situation, leading to more stress and frustration when sleep doesn't come, paradoxically making you feel more awake! A mindful approach to sleep is one in which you stop TRYING to get to sleep. This surrendering to wakefulness immediately ends the battle with insomnia, allowing you to calmly shift your attention to the immediate sensations of resting, and in doing so trusting that sleep will come eventually when the mind and body are ready.

The personal qualities developed through mindfulness practice not only help you manage insomnia at night, they also improve your resilience and capacity to regulate your emotions during the day, especially when facing demanding or challenging situations. If you can remain patient, openminded and non-judgmental, you are more likely to remain calm, non-reactive and clear-minded. Progressing through the day in this way reduces overall stress and physical tension (hyperarousal), which in turn makes for a better night sleep.

Mindfulness also increases your general self-awareness so you can better manage your mental, emotional and physical needs. This includes a greater capacity to recognise signs of sleepiness, so you can go to bed at the ideal time for sleep. The more you are in tune with your own psychological, emotional and physical needs, the greater the likelihood that you'll make the wisest decisions for your health and wellbeing. For example, if you are feeling tired or sleepy in the afternoon you could go for a quick walk, lie down for a rest or even take a short nap (if possible) rather than drink another coffee or reach for a sugar hit to stay awake. Recognising and balancing your own needs with the demands of your professional and personal roles protects you from overworking, chronic fatigue and burn out, and mindful self-compassion can help you successfully navigate this skill.

There are two components to mindfulness training: 'informal practices' such as mindfully walking in a park or mindfully taking a shower, or 'formal practices' such as sitting or lying-down meditations often practiced with guided meditation recordings. Both practices are important and time-poor doctors may find it easier to start with informal mindfulness practices (e.g., attending to any activity during the day with an intentional mindfulness awareness), and may find regular short formal practices (e.g. five mindful breaths, a three-minute breathing space or a one-minute practice of focusing on the breath between patients) a useful place to start, adding longer practices to a morning or evening routine over time.

When first learning meditation it is normal to feel overwhelmed by the sheer volume of thoughts running through your mind. When your mind is busy and overstimulated it can feel extremely difficult to stay focused on a single object, such as the breath, when it is not a goal-oriented activity. Noticing this phenomenon is an important step towards understanding your own mind and why you may feel so exhausted by the end of the day. It can also act as a motivator to keep learning, with 'mental calm' and 'inner peace' the treasured fruits of a committed practice. Structured mindfulness programs can help you navigate this process and overcome the common barriers for a smoother learning journey.

Cognitive behavioural therapy for insomnia (CBTi)

CBTi skills are a set of practical strategies that you can implement to set up the best conditions for healthy sleep, and the mindfulness training develops your mental and emotional capacity to respond calmly and wisely to each moment you face on the path to better sleep.

There are five commonly used cognitive behavioral strategies for acute and chronic insomnia (CBTi).

1. Cognitive therapy challenges unhelpful beliefs and thinking habits, which interfere with sleep cycles, such as fears of going to bed and not being able to sleep, missing out on sleep, and the consequences of poor sleep on the following day's performance. Worrying that you cannot sleep is one of the main causes of insomnia. A brain trick, called paradoxical intention, to break this frustrating repetitive thought, is to try NOT to fall asleep by keeping your eyes open for as long as you can.

2. Sleep hygiene strategies may include simple instructions such as avoiding caffeine and alcohol and reviewing environmental factors that may disrupt sleep – temperature, noise, light, etc.

3. Stimulus control strategies include avoiding non-sleep activities in bed (particularly reading, thinking about patients and exposure to screens, with the exception of sex), and getting out of bed if lying awake for more than 20 minutes, returning to bed only when sleepy.

4. Sleep consolidation or bed restriction involves limiting your time in bed to match your current average sleep time to increase 'sleep drive', provided you allow a minimum of six hours in bed each night. If sleeping patterns improve after a week, but there is a feeling of sleep deprivation, begin adding 30 minutes of extra time in bed and monitor for another four to five days. Continuing adding 30 minutes to your time in bed until feelings of sleep deprivation disappear.

5. Relaxation training involves focusing the mind on various relaxation techniques including progressive muscle relaxation, visualisation and breathing techniques, and can also reduce the anxiety associated with not sleeping. Reassure yourself you are benefitting from time taken to relax the mind and body, slow your pulse and breathing and lower your blood pressure even if you stay awake all night.

Mindfulness and CBTi interventions for insomnia are typically delivered by psychologists or clinicians with specialist mindfulness training in these treatment models. As access to other trained professionals can be difficult, online options are an excellent alternative and offer the flexibility to undertake the training in your own time and at your own pace.

A short mindfulness practice for acute and chronic insomnia

Close your eyes and take a few deeper breaths to bring your attention inwards. As you feel the breath move through your body, release any tension you may notice in the face, neck, shoulders, arms, torso, hips and legs. Allow *your breath to return back to its natural rhythm and practice observing it without needing to change or control it. If your mind starts to wander, gently bring your attention back to following the movements of the breath, releasing any judgments or self-talk during the process. It is likely that you will need to catch your wandering mind many, many times. This is completely normal and precisely the task of mindfulness meditation. The key is to be patient, kind and gentle with yourself as you practice.*

There is no need to use statements such as 'just relax' as this can set up expectations that can make you feel worse if it doesn't happen. You can start to feel stressed about feeling stressed. Instead, you can accept your active mind as normal and can experiment with creating some distance from your thoughts. Rather than trying to stop stressful thoughts, allow your thoughts to flow through your mind as you observe them from a distance. Some helpful metaphors for this technique are to imagine sitting by a river and placing your thoughts on leaves to watch them float down the river, or imagining your thoughts as text or images on a computer screen and slowly fading the screen's backlight until you can no longer see the words. After releasing thoughts, continue to bring your attention back to the present moment and notice the simple movement of the breath in your body, releasing any judgments and bringing acceptance to the moment. There is no need to achieve a particular state or even to feel calm and relaxed, though this is often an outcome, the practice is about moving from the 'doing' and 'thinking' mode to the practice of being in the moment without expectation. This experience can be deeply restful and when it boils down to it, you may come to realise that 'being in the moment without any expectations' is fundamentally an act of self-compassion, and where healing really begins.

Dr Giselle Withers[2]

A special note about shift work and sleep

Shift work can be challenging. In medicine, shift workers endure the expectation of consistent high performance despite being awake during an adverse

[2] Dr Giselle Withers is an experienced Clinical Psychologist, providing psychological therapy and counselling for adults and adolescents in Australia. She developed A Mindful Way to Healthy Sleep, an online course to help you sleep better and overcome insomnia, using the evidence-based, proven treatment approaches of CBTi and mindfulness.

circadian phase, and being subject to conditions well known to impair cognition and increase propensity for mistakes.

Shift work outside a diurnal rhythm is a major contributor to poor sleep in doctors. Acutely, it causes misalignment with our circadian rhythm, excessive sleep deprivation exacerbated by cumulative sleep loss, and impaired alertness and performance. The unconventional hours can be particularly isolating and lonely; leading to missed family and social gatherings, and even on days off, a feeling of perpetual jetlag preventing us from truly connecting with loved ones. Long term, the adverse impact of shift work can be even more serious, increasing the risk of cardiovascular disease, metabolic disease such as Type 2 diabetes, mood disorders and autonomic nervous system dysregulation.

Feelings of exhaustion and misalignment can become pathological if they develop into Circadian rhythm sleep-wake disorder (shift work type). In the ICD11, Circadian rhythm sleep-wake disorder, shift work type is characterised by '*complaints of insomnia and/or excessive sleepiness that occur as a result of work shifts that overlap with all or a portion of conventional nighttime sleep periods. The disorder is also associated with a reduction in total sleep time. The symptoms should have persisted for at least several months and result in significant distress or mental, physical, social, occupational or academic impairment*'. This under recognised yet common disorder can have serious health and social consequences, and diminish quality of life.

To protect yourself from the negative consequences of shift work:

- Be aware of how to recognise disordered sleep behaviour, and how it differs from the usual challenges of shift work.
- Do not feel ashamed to take a nap if you have downtime during a night shift. The literature suggests that those who take night-shift naps experience less fatigue and have better reaction times. Access to a clean bed for any doctor working a night shift is a basic workplace right.
- Try to practise good sleep/wake hygiene, mindfulness and CBTi, and consider an online specialised training course for insomnia before you experience problems.
- Talk to your doctor and consider seeing a sleep specialist if insomnia persists. If appropriate, there are pharmacological measures that can help under the supervision of another treating doctor.

Ultimately, shift work, like many aspects of medicine, is mentally and physically demanding – you are functioning in a hostile sleep cycle, and making difficult decisions whilst disconnected from your support systems. Be kind to yourself, and take a break if you inevitably need one.

Summary

Of all the activities we undertake in our lives, sleep is probably the least appreciated, unless, of course, we suddenly find ourselves needing it but not able to have it. In these moments we long for nothing else.

Acute and chronic insomnia are highly distressing conditions that can affect anyone at any time in their life. Doctors are particularly susceptible to insomnia due to our heavy workloads, long and irregular work schedules and limited opportunities for adequate rest and recuperation. There is no quick fix for chronic insomnia, and overcoming it requires changes to daytime behaviours and lifestyle patterns as well as nighttime routines.

We encourage doctors with insomnia to reach out for help, arrange an assessment with a treating general practitioner and undertake a formal mindfulness and CBTi program, such as A Mindful Way to Healthy Sleep (amindfulway.com.au). The combination of mindfulness training and CBTi provides the broadest possible set of skills to sleep well and function better during the day. Treatment takes time and patience, yet the skills of a structured insomnia program will have long-term benefits in many areas of life.

8

Nurturing loving relationships at home

My adult children told me that other people would often ask them if they were going to be a doctor like their dad when they were young. I wish I had known this earlier because I had deliberately avoided talking to them about a medical career for fear of pressuring them. Inadvertently, other people were placing big expectations on their small shoulders. On reflection, there are so many things I wished I had talked to them about when they were young children about my career, like why I was often late home and why I found it hard to switch off from work when I got home.

Retired Doctor

Doctors' families are of course as diverse as our profession. Throughout our busy and challenging careers, our families, including our partners, children, extended families and/or families of friends are our most important sources of love and support. And yet, unfortunately, these relationships may also be the first to suffer as we navigate the demands of our career, particularly during our long years of training. At times of excessive workloads or during the gruelling hours of exam study, our relationships may be pushed aside. This is unfortunate as talking about stress with our loved ones can be one of the most effective strategies for dealing with it. And good relationships do not just happen – they require time, communication, respect and love.

To complicate these challenges, doctors working at the front line have been justifiably concerned about the safety of those they live with, and many of us have been isolated from loved ones due to the risk of COVID-19 transmission.

In the next section, we focus on nurturing loving partnerships and parenting children. Many of these reflections can be applied to our extended families and our friends and their children.

Partnerships

The essentials of all great partnerships include love, shared values, mutual respect and the ability to compromise. Good communication, shared decision making, trust, commitment and intimacy all require time, but long working

DOI: 10.1201/9781003296829-10

69

hours can make this difficult. Understanding common sources of relationship problems can help us minimise the impact of our work on our relationships.

One of the most effective ways to resolve relationship issues is to recognise the way our personality traits can predispose us to tension or conflict. For example, an extroverted person who enjoys being with people may have to adapt to their introverted partner's need for solitude. A person who needs the security and certainty of making decisions may have to learn to compromise with a partner who prefers to be flexible and open to new opportunities. People who base their decisions on evidence alone may have to adapt to the needs of a partner who bases decisions on feelings. A healthy relationship is more important than being right all the time.

Here are some common patterns in doctors' partnerships which can lead to problems.

The driven doctor

Many doctors tend to have a personality characterised by obsessional traits, feelings of self-doubt and guilt, excessive fear of failure, hypervigilance in avoiding mistakes and an exaggerated sense of responsibility. These characteristics may be developmental in origin and reinforced during training, or a normal adaptation to excessive workloads.

A doctor's partner may feel dissatisfied with the relationship as the doctor becomes more immersed in work. As the partnership deteriorates, the doctor may immerse him or herself further into work, which of course is counterproductive.

The special doctor

'Special' doctors may work hard because of a pervasive need for status and to compete with others. Some develop overactive egos and arrogant behaviours.

At work, it is often necessary for doctors to be authoritative, decisive and in control, but these behaviours are rarely appreciated at home. Nor is it appreciated for doctors to be always preoccupied and talking about their work.

If doctors do not challenge the medical mindset of 'specialness', they risk allowing their identities to become completely defined by their work. This can only lead to unhappiness.

The career partnership

This is a partnership of two people with equally demanding careers. A common trap is when one career is valued over the other, often in unspoken ways, and parenting and domestic duties are not shared equally. Superficially, the couple live together peacefully, but there is a lack of balance in the relationship.

Female doctors are particularly vulnerable to this type of relationship. While their partner may share domestic and parenting roles, women doctors continue to carry a majority of the mental load of running a household. They juggle work and family (including extended family) responsibilities and may feel unjustified and harmful guilt at failing to meet their own and others impossible expectations.

Sexual relationships

Some of the most common but overlooked problems for any partnership are sexual problems related to differences in sexual desire. Sexual problems are commonly dismissed as the least of our problems, but they may herald the onset of major relationship issues.

The most common causes of relationship difficulties associated with sexual problems include the following:

- Inability to communicate about sex and difficulty in understanding each other's needs.
- Lack of privacy, wakeful children, after-hours calls.
- Preoccupation with the excessive demands of work.
- Fatigue or stress related to overwork.
- Anxiety about sexual performance.
- Not making time for sex.

The key is to anticipate that excessive work demands usually create discrepancies in sexual desire between partners, and to talk about this before it leads to a negative cycle of emotions.

It is important to find out specifically what increases and decreases our partner's sexual desire, and to freely express sexual needs in a loving way without pressing or rejecting our partner. Sometimes rest, relaxation and quality time are all that is required to restore sexual desire. At other times, more effort will be required to reconnect intimately.

If differences in sexual desire and needs are not communicated sensitively, they can develop into a major source of conflict within a relationship. If this negative cycle has already been established, a counsellor or a sex therapist may help to restore healthy communication.

Dealing with partner separation

Separation and divorce are among some of the most difficult experiences anyone can face. Most people survive separation and go on to live happy and fulfilling lives, but unfortunately, about half of those who remarry end up divorcing again.

Separation may not only mean loss of a partner, but loss of time with children and extended family, loss of the family home and community, loss of friends and social life, and loss of hopes for the future. It is natural to grieve over these losses and the future plans that once bought joy and excitement.

It takes time to rebuild lives and social networks. It is common to experience depression and it is important to seek support from family, friends and a general practitioner, maintain a healthy lifestyle, avoid drugs and alcohol, and try to continue normal routines and activities such as exercise and sport. It may also help to seek professional counselling and to attend partnering and parenting courses following separation.

Evidence-based parenting

There is no training for the most important job in the world – parenting. This common community myth is very wrong. There are many research-based training courses on evidence-based parenting.

What is evidence-based parenting? Research suggests that the most effective style of parenting is warm, respectful, loving, nurturing and flexible, but firm as well as appropriately autonomy-granting. With this caring but authoritative approach, parents encourage their children to make good choices consistent with their personal values, and to grow into healthy independent adults. As doctors, we are acutely aware of the protective benefits of evidence-based parenting in protecting our young patients from mental health problems and other major health issues.

Unfortunately, we may overlook some special pitfalls when parenting our own children as there is very little research on effective management of specific challenges in medical families. To illustrate some of the unique differences between medical and nonmedical families, here are a few interesting insights from doctors' young children into their parents' work:

Response from a five-year-old daughter of a female physician to a friend's question of whether her two-year-old brother is going to be a doctor when he grows up. *Don't be silly, boys can't be doctors.*

We thought he would diagnose us. Explanation by doctors' children about why they had avoided a psychiatrist guest at their family home.

When asked by her teacher what her breast surgeon mother does, a five-year-old responded, *Mummy cuts off sick boobies and puts new ones back.*

Mummy helps babies breathe and when she doesn't come home at night, a baby has died. Child of a neonatologist.

My mum is changing the world. Eight-year-old's response to his teacher about why his doctor mother can't attend the parent's open day at school with the other mothers.

When you ask a child or adolescent what they think about our work as doctors, their answers can be surprising, funny, flawed and sometimes sad. Their responses can reveal what often goes unsaid in doctors' families and why we need to continually talk to them about our work and why we do it.

Our children also absorb and learn from everything we do and say from a very young age – the way we deal with stress and sadness and interact with others, our physical and mental fitness, our attitudes toward people and our help seeking behaviours. They are highly intuitive, and if we have a distressing day at work, our families will sense a problem despite our best attempts to suppress our emotions at home. To address these issues, it can be helpful to consider how we are modelling our attitudes and behaviours, particularly in relation to our own mental and physical health. It can also help to talk to children openly about the challenges of our work, but also how much it means to have a loving family and sanctuary at home to sustain us.

What style of parenting raises happy, well-balanced and independent children and adolescents?

The following reflections on healthy parenting comes from the book *I Just Want You to Be Happy: Preventing and Managing Adolescent Depression* by Professor David Bennett, Professor Bruce Tonge and Clinical Professor Leanne Rowe, published by Allen & Unwin:

> Warm and respectful parents listen and reassure, but also make it clear when they disagree and for what reasons. They are high on warmth and mutual respect, but firm on consistent boundaries and family rules, while being sufficiently flexible to take account, within reason, of their child's level of maturity and development. Mindful parenting is about being fully

present with our children when we are with them by listening fully with our eyes as well as our ears.

> When I look back on my school years, the most important thing that helped was that my mum really listened to me. I just wanted her to understand but not to worry, or overreact, or do anything, or give me advice. She would sometimes stop the car and give me her full attention, or stay up late with me just talking on my bed. Most of all she would listen with her kind eyes. She didn't even have to tell me. I knew when she did this she really loved me.
>
> 18-year-old, reflecting on how her mother supported her most

Like all parents in senior positions at work, it is easy to adopt an ineffective, overly controlling authoritarian approach to parenting. At the other extreme, parents who juggle excessive work demands sometimes take a permissive approach to parenting to avoid conflict and to keep the peace at home. Sometimes parents swing inconsistently between the two extremes.

At one extreme, pressure cooker parents are low on warmth and high on control, frequently interfering in minor issues that, in the overall scheme of things are insignificant. Pressure cooker parents tend to believe that 'molly coddling' a child will interfere with their growing up into a successful, appropriately independent adult, and they often create a damaging emotional distance. At other times, parents can be overly intrusive, giving advice before listening and either squashing or inflaming conflict. Discipline and punishment are features of pressure cooker parenting, generally of the 'do as I say, not as I do' variety.

> My mum hates work and takes it out on us and then says, 'I'm doing all this for you'. I feel like saying, 'What exactly are you doing for us?' My parents get up, go to work, get dinner, clean up, get ready for the next day. I feel I should be grateful, but this doesn't feel like it's enough.
>
> 16-year-old, commenting on her distant relationship with her parents

In response to parenting that is meddlesome, inconsistent and lacking in warmth, children often withdraw in quiet resentment, give up seeking their parent's approval or display behavioural problems. The resulting fear of loss of control drives the pressure cooker parent to interfere more in their child's life. They may frequently comment on their child's friends and future ambitions as well as what their child should eat, drink, wear, study and do with their leisure time. These parents tend to believe that if they lose the small battles on the home front, they will lose total control. Unfortunately, they often lose a great deal more than control – it is the child of a pressure cooker parent who will find it very difficult to develop a sense of autonomy or identity, and is at higher risk of depression.

The anything goes parent, who is generally high on warmth but far too low on control, tends to raise children with poor social skills, insecurity and other similar behavioural traits. Without clear rules and boundaries to test out against, adolescents tend to seek their role models and guidance elsewhere, not always with satisfactory results. The anything goes parent is not only permissive, they usually use material rewards in a futile attempt to keep their children happy.

And, finally, uncaring parents are low on both warmth and control. In this neglectful or chaotic style of parenting, it is easier to give in to the child's demands to keep them quiet in the moment than to set healthy consistent limits, which may take time to negotiate and understand. In this type of family, the child is adrift without the support of secure attachments to their parents, and is at risk of mental health problems.

In summary, evidence-based parenting is warm, respectful and:

- *Nurturing: Loving, mindful parental involvement makes a child more responsive to parental influence, creates a secure sense of self and a kind inner voice that enables them to socialise effectively and withstand our harsh world.*
- *Firm: The combination of predictable support and clear limits helps with self-discipline. It allows the child to function as a responsible, competent individual, reduces exposure to risk and protects them from harmful, damaging experiences.*
- *Autonomy-granting: The negotiation of rights and responsibilities at appropriate ages through the journey of childhood and adolescence allows for a healthy independence, at the same time fostering social cohesion and strong connections with peers and community.*

Parenting pitfalls for doctors

I don't mind my dad working long hours. His work is important and it gives our family financial security, but it feels more important than us. What shits

> *me is the way he is always rushed, in a bad mood and preoccupied with tick-*
> *ing off his endless to do list. He feels guilty about being home late and then is*
> *not listening to us when he is home. He either overreacts to small things, or*
> *we get away with murder when he is tired – so I avoid him.*
>
> *17-year-old reflecting on his labile relationship*
> *with his father*

The children of medical practitioners are often assumed to have an absent doctor parent and an over-involved, unhappily married, non-medical parent. Doctors are increasingly changing this stereotypical view, and doctor parents are increasingly seeking better work-life balance to spend more time with their children for all the right reasons.

Unfortunately, the health system and our training programs can be intolerant of applications for part-time work or time off. This can be particularly challenging for doctors with babies and toddlers and when sleep deprivation is common. We must all continue to advocate at our workplaces and our colleges for more flexibility with working hours, competency-based medical education and appropriate study and parental leave. In the meantime, we must enlist as much support as we can from family, friends, like-minded work colleagues, child care and home help.

When feeling torn between work and family, any parent can feel a lot of unwarranted guilt, which in turn negatively impacts relationships at home and work performance. No parent should apologise or feel guilty for working hard. If we talk about what we are doing at work in a positive way with our children, we can encourage them to develop a strong work ethic and to become independent and autonomous. Working long hours is only damaging when a parent has poor boundaries between work and home, fails to convey how much they love their children, is emotionally distant from them, or displays an inconsistent parenting style because of their mental exhaustion as the quote above suggests.

Children of doctors can develop common mental health problems for the same reasons the general population does. This is another important reason for all doctors, not only those treating mentally unwell patients, to improve their mental health literacy and seek early professional help for their own mental exhaustion, burnout or mental illness (Chapters 20–22).

Medical regulatory bodies generally recommend that doctors should not treat themselves or their families, due to a lack of objectivity and discomfort with asking about sensitive topics or doing full physical or mental state examinations. On one hand, doctor parents can fail to seek independent medical or psychological attention for their children for fear of appearing over-concerned or neurotic about their offspring, and at the other extreme, bypass an independent treating general practitioner, referring directly to a specialist friend, who may tend to over investigate/treat for fear of missing something serious in a colleague's child. Our choice of a family physician or general practitioner could not be more important for these reasons.

Summary

Nurturing loving relationships with our partners, children, family and friends enrich our lives and sustain us throughout our long medical careers. Healthy relationships based on love and mutual respect can be an immense source of joy and support, but relationships do not just happen – they require time, communication, respect and love.

There are a number of common pitfalls and damaging behavioural patterns among doctors which can predispose one to dysfunctional family relationships. As medicine inevitably spills into our home lives, we need to make conscious choices about our priorities, including the care of our families, friends and our own health.

Our parenting style also matters and influences how children to grow into mentally and physically healthy, independent adults who are resilient in adversity. Evidence-based parenting is warm, respectful, nurturing, firm and appropriately autonomy-granting.

Trusting our own treating doctor

I called in sick because I had been vomiting and I was told, 'You don't sound that bad – you need to toughen up, princess'. After I gave myself an anti-emetic injection, I went to work, and it was implied that I wasn't pulling my weight. I'm a doctor and I don't have the right to take sick leave when I need it.

Anonymous Doctor

Traditionally, doctors have been staunchly reluctant to take sick leave. Although this was multifactorial, we overwhelmingly and justifiably felt that we just could not. It places burdens on colleagues and we feared our patients may suffer, particularly in workplaces where there is no redundancy plan for the absence of a team member, or in small self-employed medical practices. There is now a greater acceptance of the need to protect our own health and our patients' health to enable us to care properly for others. Nevertheless, many doctors continue to feel guilty for taking time off work and are unfairly expected to 'make up' for an absence from work.

We must have our own trusted treating general practitioner or family physician to help us make good decisions about taking sick leave, particularly when we are feeling vulnerable. No one will thank us for making a clinical error when we are unwell. It is also essential to have our own doctor to ensure we have access to comprehensive evidence-based preventive health assessment, early intervention for any medical or psychological problems and timely crisis management.

Despite this, many of us, if asked, will admit that we don't have our own doctor. Why do we often ignore the need to prioritise our preventive mental and physical health care? What are the reasons for this and how can we encourage doctors to seek help?

In the words of Sir William Osler:

The doctor who treats himself (or herself) has a fool for a patient.

DOI: 10.1201/9781003296829-11

Many doctors have fears about breaches of confidentiality, a dislike of waiting in other doctors' waiting rooms, and experience embarrassment when in the patient role. Some experience difficulty relinquishing control and fear being judged by colleagues as weak or unable to cope. Most do not like feeling vulnerable with a colleague.

Doctors may be particularly concerned about presenting to a colleague for a mental health problem and many accept poor levels of wellbeing, chronic stress and fatigue as the norm. Sometimes, it seems as if 'everyone feels like this', so why complain?

In corporate life, many professionals in senior positions routinely seek coaching, mentoring, leadership training and health assessments to maintain optimal performance. Many healthcare professionals, particularly psychologists, regularly debrief with a trusted mentor to ensure they maintain their wellbeing, particularly if exposed to trauma and grief. Unfortunately, doctors do not usually avail themselves to this level of support to stay healthy, despite facing significant challenges.

Sometimes, doctors underestimate the impact their mental ill health can have on themselves, their families and their patients. We may continue to work and function adequately while anxious and depressed, and we may not seek help until a crisis forces us to do so.

We know that some doctors will self-medicate and seek ad hoc treatment from medical friends, rather than accessing the optimal support, evidence-based management and ongoing monitoring they would recommend for a patient with mental health problems. Clearly, doctors should never self-prescribe, particularly with psychotropic medication as this is against medical regulatory authorities' guidelines. However, our main point here is that doctors too, deserve better mental health care.

An independent treating doctor is a necessity not an option

From early in our careers, we must develop a trusting relationship with our own family physician or general practitioner, and seek routine comprehensive preventive healthcare, including cardiovascular and diabetes risk screening, cancer screening and mental health screening. Regular health assessments provide an opportunity to develop a professional relationship with another independent doctor. When such a relationship exists, a doctor is likely to feel more comfortable attending early with mental or physical health problems, or for regular debriefing. An existing trusted relationship is even more important in a crisis situation or for trauma counselling.

This level of care is a basic requirement for all doctors and should not have to be mandated by medical regulatory authorities before being accepted as an essential part of a healthy medical career. Workplaces that employ doctors must allow them to take time off work when unwell to attend their own doctor. Having our own doctor also means we have an effective advocate if we need time off work.

The following suggestions about establishing a relationship with a general practitioner or family physician is authored by Dr Margaret Kay, an Australian doctor and researcher with a special interest in doctors' health.

Your relationship with your treating doctor

Being a doctor can make it difficult to accept the patient role. We are no longer talking as a colleague, nor as a friend. Instead, we are engaged in a therapeutic relationship and both treating doctor and doctor patient need to maintain that focus. Both doctor and patient need to set comfortable boundaries. Here are a few tips for making the relationship work:

- ***Accept the new role as patient**. Be honest about the fact that you are a doctor. It is common for doctors to feel that they need to hide the fact that they are a doctor to ensure that they receive 'normal care'. However, conversations about health inevitably declare our health literacy, so it is better to acknowledge your training. Telling your treating doctor that, even though you are a doctor, you would like to be treated as a 'normal patient' can help reassure your doctor that you are stepping into the patient role, enabling them to normalise the care they provide.*
- ***Be prepared to be uncomfortable**. All patients are! Patients are uncomfortable about the questions, about the examination, about the recommended investigations. This discomfort should be resolved through dialogue. If you don't understand something, or if you prefer to decline a specific test being offered, then it is best to have that conversation rather than simply not go back.*
- ***Establish your relationship** with your general practitioner or family physician before you develop health issues. Everyone needs*

a general practitioner for their physical and mental health, even when they are well. Developing that relationship requires the investment of time and energy. As a health literate doctor, it can be difficult to prioritise the time to establish this relationship, however it can be invaluable to establish a comfortable relationship with our general practitioner before we are facing complex health issues.

- **Address basic assumptions** that may arise within the doctor-doctor consultation. Self-prescribing, self-referrals for pathology, radiology and routine specialist care have been common practices within the profession. Be aware of the current regulations and codes of conduct governing such practices. Discuss your expectations with your general practitioner to avoid misunderstandings.

- **Strengthen the relationship**. Once we have established a relationship, we need to attend our general practitioner regularly. It may not be necessary to go often, but you should attend regularly. Give your general practitioner an opportunity to get to know you better to enable the development of rapport and the delivery of whole-person care and preventive medicine. This makes it easier to engage with the shared-decision required when health issues are complicated.

When choosing your treating doctor, here are some issues to consider:

Independence: If the doctor is related to you, someone you work with, or a colleague you interact with on a close personal basis, then this is not the best person to be your general practitioner, even though you trust them. They have an important, but different, role in your life.

Confidentiality: Do you feel that your confidentiality can be assured? If you have any concerns, then you should discuss how your confidentiality will be maintained with your general practitioner.

Geography: Consider how easy it is to get to the doctor you have chosen. Is this a reasonable journey to make if you are unwell?

Age: Does it matter to you how old your doctor is, whether they are younger than you, or older than you? Consider how you will manage the dynamics if there is a significant age difference.

Gender: Does it matter to you if the doctor is the same or a different gender to you, especially if they need to ask intimate questions or perform a more intimate examination?

Religious beliefs/Cultural background: Does it matter to you whether the person has specific religious beliefs or is of a specific cultural background? These issues can be important for some people while of no importance for others. When cultural dissonance is avoided, understanding and rapport may develop more easily, but sometimes confidentiality and independence can be more difficult to navigate.

Special interests: Sometimes we prefer a doctor who has a strong interest in a specific area of medicine such as mental health or women's health. However, we usually want our general practitioner to be ready to address a breadth of issues over the years.

Hours/after-hours backup: If you choose a doctor who works very part-time, then it may be difficult to get an appointment at a time that suits you. If you can't see your usual doctor, are you happy to see the others who work at that practice? Does your general practitioner have any after-hours arrangements and do you know what they are?

Cost: A frank discussion about costs is important to avoid misunderstandings. Do you have expectations about the cost of the consultation? Are you assuming that 'professional courtesy' will mean that you will not need to pay? Have you discussed the fee with your treating doctor rather than find your assumptions were wrong?

Style: Have you considered that your treating doctor may have a different style in their practice of medicine compared to you? Even if you enjoyed a friendly conversation at a meeting, this does not mean that your approach to a consultation will be the same. Be prepared for things to be different to your expectations. If you are worried that an issue is not being considered by your general practitioner or your general practitioner has not taken a full history, then be proactive and discuss this openly to ensure that these issues are addressed. Your doctor can't read your mind.

Dr Margaret Kay[1]

[1] Dr Margaret Kay is a General Practitioner, Fellow of the Royal Australian College of General Practitioners and holds an academic title as Senior Lecturer with the University of Queensland. Her PhD in Physician Health focused on doctors' access to healthcare and she continues her work in doctors' health as Academic Lead with Doctors' Health in Queensland.

Tips for doctors caring for doctor patients

- Be kind, listen and reassure your doctor patient about strict confidentiality.
- Take a thorough physical and mental health history, and perform a thorough physical and psychiatric examination if appropriate.
- Maintain empathy with objectivity and be aware of the risk of countertransference (this is when a doctor/therapist takes on the suffering of their patient often because they overly identify with their experience).
- Provide the option of a long consultation but avoid treating your doctor patients as VIPs. Ask them what their self-diagnostic ideas are, as you would any patient. 'What do you think is wrong?' is a reasonable question, but be objective and feel free to disagree with their conclusion.
- Do not assume the doctor as a patient understands all aspects of their own medical condition. Always explain management options fully.

Summary

It is critically important for each of us to have our own trusted doctor, given the many barriers we face in looking after our own mental and physical health. We are often under pressure to forego our own healthcare needs to fulfil our daily work demands. Unfortunately, all too often, we are also more willing to accept chronic stress, fatigue, depression and poor wellbeing as our normal functional state. Other barriers deterring help-seeking include fear of judgement and confidentiality breaches.

It is beneficial to develop a strong relationship with our own general practitioner/family physician before we become sick – for example, for regular preventive health checks, routine mental health screening and debriefing. Developing a strong therapeutic relationship with our own doctor means we have an advocate and a source of support in times of crisis.

Caring for doctors as patients does not necessarily require special skills. As with all patients, we must uphold confidentiality, listen carefully, provide optimal physical and mental health reviews and respond appropriately to our patients' high level of health literacy.

Every doctor promoting healthy workplace cultures, fairness and safety

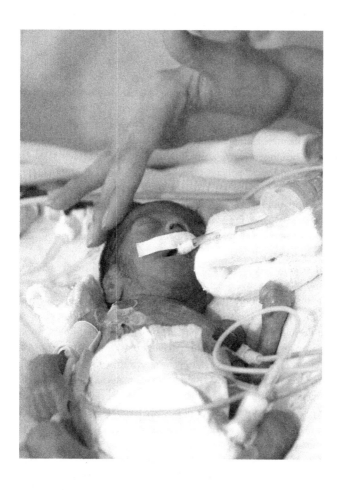

DOI: 10.1201/9781003296829-12

There are many examples of positive medical workplace cultures and healthy clinical teams that we can all learn from. Many extraordinary stories have emerged during recent public health crises in which doctors and other health professionals united to tackle impossible challenges and upheld professionalism throughout prolonged and extreme adversity.

Unfortunately, there are common human resource failings and administrative failings in every corner of our health systems. For too long, our chronically underfunded, fragmented and inefficient health systems have relied on the good will and altruism of clinicians to work in unfair, inequitable and unsafe environments at great personal cost. This has never been acceptable and it is no longer tolerable.

There are many reasons why health services often have inadequate human resource systems. From large hospitals to private clinics to remote community health services, human resources and technologies are underfunded and deprioritised compared with other pressing needs. As a result, basic human resources processes are often not in line with contemporary thinking or legislation. The most blatant examples of this are the chronic failures of hospitals and other health services to keep clinicians and non-clinicians safe by properly implementing robust policies on sexual harassment, discrimination, racism, bullying and whistleblowing. When health workers experience mental illnesses such as post-traumatic stress disorder and adjustment disorder as a result of being exposed to unsafe and traumatic environments, there is a harmful stigma deterring reporting of 'workplace mental injury' and a failure to adequately support them.

Other common examples can include biased or discriminatory application and interview processes resulting in lack of diversity in medical appointments; inadequate induction for new recruits; failure to provide well-fitting PPE; untenable and unsafe rosters including inadequate notice of rostering and inflexible shifts; failure to pay for on-call and after-hours work; unsafe clinician-patient ratios; expectation to work outside the scope of practice with inadequate supervision; expectation to return to work too soon after illness; poor approach to sick, study, compassionate, maternity and/or parental leave; inadequate education and training, mentoring, debriefing or communication about role expectations and lack of positive feedback; scapegoating of individuals for clinical incidents when health systems are at fault; and lack of security of tenure, to name a few.

Many of these issues impact junior doctors disproportionately because they are disempowered from complaining by senior doctors who are often quick to point out that this would be a career-limiting step, and 'things were much worse in the past'. Senior doctors therefore have a special role in advocating for contemporary human resources practices and humane treatment of early career doctors (Part 3 and 4).

Many countries are currently concerned about health workforce shortages, which have arisen from the reduced participation or mass departure of doctors and nurses. As a result, governments and health leaders are considering new strategies to address challenges in education and training, recruitment and retention. Unfortunately, one of these strategies is for comparatively wealthy countries to poach health workers from other nations who need them most, without first addressing common human resources failures in their health systems to retain existing clinicians. This is unethical and unacceptable.

As a profession, we have a responsibility to unite and advocate in our workplaces for human resources, fairness, equity and safety. We also have a responsibility to work together to address the issues we can influence at a local level, including:

1. Co-creating kinder cultures and clinical teams
2. Responding to challenging interactions with patients
3. Learning from mistakes, complaints and clinical incidents
4. Calling out conscious and unconscious biases
5. Eliminating discrimination, racism, sexual harassment and bullying
6. Confronting narcissistic personality disorder
7. Preventing and managing patient initiated violence

10 Creating kinder cultures and clinical teams

A wonderful, diverse and highly skilled team

As a newly graduated doctor, I worked in a community clinic providing care to people with HIV. This was in the early 1990s before effective treatments transformed HIV from being an inevitably terminal condition to a chronic manageable condition for many people. Working in general practice with people affected by HIV, I discovered something new about human existence every single day. I couldn't provide everything that my patients needed, but I could do so much more by working as a member of a wonderful, diverse and highly skilled team of healthcare professionals and volunteer carers. I experienced and valued the camaraderie between general practitioners that supports us in our important work. Being able to assist someone who trusts you and to care for them while they are supported to die with dignity is a very special privilege. I learned it is okay to cry with people who call you their doctor. I also discovered that wisdom came with experience. My patients of course knew more about their experience of their own condition than I did, and they became my greatest teachers.

Dr Michael Kidd

Those of us who have worked in healthy clinical teams will recognise the essential ingredients of strong collaborative clinical leadership and culture. Functional clinical teams recognise that this involves open, honest, constructive debate and feedback, based on objective analysis and clinical experience. They value healthy communication and diversity of thinking, recognise equal opportunity, treat people fairly and help them reach their full potential, continually investing in ongoing training and education.

Healthy clinical team members work in the best interests of the team rather than for the status of a few individual doctors. Effective clinical meetings have planned agendas and result in clear outcomes as meeting discussions encourage the participation of the whole multidisciplinary team. Clinical decisions are based on evidence and reasoning. High standards are expected but personal blame is not attributed to mistakes or errors, which are appropriately attributed to issues related to systems of care and regarded as opportunities for learning and continually improving.

Unfortunately, many of us have also worked in dysfunctional clinical teams, which are renowned for the arrogance and egos of a few doctors, and the quiet despair of their junior people who are competing to stay on the team. Dysfunctional clinical teams have a tendency to 'drown in their work' because they do not effectively tap into the knowledge and skills of all team members. There is often a lack of trust between team members, who struggle to solve complex clinical problems alone as they do not engage in debate or listen to diverse clinical opinions. Team members who express vulnerabilities are regarded as weak and blamed individually for poor patient outcomes.

> *The brutality of the medical culture needs to be addressed – the lack of support mechanisms and the sniping, the attitude that anybody with a mental illness is too weak, they're not fit to be a doctor. The caring profession needs to care for itself.*

> *Dr Mukesh Haikerwal*[1]

Superficially, there may be a veil of politeness, but team members behave in passive-aggressive ways, blame others, hold grudges and avoid or become defensive during difficult conversations or conflicts. Consequently, team members usually dislike or fear clinical meetings, especially junior members of the team who may be humiliated for their knowledge and skill gaps. Often there is a toxic culture where unconscious and conscious biases, bullying, discrimination and harassment are not called out.

Does your team display any of these traits?

Try this exercise

Here are some questions to ask yourself about the way you interact with your team at work. In the last week:

- What did you do to help or support a colleague, particularly if they are unwell?
- What did you do to acknowledge the good work of a colleague?
- What did you learn from a mistake?

---

[1] Dr Mukesh Haikerwal is an Australian General Practitioner, Past Chairman of the World Medical Association and Past President of the Australian Medical Association.

- Did you ask for advice from a trusted colleague?
- How did you improve your care of patients in response to their suggestions or complaints?
- Did you take time to say good morning and goodbye every day, welcome a new colleague, congratulate a colleague's achievement, celebrate a colleague's significant work anniversary, or say a special farewell to a colleague who is leaving?

Five ways I know when I have had a good day in my practice

I've asked the right questions and at least one person has cried and at least one person has laughed in my consulting room.

I've had at least one person tell me the real reason why they have come to see me.

I've learned something new about human existence.

I've increased my medical knowledge.

I've cared about what happened to each patient and each colleague I have seen today.

Dr Michael Kidd

Responding to inevitable conflict and criticism

Our medical practice is a deeply dysfunctional, unhappy place, where most doctors don't say good morning and avoid contact in the staff room. Some of us disagree about patient care. Others about practice management and money. But the real problem is that we avoid debates and disagreements, and tension festers.

Anonymous Doctor

Objective peer review, constructive feedback and robust debate are essential to continually provide the highest standard of patient care. Differences of opinion are healthy in medical practice. This is how we learn. For all these reasons, we must become as expert in communicating and managing inevitable disagreements and conflict as we are in our clinical knowledge and skills.

We all know this academically, but in practice, egos and conflict over differences of opinion can be difficult to manage. During times of intense stress, working long hours and dealing with angry, anxious patients and exhausted colleagues, clashes with peers are inevitable.

How can we respond to workplace disharmony with colleagues constructively?

Try this exercise

Next time you are involved in a conflict with a colleague or group of colleagues, try to:

- Leave your ego at the door.
- Regard the experience as an opportunity to build a stronger relationship with your colleagues, rather than avoiding conflict or disagreements.
- Remain calm and appropriately assertive. Ask if it is possible to have healthy differences of opinion and express them respectfully.
- Begin the conversation with statements like 'I hope we can create a trusting relationship where we can give each other constructive feedback'.
- Or statements like 'Thank you for the feedback', 'I can see we both want what is best in this situation', or 'I appreciate you have high standards'.
- Objectively establish the facts of the situation to ensure there is no mis-understanding. Try to understand if the conflict has arisen as a result of misinformation, poor communication or personal differences.
- Listen to understand, without interrupting. Understand the other person's intentions. Are they being constructive? What is really behind the conflict? What are they really trying to say?
- Reassure your colleague that you understand why the conflict has arisen by saying 'I can see why you would be concerned/upset over this. I'll bear that in mind in the future to prevent any misunderstanding'.
- Ask for specific examples so that you can better understand the issue. Try: 'Thanks for raising these issues so we can talk about some solutions'.
- List all the possible solutions to a conflict or problem together and then weigh up the advantages and disadvantages of each solution objectively. Choose the best solution together – if it does not work, try negotiating again.
- Agree on finding an outcome that you can both support. This may require mutual compromise.
- Be clear on the issues that you cannot compromise on. Be open to changing your opinion as more facts emerge.
- Implement the agreed solution, and agree to review it later to determine if it is working.

Ask later: 'Is everything OK now? How can we work together to prevent any misunderstanding happening again?' If the conflict becomes heated or personal despite these strategies:

- Acknowledge any strong feelings on either side.
- If you are being interrupted, ask if you may finish your sentences.
- Refer back to the issue at hand if there is any personal attack.
- Take responsibility for your own feelings by using 'I' statements like 'I feel hurt . . .' and 'I feel distressed . . .', rather than 'You make me . . .'
- Also try: 'I do not agree with your assessment', 'It is unprofessional to attack me personally', and 'I'll discuss this with you when you are ready to communicate calmly'.
- If the conflict becomes destructive, it may be best to engage professional mediation.

Think about a recent difficult conversation and your reaction. Did you cut it short? Did you acquiesce when someone showed a display of authority, attacked your integrity or yelled? Did the encounter trigger something from your past? Did you back down?

Try experimenting with your next conflict by remaining professional, listening fully and stating your rationale without emotion. Persevere with your point of view even if others behave inappropriately. Try reviewing your response using the points above. What did you find helpful?

> *Honest differences are often a healthy sign of progress.*
>
> *Mahatma Gandhi*

A harm minimisation approach to negative behaviours

Healthcare is increasingly complex. One of the contributing factors to negative behaviours and poor cultures in medicine is the complex interplay of different personality types in very stressful situations. Some doctors have personality traits that predispose them to having interpersonal conflict and being unable to see the situation from the perspective of others.

In this challenging environment, it is critical to understand what constitutes poor behaviours and bullying, and what doesn't. Routine performance review, justified criticism of suboptimal clinical management or an occasional short temper due to sleep deprivation are clearly not bullying. As we will explore further in Chapters 14 and 15, bullying is repeated, unreasonable behaviour directed towards someone that creates a risk to their health and safety. Sometimes this is difficult to prove.

For an effective complaint of poor behaviours or bullying to be made, evidence of the following should be documented: repetitive verbal abuse, threats or yelling; unjustified criticism; physical or mental intimidation; repetitive behaviours such as excluding, ignoring, isolating or belittling; giving people impossible tasks or timeframes; deliberately withholding information that is vital for effective work performance; spreading false rumours or lies or back-stabbing.

In an ideal world, poor behaviours in medicine wouldn't exist, but if they occurred, they would be dealt with quickly and constructively by the clinical team with an optimal human resources intervention. In an informal or formal complaints process, a senior member of staff would try to mediate the situation and meet with the complainant, alleged perpetrator and witnesses separately to ascertain the facts and to take appropriate action.

Unfortunately, we live in a less than ideal world. Sometimes, a perpetrator and their target are brought together for mediation at the outset, which is inappropriate if the behaviour has been abusive. At these meetings, perpetrators usually deny bad behaviour and question the competence, mental stability or integrity of their victim, which adds to the trauma. Alternatively, a mediation may appear to resolve issues, but the whistle-blower is later 'punished' by the perpetrator in passive-aggressive ways.

To avoid being held to account, perpetrators often conduct their abuse privately or in subtle repetitive ways that are difficult to document. Unless there is written or other evidence of bullying, it can be difficult for a complainant to prove damaging behaviour without witnesses. But others may prefer to stay neutral for fear of career damage. Bad behaviours and bullying thrive in environments where good doctors say nothing.

How can we respond early to poor behaviours or bullying before they become harmful and without being unfairly accused of being sensitive or vexatious?

It can help to speak privately to the most senior person you can trust and say something like:

> *May I speak to you confidentially? I have noticed these unacceptable behaviours in X. I am not going to make a formal complaint, I can deal with them, but I am*

concerned that someone else will. Please talk to X privately to make them aware of the impact of their behaviour. These behaviours need to stop.

The most senior person may be another doctor, a medical director, a human resources or practice manager, a chief executive officer or a board member. It must be someone who can influence change. Then, here is the important part: Remain objective when your trusted senior confidant tries to dismiss your concerns. Pre-empt their resistance, which usually comes in the form of questions such as this:

Are you being oversensitive? Did you do anything to provoke this behaviour? Can't you stand up for yourself? Why has no-one else made a complaint about this?

Or comments such as:

You need to muscle up. I would never let that happen to me. I have never seen those behaviours.

Respond calmly and professionally to any inappropriate responses like those above, with statements such as this:

I am very tolerant but I will not tolerate these negative behaviours because they are harmful to other doctors, staff and patients. As I said, I will not make a complaint but someone else might. Do we want that to occur on our watch?

X's behaviour usually stops with a quiet word and no-one gets hurt.

For more information on responding to challenging behaviours together, refer to Chapter 13: Calling out conscious and unconscious biases, Chapter 14: Eliminating sexual harassment, discrimination and bullying and Chapter 15: Confronting narcissistic personality disorder.

Summary

Healthy clinical teams centre around strong collaborative leadership, honest communication, robust debate and an overarching goal to provide excellence in patient care while caring for colleagues and promoting positive workplace cultures. Disagreements and conflicts are inevitable in medicine and require a calm, professional response.

In creating healthier clinical teams, we challenge the stifling hierarchies and unforgiving cultures perpetuated by some medical workplaces. Despite the medical profession's commitment to care for others, caring for colleagues can often be lacking. This may manifest through unrealistic work expectations and teaching by humiliation.

Dysfunctional clinical teams may be dominated by egotistical individuals, where there is a lack of collaboration, trust and listening between members. As a result, these teams are often overworked and demotivated, creating a toxic work environment with high levels of unresolved conflict and poorer outcomes for patients. This must be confronted.

11 Responding to challenging interactions with patients

This woman had no real medical history but was simply suffering from the depredations of antiquity and abandonment and she was monosyllabic in her responses and gave a history of no substantive content. Nothing it seemed had ever really happened to her. She had lived a singularly unexciting life as a hotel maid. I asked the woman how long she had lived in San Francisco and her responses went like this:

Years and years.
Was she there for the earthquake?
No, she came after.
Where did she come from?
Ireland.
When did she come?
1912.
Had she ever been in hospital before?
Once.
How did that happen?
Well, she had broken her arm.
How had she broken her arm?
A trunk fell on it.
A trunk?
Yes.
What kind of trunk?
A steamer trunk.
How did that happen?
The boat lurched.
The boat?
The boat carrying her to America.
Why did the boat lurch?
It hit an iceberg.
Oh, what was the name of the boat?
The Titanic.

I believe it is our duty as those who teach young physicians to identify medical students with a gift for curiosity and take infinite pains to encourage that gift. Not only will patient care be enriched, but so will the lives of

DOI: 10.1201/9781003296829-14

these physicians and the vigor of our art and science. Besides, it will be much more interesting.

Emeritus Professor Faith Fitzgerald[1]

The late Emeritus Professor Fitzgerald's story provides us with a powerful message about the benefits and joys of truly listening to our patients' stories.

Communication skills

From early in medical school, we are taught that good communication skills are critical to quality patient care, preventing patient complaints and avoiding medicolegal action. Doctors receive communication skills training throughout medical school, in specialist training programs and through medical defence organisations.

Most doctors therefore know that the basics of active listening involve:

- Trying to understand what the person is really trying to say by fully listening first.
- Restating what you have heard from the other person in your own words, beginning with something like this: 'Let's see if I understand what you're saying . . .'.
- Trying to be neutral and non-judgmental in your answer and your body language.

Professor Emeritus Philip C. Hébert describes this beautifully in his reflections on the art of medicine:

You Talk and I Will Listen. The art of medicine, the art of caregiving, means learning the art of 'presence'. Presence is looking into someone's eyes, placing your hand in solidarity on their arm, speaking to them directly and with authentic feeling. To be ready to respond to human suffering – to learn how to care – you have to learn how to listen. And active listening strengthens the bond between physician and patient; it makes it more likely that the bond will hold – will be resilient, bend but not break – in bad times as well as good.[2]

---

[1] The late Faith Thayer Fitzgerald was an Emeritus Professor who devoted nearly four decades to educating the next generation of physicians at the UC Davis School of Medicine.

[2] Professor Emeritus Philip C. Hébert is a Canadian family physician, bioethicist and the author of *Doing Right: A Practical Guide to Ethics for Physicians and Medical Trainees* and *Good Medicine: The Art of Ethical Care in Canada.*

Unfortunately, the reality of medicine is such that there is limited time to do this. Instead, it is common to see many doctors avoiding eye contact, interrupting, dismissing and ignoring patients and colleagues. If we take short cuts while listening, we are prone to mistakes, which are likely to be time consuming when other consequences emerge.

It is important to remember that our underfunded healthcare systems and health workforce shortages impact both patients and doctors, and set us up for relationship tension. A challenging interaction often results when a patient who fears a serious diagnosis has experienced a long wait or has been treated poorly in the past. A doctor who has been forced to 'squeeze in' additional patients over meal breaks or after hours to cover chronic workforce shortages may be more likely to appear brief, rushed and defensive when questioned or criticised. In these situations, it is the underlying health system dynamics that are challenging, not because the patient or their doctor are unreasonable or poor communicators.

While a masterclass course in communication and empathy training may assist, it is our genuine willingness to explore the root cause of our patients' justifiable tension or anger which will help us to manage challenging interactions in crowded hospitals and consulting rooms.

Being 'terminated' by a patient can be one of the most difficult interactions in medicine. Here is a story from Tim Baker, author of *Patting the Shark*, which describes why he terminated his treating oncologist and what we can learn from our patients about what matters in our interactions.

Physician heal thyself? After four years of treatment for stage 4 cancer I just wanted some encouraging words from my oncologist

My oncologist has one of those little motivational prints hanging on his waiting room wall, with the simple statement, 'Trust Your Instincts'.

One day, bored with the long purgatory of the waiting room, I tweet this news to the world with the observation: 'If I trusted my instincts, I'd run screaming from this place and never come back'.

I'm only half-joking. I don't wish to appear ungrateful for the miracles of modern medicine, without which I very probably would not be alive. Yet the routine of the oncologist's visit feels deeply dispiriting.

I sit and wait for anywhere up to an hour or more, in an atmosphere thick with dread and stress and anxiety, whiling away the time on my phone *or with a trashy magazine, until my name is called. My oncologist takes a cursory glance at my latest blood test results, usually tells me to continue the medication I'm on, writes me a script for another blood test and tells me to come back in four to six weeks.*

The final straw comes about four years after my diagnosis of stage four metastatic prostate cancer, as I stand up to leave another perfunctory 10-minute consultation after an hour's wait.

Something just doesn't sit right about all this. It's my life hanging in the balance. I have been through radiation therapy (reasonably tolerable), chemotherapy (seriously debilitating), hormone therapy (made me almost suicidally depressed) and surgery (harrowing but quickly over with).

The lack of opportunity for a more wide-ranging conversation about treatment options, how I'm holding up emotionally and strategies to miti- gate the life-sapping side effects of treatment just feels wrong.

I walk towards the door, pause, turn and announce, 'Oh, one more thing.'

My oncologist does not appear pleased by this development. He has a waiting room full of patients and is already running an hour behind schedule.

'It's been four years now. I work really hard at this,' I begin tentatively. We're entering uncharted territory. I'm talking about my feelings and expect- ing him to respond, a betrayal of our unspoken doctor–patient contract up to this point. I press on regardless.

'I follow a strict diet, exercise and meditate daily, do everything I can to support my health. How do you think I'm doing?'

I pause, opening the way for him to offer some soothing words of encouragement. He briefly ponders this unscripted moment, as if I've just told a joke he doesn't quite get.

'About average,' he eventually declares, coolly. 'Some of my patients are doing better than you, some worse. You're about average.'

His response seems designed to ensure I never again have the imper- tinence to ask such a question, or to attribute any therapeutic powers to my own lifestyle interventions. Even if this was his sincerely held professional view, would it have killed him to say something vaguely positive like, 'It's great that you are being so proactive about supporting your health'? Or a kind-hearted white lie, even if he didn't actually believe it: 'You're doing great. Keep it up.'

I have no reason to doubt my oncologist's professional expertise and deep knowledge of his chosen field. But I've become frustrated by his uninter- est in anything I might be doing to support my own health, or any research or suggestions I've come across for credible supportive or adjuvant treatments, all of which are swiftly dismissed.

More than anything, I'd like a bit more evidence that he cares, which must be hard to deliver when he's seeing dozens of patients every day at roughly 10-minute intervals, many with conditions far more dire than mine, most of whom he won't be able to cure. Compassion fatigue is real.

I eventually took the advice of that wall-mounted print in my oncologist's office and trusted my instincts.

I sacked my oncologist and found a new one more open to discussing my own lifestyle strategies, showing empathy and concern for my mental struggles and quality of life along with my cancer.

Research has shown doctors in general, and oncologists in particular, suffer from poor mental health and are less likely to seek evidence-based treatment for it than the general population. Does it strike anyone else as sadly ironic that one of the most dire health issues of our times is presided over by a profoundly unhealthy physician population?

The current model of cancer care serves no one's best interests, leaving complex patient needs unmet and exacting a cruel toll on clinicians. We are all – patients and doctors alike – casualties in the war on cancer.

Tim Baker[3]

Valuing all patients' voices

What is required is a pause to value the voices of patients and their carers, particularly those who are frequently unheard, such as a parent with a terminal illness who has young children, a child with a disability, a woman with poor literacy or an elderly man with morbid obesity. Older people with cognitive issues may require extra time to ensure they can make informed choices, and people from culturally and linguistically diverse backgrounds may require increased sensitivity to cultural beliefs about treatment. Often, a doctor may be the only person someone feels they can completely trust and confide in, and we need to be conscious of this. In all our interactions with our patients, we need to remember the healing nature of kindness and focused attention in all our interactions with patients.

---

[3] Tim Baker is an author, journalist and PhD candidate at the School of Philosophy at Griffith University. This is an edited extract from *Patting the Shark* by Tim Baker, published by Penguin Random House Australia.

Professor Ronald Epstein,[4] at the University of Rochester School of Medicine and Dentistry in the United States, describes mindful practice like this:

Mindful practice in medicine is more than meditation and personal growth. Being mindful is when I know to stop briefly, look at a patient in the eye, and ask, 'Have I got it all, or is there more?' and the patient, whose previously well-controlled diabetes is now uncontrolled, then tells me he hasn't been taking care of himself since his wife died six months ago. It's when I inject an inflamed shoulder joint – with focused attention, visualising the bones, tendons and muscles – and the needle slides in easily and painlessly. I'm being mindful when I notice that a patient doesn't look quite right, not her usual self, and then I notice a fatigued expression and a faint rash that are clues to her new diagnosis of lupus. Attending to each patient means that I remember that, although the last patient I saw only has days to live, the next patient – with a stubbed toe – needs the same focused attention.

If you think you don't have time to pause and listen, remember that you will save time if you communicate effectively because you are more likely to make the right diagnosis and make optimal decisions about patient management. If you think you are too busy to be kind, it is time to talk to your own treating doctor about the negative impact of your burnout on your patients and your life.

Why are our patients angry?

Anger is a common emotion in healthcare. This health service sign sends an important message to patients, their families, and all healthcare workers including doctors as well as health administrators:

Please take responsibility for the energy you bring into this space.
Your words matter. Your behaviours matter. Our patients and teams matter.
Take a long slow breath and make sure your energy is in check before entering.
Thank you.

Health service sign designed by Indiana University Health

---

[4] Dr Ronald Epstein is a Professor of Family Medicine, Oncology and Medicine (Palliative Care) at the University of Rochester School of Medicine and Dentistry in New York. He is a family physician and palliative care physician, writer, researcher and teacher of communication and mindful practice in medicine, as well as author of *Attending: Medicine, Mindfulness and Humanity* (www.ronaldepstein.com).

As mentioned above, patient anger may relate to prolonged waits or lack of access to basic healthcare – or intense fear, grief or a past negative experience in another health service or with another doctor. It may be in response to a serious diagnosis, rudeness from other members of staff, an adverse event, or a perceived lack of support from family, friends and doctors.

Recent public health crises have left many of our patients even more vulnerable than before. With elective surgery delayed, follow-up appointments deferred to telehealth, chronic illness management neglected and resources devoted to managing coronavirus at the expense of other essential services, patients have waited longer than ever before for their basic healthcare needs to be met. It is important to acknowledge this, and reassure patients we understand their resentments.

When we bear the brunt of patient anger, we need to react without taking this personally or criticising another colleague. It is rarely helpful, and usually destructive, to openly criticise another doctor's management to a patient because the facts of the past can be unclear. When a patient is angry or a patient arouses anger in us, it is important to listen carefully, objectively assess the situation and consider the underlying cause. A calm question like 'I sense you are angry. Can you tell me what is happening?' will often diffuse the situation and help our patients articulate very significant fears. Statements such as 'That must be very difficult for you', 'I am sorry you are feeling like this', and 'What can I do to support you?' can help our patients communicate their justified anger without directing it at us.

Sometimes patients with specific personality types are more likely to display anger and frustration because they feel misunderstood and they are unable to assertively communicate their needs. Here are a few examples of common personality types:

- A patient who is preoccupied with details may have a tendency to be rigid and only undertake treatment with excessive cautiousness.
- A patient who is hypersensitive to disapproval may have difficulty presenting for healthcare because of their fear of negative evaluation or rejection.
- A patient who has a strong need for reassurance may have a tendency to seek frequent consultations.
- A patient who displays a lack of emotional responsiveness may be reluctant to talk about their problems.

> *As doctors we are as diverse as our patients. Those patients we find difficult can push our individual buttons in different ways. I have often discovered that one doctor's 'heartsink' patient can be another doctor's joy.*
>
> Dr Michael Kidd

Vexatious patient behaviours

Doctors must recognise when a patient or a colleague's behaviour is sociopathic or vexatious because an effective response requires a different approach from managing justified anger.

Unreasonable complainant behaviours are demanding, persistent, uncooperative or aggressive through unreasonable anger, abuse, intimidation, threats or violence. Their communications are often relentless, out of proportion, voluminous but vague, and they often misconstrue communication from others. They seek reparation and retribution, but are rarely satisfied with offers of resolution. In these situations, it is particularly important for doctors to support each when personally targeted by a querulant or vexatious complainant.

Querulant (morbid) complainants are relentlessly driven by a 'pursuit of justice' or 'perceived injustice', and their complaints cascade over years, often devastating the lives of their victims and their own lives. Vexatious litigants often repeatedly institute a diverse range of legal proceedings without reasonable grounds.

Doctors who are targeted by unreasonable complainants require the support of their colleagues, workplaces and skilled mental health professionals to help them set firm boundaries and limits, and to debrief after encounters and attacks. Medical defence organisations can also help doctors manage the legal aspects of vexatious or sociopathic attacks.

For more information about de-escalating patient anger and preventing and managing patient violence, refer to Chapter 16.

Summary

Good communication skills are critical to quality patient care, preventing patient complaints and avoiding medicolegal action. Despite our best efforts, some patients carry vulnerability and anger with them due to past experiences and may have difficulties establishing a trusting relationship with their treating doctor.

While a masterclass course in communication and empathy training may help, it is our willingness to understand and accept our patients' frank feedback which will assist us with challenging interactions most. Many patients are justifiably angry with the access blocks in the health system and being rushed in consultations.

Other patients may possess challenging personality traits and behaviours that may predispose them to making complaints. We will all meet vexatious litigants and patients with antisocial traits, and need to identify them and respond appropriately with the assistance of our medical defence organisations. In these situations, it is important to seek the support of our colleagues, work cooperatively with our peers and have access to a treating family physician, general practitioner or a skilled mental health professional with whom to routinely debrief.

Learning from mistakes, complaints and clinical incidents to improve care

I presented a complex patient history on a Zoom call to 15 other doctors. One by one they criticised my treatment, using a condescending tone, as if 'it should be obvious' I had made an error of judgement. Each of them also disagreed with each other, without coming to any agreed consensus on a way forward. This confirmed to me that treatment decisions in this case were not black and white and there were multiple options rather than mistakes in management. None of them seemed to realise that the goal of our meeting was to engage in constructive peer review in the best interests of my patient, not a clash of egos about who was the smartest person on the call. The only thing I learnt from this was to stay under the radar and to battle on with complex cases alone.

Anonymous Doctor

Healthcare is complex. There are many thousands of diagnoses and treatments – it's a lot to get wrong, which is why peer review is so important. But too often, doctors are quick to criticise the clinical management of colleagues rather than engage in constructive feedback or debate about the pros and cons of treatment professionally. It is usually easy to see clearly in retrospect with a full analysis of the patient outcome what should or should not have happened in the past. This is much easier in the light of day, and much harder in the fog of a difficult presentation or during the dark of night.

Despite knowing all this intellectually, mistakes can be harrowing experiences for doctors, and made much worse by harsh or humiliating responses from colleagues. Perhaps because we pride ourselves in maintaining very high standards, one of the most stressful situations in medicine is if we are suddenly on the receiving end of a patient complaint or medicolegal action.

Patient complaints

It can be difficult to uphold a caring approach to all patients, particularly in a crowded public healthcare setting or when patients challenge us. It is impossible to be the kindest doctor every single time, especially when juggling time and administrative burdens, all the complex demands of patient care. When we fail to live up to the high expectations and complex needs of our diverse patients, we will inevitably receive complaints. We are not superhuman.

Tips for responding to a patient complaint

- Try to re-establish patient trust by having a prompt face-to-face meeting. Listen fully. Use a concerned, sincere tone, take your time during the meeting and offer to work with the patient to address the situation together.
- Establish the facts behind the complaint and the factors that led to the complaint, to deal with the patient's concerns and identify any changes that can be implemented to prevent this happening to another person.
- Establish what the patient expects to happen after the complaint. Apologise if this is appropriate.
- Validate a patient's anger by saying 'It must be very frustrating for you'.
- Provide relevant clinical information and document the process of dealing with the complaint. Ask if there is anything else the patient needs to know about or if the patient requires any other support.
- Discuss appropriate ways of dealing with the payment of accounts. For example, it may be appropriate to waive payment. Do not send accounts for incorrect treatment.
- Provide options for ongoing medical care and consider referral to another doctor if required.

It is also worth taking time to observe what is really happening in our waiting rooms and on our front desk telephones. Poor communication at medical reception is a common cause of patient dissatisfaction and may be another source of complaints. Staff training on customer service is especially important in a medical context where patients may feel sensitive and anxious.

Clinical incidents

The human body is not a machine, and it does not always operate in predictable ways. Clinical incidents and treatment complications are therefore inevitable. Open, honest, timely and caring communication with patients and their families is encouraged in this situation. Patients need to be reassured that any clinical incidents are being taken seriously and responded to by the doctor concerned to prevent a recurrence.

Medicolegal action is more likely if a situation has been handled insensitively, or if there has been delayed or poor communication. To lower the risk of medicolegal action, we must contact our medical defence organisations immediately after a clinical incident, and before open disclosure or an apology is offered. Medical defence organisations will usually advise against making any admission of liability or error of judgement, particularly before all the facts of the case are known.

Expressions of sympathy do not constitute an admission of fault. We can say to our patients, 'I am upset about this outcome' without admitting negligence. We may express regret for what has happened by saying 'I am very sorry this has happened'. Many patients wish to be reassured that an error will not be repeated and may seek compensation if they believe this is the only way to raise awareness about a medical mistake. Others may take medicolegal action to punish the doctor or to raise money.

Whether a clinical incident involves a near miss, an adverse event or a sentinel event, we must also recognise the way the system in which we work might predispose us to making mistakes, by requiring us, for example, to work long hours or without adequate supervision and training. After any clinical incident, it is important for a hospital or practice team to undertake root cause analysis to determine the cause and contributing factors, in order to identify and manage systems issues and avoid repeat incidents.

Sometimes this involves identifying clinical training needs, performing clinical audits and examining the systems that have contributed to a failure such as processes for reviewing investigations, infection control procedures, and the management of confidentiality and privacy. While being involved in these investigations and peer reviews can be personally challenging, they are a routine process to maintain the highest standards of safety and quality in healthcare.

Doctors have become more aware of the importance of proactive clinical risk identification and the management of quality and safety in everyday practice. It can be a time-consuming process to be involved in clinical governance, but most doctors understand the importance of regular formal meetings with colleagues to continuously improve the quality and safety of patient care and to prevent future clinical incidents.

Because we care about high standards, we can be overly harsh with ourselves and other colleagues after a clinical incident. Unless we receive support in these situations, we can be more likely to practice defensively and order unnecessary investigations, refer to other specialists for minor issues and consider leaving our practice or retiring early. Doctors can also suffer high levels of depression and anxiety following a significant clinical incident, even if there is no wrongdoing.

It is essential to seek supportive debriefing from trusted colleagues, treating doctors or psychologists and medical defence organisations. Sometimes the best response to a colleague who is devastated by an error is 'I have made mistakes and recovered and you will too'.

Professor Cynthia Haq, an American family physician and Chair of Family Medicine at the University of California Irvine, describes her harrowing experience of making a mistake with some profound lessons about forgiving, hoping, living and dying with courage and dignity.

Nine words

I'm sorry

> As I reviewed the small mountain of reports on my desk, one gave me pause. I had just returned to my small-town family practice after an extended leave of absence. Pat had lung cancer.
>
> Pat was a 78-year-old beloved patient for whom I had cared for more than a decade. She was a dairy farmer, mother of six, interior designer, and one of the best pie bakers in the county. Reports from the hospital and oncologist confirmed widespread metastases. Pat had declined aggressive treatment. She was receiving palliative care from hospice under the supervision of an oncologist. I called Pat to express my concern. Her response was lukewarm. I offered help if she desired.
>
> A few days later I spoke with the oncologist. He provided details and added, 'You might want to check the records. The primary lesion was detected years ago, but there was no follow-up. Someone dropped the ball'.
>
> What had happened? I reviewed Pat's electronic record, including reports from a hospital stay more than three years ago for pulmonary emboli following knee surgery. The computerized tomography (CT) report described extensive bilateral infiltrates and a possible small nodule in the base of the left lung. Follow-up was recommended, but no follow-up was obtained. A chest X-ray report from a visit more than a year ago with one of my partners revealed a left lower-lobe pneumonia and suggested follow-up to ensure resolution; no follow-up was obtained.
>
> Pat presented infrequently for care and usually only if something was wrong. There was no indication in any of the notes that the abnormality was noted. Pat had not been informed of the findings. Who was responsible for identifying, discussing, and following these issues – the hospital team, my

partners, or the radiologists? None of these was to blame. As Pat's family physician, it was my responsibility to follow up abnormal tests. I had made a serious mistake.

I was afraid, ashamed, and confused. Had Pat rejected me because of this mistake? Was she angry? Would she sue me? What was wrong with me? Was I a bad doctor? Could I be trusted? Had I made other serious mistakes? What was wrong with our healthcare system? Was the mistake due to pressure to see more patients more quickly? Did the conversion from a paper chart to an electronic medical record contribute to the error? Would early detection and treatment have changed the outcome? What should I do?

Forgive me

Discussion with a trusted colleague helped me sort out my thoughts. Yes, I had missed a finding. No, we will never know if early detection would have changed the outcome. Yes, I should share this information with the patient and apologize. I took a deep breath, called the patient, and asked permission to visit her at home. She agreed. It was a quiet, bright, sunny day.

Pat was lying in bed in a darkened room with mildly laboured breathing. I kneeled at the bedside and took Pat's hand. She wept when she saw me. She said she had no pain but was very tired. She was worried about her husband of nearly 60 years, who had also been ill, and distraught about conflicts with many family members who were not on speaking terms. I listened.

Finally, I shared what I had come to disclose. I had made a mistake. I did not note the possible nodule on the CT scan. I was sorry that Pat had cancer. I was sorry that I had not fulfilled my responsibility to provide her with as much information as possible so that she might have taken action sooner. I did not know if this would have made a difference in the outcome.

Pat's immediate response was, 'It's not your fault that I have cancer. If you had found this earlier, I might have had four terrible years, instead I had four good ones. You did nothing wrong.'

I emphasized that yes, I was indeed responsible for not noting the nodule on the report, for not discussing it with her, for not providing options for further evaluation and management. She repeated that no, I was not to blame. I was forgiven.

A tremendous load was lifted from my shoulders. Since Pat had forgiven me, perhaps I could forgive myself and continue as her doctor through the end of her life.

I love you

I took another deep breath and continued. 'Pat, I have known you and your family for many years. I care about you. May I continue to be your doctor?'

I wondered if Pat could trust me with my imperfections. Pat immediately responded, 'Of course. You're my doctor. You know me. I want you to care for me. The oncologist is fine, but he doesn't know me.'

One week later we conducted a family meeting in Pat's home with her husband, children, and the hospice team. Another deep breath: 'We are here because we love Pat. None of us is perfect. There are no perfect families. Yet because of Pat's love, forgiveness, and courage, we have this precious gift of time together.'

We discussed Ira Byock's four things that matter most at the end of life (saying 'Please forgive me', 'I forgive you', 'Thank you' and 'I love you'). Pat expressed her love and hopes: for the family to be at peace, to celebrate the good times, and to support one another in the difficult times to come. Pat died less than two days later.

Thank you

In her quiet and simple way, Pat taught us profound lessons about accepting the unexpected, forgiving, celebrating, hoping, and living and dying with courage and dignity.

I'm sorry. Forgive me. I love you. Thank you.

Professor Cynthia Haq[1]

Summary

Despite our best efforts and intentions, we can make mistakes that can leave our patients unhappy and adversely affected. Facing review of complaints and clinical incidents can be difficult and stressful, and subsequent medicolegal action can have serious consequences on our confidence, mental health and performance.

It is important to engage in open and honest communication with patients and make time for a sincere face-to-face conversation with them to offer open disclosure. Such interactions allow us to clarify the relevant facts about why an adverse event has occurred by earnestly listening to our patient to understand their expectations, validating the patient's frustration, expressing regret and sympathy and discussing mutual goals to help re-establish a trusting professional relationship.

---

[1] Professor Cynthia Haq is an American Family Physician and Chair of Family Medicine at the University of California Irvine. This extract was first published in *Family Medicine* 2006;38(9):667–668.

It is also important to recognise that many clinical incidents are the manifestation of systemic failures in the health system, which need to be identified through root cause analyses and rectified with supervision, training and systems changes rather than blaming individuals.

We must confront the realities of the risks associated with practising medicine and reach out to supportive colleagues for debriefing after inevitable mistakes, patient complaints and clinical incidents. We can also contact our medical defence organisation early as this can be a major source of support.

Saying sorry can be powerful. In most situations, patients forgive us for our errors. We can also practise self-forgiveness for being human.

Calling out conscious and unconscious biases

Cultural awareness is the recognition and acknowledgement that we are all cultural beings, and that this may affect our interactions with patients, their families and our colleagues. Cultural sensitivity is the conscious attempt to understand the possible influences of culture and cultural differences on interactions between patients, their families and ourselves. Cultural competency is the ability to identify and challenge one's own cultural assumptions, values and beliefs, the development of empathy for people viewing the world through a different cultural lens and the application of specific communication and interaction skills that can be learned and integrated into clinical encounters. There is a growing body of evidence to support the need for cultural competence among health professionals to positively influence clinical consultations and health outcomes.

Professor David Bennett[1]

There is extensive medical literature on the patient harm, including health disparities, caused by unconscious and conscious biases of health professionals in relation to gender, age, sexuality, race, culture, physical and mental disability and certain characteristics such as obesity. In this chapter, we focus on the common conscious and unconscious biases of doctors towards other groups of doctors.

Conscious or explicit bias occurs when there is a deliberate attempt to discriminate against a person or a group of people based on certain differences. Unconscious or implicit bias involves a lack of awareness of inadvertent prejudice, and although it may be unintended, it can be more harmful than explicit bias and result in disparities in healthcare. No one is exempt from unconscious or implicit bias. It is an automatic form of cognitive processing which draws on

---

[1] Professor David Bennett is an Emeritus Consultant in Adolescent Medicine at the Children's Hospital at Westmead and an Adjunct Professor with the University of Sydney. He established Australia's first hospital-based adolescent unit at the Royal Alexandra Hospital for Children in 1977 and developed innovative community-based services for young people at risk, advocating strongly for the health and medical care of children at this formative stage of life.

DOI: 10.1201/9781003296829-16

our attitudes to shape our pre-conceived perceptions and assumptions about people. It is extremely dangerous to assume that we, no matter how open-minded and educated, are immune to unconscious bias, and needn't be constantly working on recognising and challenging it.

Doctors often regard themselves as being proudly egalitarian and ethical. We increasingly understand how to effectively deal with overt bullying, sexual harassment and discrimination between colleagues at work (Chapter 14), but sometimes we find it difficult to respond to insidious biases or subtle exclusion between colleagues.

Training is recommended to help all doctors become more aware of the dangers of stereotyping certain groups of patients and colleagues, and to commit to treating everyone with understanding and respect. Doctors cannot be experts in all the intersecting cultures they encounter in their professional lives, but we must display an ongoing cultural curiosity, sensitivity and humility, as well as an ongoing commitment to learning about diversity and inclusion.

Despite our awareness of the benefits of recruiting and retaining a diverse medical workforce, doctors from racial and ethnic minorities continue to report feeling isolated, experiencing microaggressions and being tasked as race 'ambassadors' to represent their entire demographic group. We clearly require more than lip service and diversity committees to overcome these common experiences of bias and discrimination.

As individuals, we can diversify our circles to include people with disabilities or people of other racial groups, gender identities or sexual orientations. We can read books by diverse authors. We can try to focus on individuals, put ourselves in other's shoes and challenge our stereotypes. Most of all we can call out any conscious or unconscious biases, instead of walking past and turning a blind eye.

Practical tips for responding to unconscious bias

- Value all voices.
- Challenge outdated role stereotypes and labelling.
- Focus on capability and competence not superficial appearance.
- Call out disrespectful language and jokes.
- Be aware that seemingly harmless comments may trigger painful feelings in people who have been subjected to chronic low-grade bias.

Bias is a big topic. There are so many forms of conscious and unconscious bias that it would require another book to cover them all. In this section, we focus on examples of common conscious and unconscious biases by doctors towards other doctors in relation to gender and sexual orientation. In the next chapter, we comment on racial stereotypes.

Gender bias

Cultural stereotypes often characterise women doctors as kind, helpful, supportive, nice, modest, collaborative, self-deprecating, gentle, soft spoken, compassionate, understanding, compliant and nurturing. In their role as doctors, women may receive push back from both male and female colleagues and other staff when they display behaviours usually attributed to male stereotypes. Women who are authoritative, strong and efficient violate their gender stereotype and may be unfairly accused of being controlling, bossy or dominating. At the other extreme, they may be told they are too weak or emotional if they show sensitivity. They walk a tightrope of labels, as they are perceived to be either too assertive or too passive, too aggressive or too soft.

More commonly, female doctors are unconsciously held (and perhaps hold themselves) to higher standards than men and are expected to prove themselves time and time again. They may be asked about their plans to have a family in job interviews and unfairly labelled as less committed to their work after they have children. Women are often invited to join committees to provide a gender balance, but find their opinions are not welcome, particularly if they do not agree with the status quo. Women doctors are more likely to experience income inequity and fewer opportunities to be promoted to medical leadership roles than men although they have equal qualifications.

The slow grind of 'everyday sexism' is difficult to tolerate, and can accumulate to exhaustion and burnout. Very often, the biases may seem too trivial to call out, and if women complain, they risk being labelled as overreactive or difficult. The repetitive nature of unconscious gender bias may be harmful as the stereotyping of women interferes with their full participation in the workplace and the advancement of women at all career stages in medicine.

Unfortunately, gender bias training may not be effective, particularly when it places the onus on women to change in order to overcome negative stereotypes, attitudes and barriers. It has to be called out by others. What we have to ask ourselves in our everyday work is: 'would this comment, attitude or behaviour be appropriate if it were directed towards a man?'

Medical women also experience high levels of anxiety, depression, bullying and violence, compared with the general population and male doctors. These issues are at the tip of the iceberg of gender bias, sexual harassment and discrimination and have been prominently documented in the medical literature for decades, without significant progress.

Sexual orientation bias

Sexual and gender minority groups are underrepresented in medicine and commonly individuals do not disclose their sexual identity for fear of discrimination. Although difficult to prove, a degree of unconscious bias and lack of recognition for achievements of doctors of sexual minority groups persists, which is in some ways more difficult to challenge without being labelled as 'over sensitive'. Here is a story by Michael Kidd to help us understand this experience from a personal perspective.

> *I found my first year at university was a real challenge. I was used to being one of the clever kids at high school but at university I was swamped by really clever people. I had moved out of home, was working part-time and trying to keep up. It was a tough year. I started to feel really anxious. It all seemed too hard. I started to spend the day hiding under the blankets rather than heading to uni for lectures or prac classes.*
>
> *Fortunately, I had made some great new friends at university who rang me to find out where I was. They tried to tell me that what I was experiencing was normal. They were all feeling anxious about exams and their progress as well. They were all finding it hard, even the people I thought were brilliant and knew all the answers. I went to see a doctor at the university health service, a great young woman, who immediately diagnosed that I was depressed and together we started some treatment which helped me turn the corner. I had a couple of sessions with a counsellor but we didn't hit it off, mainly because as a young person, I thought if he wasn't going to ask the right questions, I wasn't going to own up to what was really worrying me.*
>
> *One of the main reasons that I was having trouble coping was because I was coming to realize that I was gay. It was something which had been obvious to many of my family members and friends since I was a toddler but it was a part of me that I had always denied. I eventually decided during my first year at uni that it was time to come out as a gay man although several of my friends advised me to keep quiet about this, because, believe it or not, having sex with another man in Australia in the 1970s was against the law and if I was charged and convicted, it could mean the end of becoming a medical practitioner.*

I have to tell you that my years as an openly gay guy didn't last long. A couple of years later there were newspaper reports about gay men in the United States starting to die from a new disease called Gay-Related Immune Disease, or GRID. A huge wave of fear gripped the world. In Australia we had the Grim Reaper campaign which whipped up fear. A group of babies were found to have contracted HIV through blood transfusions taken from a donation from an HIV positive gay man. One Member of the Australian Parliament stood up in Parliament and recommended that all homosexually active men in Australia be quarantined on an island. It was not a time to be openly gay if I wished to graduate as a doctor in a very scared and homophobic society.

It's amazing where our careers as doctors can take us. In my first year at university as a young gay medical student I had no idea that I would become a general practitioner working mainly with people with HIV, that I would spend time working with child victims of the Chernobyl nuclear disaster in the former Soviet Union, that I would have the opportunity to teach in countries like Uganda, Sri Lanka, Malaysia and Saudi Arabia, that I would give a talk in the grounds of the temple where the founder of western medicine, Hippocrates, had his own clinic and taught his own students, that I would become a consultant to the World Health Organization and have the opportunity to influence health programs and health policy around the world, that I would spend time working in South Africa setting up clinics to test and treat people with HIV living in some of the poorest rural communities in the world, that I would become an advisor to a succession of Australian Health Ministers, that I would find love and be able to marry my beautiful same-sex partner and live together as openly gay men, that 20,000 doctors would vote for me to become the President of their Royal Medical College, twice, and that doctors from over 100 countries would vote for me to become the President of their Global Organization.

If things get tough, and you feel more like hiding under your blankets than going to lectures or prac classes, please don't give up. If you are feeling sad or anxious or exhausted or just can't cope, please go and speak to one of the doctors or counsellors at your university health service. It is normal to have good times and bad times as a medical student. If you find that you are drinking too much for your own good, or engaging in other risky behaviours that put your health at risk, seek some support from your friends or from a trusted doctor or counsellor or from a member of staff. You may feel alone at times but you are never alone. You are part of a wonderful community of people who care about you and your wellbeing.

Remember each of us is able to make a positive difference to our world every single day, through the way we live our lives, through the care that we show to other people, through the passion that we have for doing what is right. Don't lose your passion. You are going to make a difference.

Dr Michael Kidd

Summary

Medicine is certainly not exempt from harmful stereotyping and conscious and unconscious biases. While incidents of explicit harassment and bullying are increasingly identified and addressed as they are unlawful, subtle repetitive everyday bias often goes unchallenged and can result in harm to the health and career outcomes of those affected.

Displays of conscious or unconscious bias by doctors towards other doctors or anyone else in relation to gender, age, sexuality, race, culture, disability and physical characteristics such as weight have no place in medicine. Please do not walk past bias – it must be called out.

14 Eliminating discrimination, racism, sexual harassment and bullying

Healthy workplaces provide caring, inclusive cultures that do not tolerate poor behaviours, discrimination, racism, sexual harassment or bullying (also see Chapters 10 and 15). Unfortunately, because they know overt discrimination, racism, sexual harassment and bullying are unlawful, perpetrators tend to target their victims with low-grade, repetitive abuse and coercive control, which is difficult to document. It can therefore be difficult for victims to make sense of what is happening over time or to prove recurrent negative behaviours, particularly if there are no witnesses to verify incidents.

All organisations, including hospitals, clinics and health services, have a legal responsibility to ensure that their workplace is safe and free of discrimination, racism, sexual harassment and bullying. Vicarious liability means that an employer may be found to be liable for the damaging behaviours of its employees. For all these reasons, doctors must be aware of safe workplace policies and undergo routine occupational health and safety training.

Here are some steps to take if you believe you have experienced discrimination, racism, sexual harassment or bullying:

- Know the definitions of discrimination, racism, sexual harassment or bullying, and document your experiences over time. This may be in the form of emails or personal records of telephone calls or meetings.
- Write a formal letter detailing the facts of repeated incidents to the most senior person in the workplace, which is usually the chief executive officer, people and culture manager or the practice principal. If you do not wish to disclose your identity, you can submit an anonymous whistle-blowing complaint.
- It is the responsibility of the person who receives the formal complaint to meet individually with the person making the complaint, separately from the alleged perpetrator to establish the facts.
- If the evidence is clear, a formal apology must be offered by the perpetrator, and it may not be appropriate for this to occur face to face. Sometimes the

DOI: 10.1201/9781003296829-17

complaint results in the termination of the employment of the perpetrator and it may be appropriate for the complainant to remain anonymous to avoid retribution.

- The organisation or practice must ensure that the person who has made the complaint and other staff are not subjected to recurrences of discrimination, racism, sexual harassment or bullying. This can be achieved by revising policies and procedures and providing mandatory training to staff.

Here are some definitions of discrimination, racism, sexual harassment and bullying.

What is discrimination?

Discrimination includes direct discrimination and indirect discrimination. Direct discrimination occurs if a person is treated less favourably than others because of a personal characteristic such as race, age, gender, disability, sexuality or a medical condition such as obesity.

Indirect discrimination occurs if a requirement, benefit, condition or practice is imposed that treats everyone in the same way and appears neutral, but which significantly reduces the ability of people with a particular personal characteristic to comply with or benefit from it.

Discrimination in any form is unlawful. It has no place in medicine, or anywhere else in the community.

Racism is often defined as the belief in the superiority of one race over another, which results in discrimination and prejudice towards people based on their race or ethnicity. However, this definition has limitations, which are discussed in the following story on implicit systemic racism in medicine by an anonymous medical student.

> As a medical student, every eight weeks I rotate through a new specialty in a new hospital or health service. This means every eight weeks I flick over to a new chapter in my textbook, learn a new set of medical lingo, meet a new team of doctors, and a new cohort of patients. As a person of colour, however, this translates to something far more challenging yet predictable. It means responding to 'where are you from?' followed by 'but where are you really from?' when the answer fails to adequately explain my brown skin. It often means responding to 'your name is too hard to remember; do you have a nickname?' with something conveniently anglicised for my supervisors to remember. It means constantly dispelling the notion that anything other than a white culture is homogenous; no,

I don't love cricket and no, my mum does not exclusively cook curries. It means feeling confused when my white colleagues can simply introduce themselves as medical students and be judged in a professional capacity while I am frequently in the background still justifying the colour of my skin.

To many, these conversations may sound perfectly benign and even well intentioned. They don't make your skin crawl and your stomach churn like blatant racial attacks. I could write about the patient who insisted I leave her room during morning rounds because she only speaks to white doctors. Or the patient who demanded my Muslim colleague remove her hijab before beginning a consult. Or the patient who asked me if I could even speak English while I wrote in his chart. While these experiences are traumatising, overt racism is paradoxically easy to distance oneself from. We let ourselves simply implicate the ignorance of individuals, rather than challenge the overlooked systemic nature of implicit racism.

I have always thought that racism stems from ignorant assumptions. In my experience, overt racism seldom occurs amongst educated health professionals. But implicit systemic racism persists, impenetrable to the protections of a higher education or the health system.

My most hurtful experiences as a person of colour have come from medical colleagues far more learned than me. From the residents, registrars and consultants who reject the notion that they can be racist, because they assume that racism is about subscribing to the idea of biological white superiority, which they do not. And from my white colleagues who feel the need to assure me that racism plays no part in medical workplaces or medical schools.

Morally rejecting the idea that white people confer biological superiority to non-white people is not enough. There is a general lack of acknowledgement that white privilege is omnipresent in medicine; that naïveté alone acts to discriminate against people of colour. In fact, if we do not understand racism as a social construct underpinning our everyday behaviours, we continually underdiagnose what it means to be racist. We continue to be complicit, through our daily actions or inactions, in the reproduction of systemic racial inequity.

Daily actions like staying silent when our colleagues face racial slurs from patients, or defining our colleagues by their skin colour before their medical skills and accolades. Daily actions like forming generalisations about racial groups and leaving it up to members of those racial groups to prove otherwise or defend themselves.

I recently sought guidance from an Indian-born physician on how to succeed through these daily challenges that grind away at my professional and emotional sense of worth. I thought that given his success in medicine, he could offer some advice. My heart sank when his response was to simply ignore it.

I refuse to ignore the racism masked within the foundations on which our medical workplaces operate. We all deserve a work environment in which we can feel truly accepted and thrive – a work environment where we stand out for our professional abilities rather than our perceived otherness.

But people of colour cannot succeed alone in quiet defiance. Our voices require the amplifying volume of the majority. Everyone must acknowledge and challenge everyday implicit racism and break the silence of white complacency in our workplaces whether they be medical schools, hospitals, general practices or other community health services. And when I feel safe to attach my name to my views without fearing career repercussions or racial vilification – I know we will have achieved this.

Anonymous Final Year Medical Student

What is sexual harassment?

Sexual harassment is any unwanted or unwelcome **sexual** behaviour which makes a person feel offended, humiliated or intimidated. Examples of sexual harassment may include:

- Offensive verbal comments and offensive jokes with sexual connotations
- Propositions or lewd gestures
- Making promises or threats in return for sexual favours
- Displays of sexually graphic material including posters, cartoons or messages left on notice boards, desks, computer screens or common areas
- Repeated invitations to go out after prior refusal
- Sex-based insults, taunts, the spreading of rumours, teasing or name-calling
- Unwelcome physical contact such as massaging a person without invitation or deliberately brushing up against them
- Sexually explicit conversations
- Offensive phone calls, voicemails, letters, emails or text messages or computer screen savers

Sexual assault is defined as a sexual act in which a person is coerced or physically forced to engage in a sexual act against their will or non-consensual sexual touching of a person.

The following piece by Dr Leanne Rowe is a sad reflection on some outdated and unacceptable attitudes to sexual harassment in the medical profession.

Things we don't say or do in medicine anymore

'. . . in a multiple-hour hernia repair surgery, I was told that since I am the only female in the room that it is my job to hold the patient's testicles throughout the entirety of the procedure'.

This was written by an anonymous female physician who said she was squeezed by the cheeks, kissed and endured other forms of unsolicited touching and inappropriate sexual advances by consultants as a medical student. She called for other doctors to speak out about sexual harassment in her article, but there was a poor online response from only four male doctors. Among their public comments were the inappropriate 'joke' – 'Sorry but what "cheeks" are we talking about?' and 'My opportunities have been gazumped by confident flirtatious female colleagues'. Another doctor wrote: 'There is a large contingent of female grads coming out of med schools now, that enter the workforce with girded loins and judging everything through an irritating gender lens – sometimes even infantilised by "trigger alerts"'. The thread continued on the topic of women doctors not pulling their weight and taking time off work to care for their children with the comment, 'Clearly the biological imperative of who bears the children is never going to go away, so we just have to deal with it.' The final response to the story was about 'standing up for yourself' with this conclusion, '. . ., when it comes to being harassed, one has to learn to stand firm, which is something no-one else can do, or be, for another'.

Let's be clear, sexual harassment, bullying and discrimination are unlawful and should never be tolerated by anyone. Despite this, we continue to hear stories of unacceptable behaviours by doctors, which may be why subtle repetitive forms of everyday bias are commonly overlooked in medical workplaces. Perhaps perceived as too small or stupid to waste precious time on, doctors may let them pass.

At other times, there is no question when unacceptable comments overstep the mark, such as in the anecdotal comments above from the four male doctors, which ignore what the medical and other literature tells us about the prevalence of sexism in medical workplaces.

Repetitive everyday sexism is sometimes difficult to call out. Sometimes there is 'eye rolling' when women speak, or we may hear 'she talks too much' when the reality is that women are often less likely to dominate workplace discussions as much as men because fewer women hold leadership roles or chair meetings. Many women can also report being repeatedly

*ignored, dismissed or misconstrued, such as what happened to the anony-
mous female physician writing on an important topic.*

*We can no longer ignore the medical literature on the resulting
high rates of stress, depression and suicidal ideation amongst women
doctors, and the disproportionate lack of women in medical leadership
roles, although females represent over 50% of the medical cohort in many
countries.*

*It's time for the medical profession to consider Duke University's cam-
paign on 'Things You Don't Say', encouraging staff and students to identify
inappropriate comments in everyday language which stereotype and discriminate against both women and men based on gender, age, sexuality,
culture, religion, disability and even obesity.*

*What are the things you don't say or do in medicine? Will you call out
major and minor harmful comments and behaviours regardless of a doctor's
status or gender? Will you stand firm and can you do that for another?*

Dr Leanne Rowe

What is bullying?

To sin by silence, when they should protest, makes cowards out of good men.

Abraham Lincoln

Workplace bullying is repeated, unreasonable behaviour directed towards an
employee or volunteer that creates a risk to their health and safety. The following types of behaviour, where repeated or occurring as part of a pattern of
behaviour, could be considered bullying:

- Verbal abuse
- Constant criticism
- Excluding or isolating an individual
- Psychological harassment (for example, isolating someone by preventing
  others from befriending them)
- Intimidation
- Derogatory comments
- Assigning meaningless tasks unrelated to the job
- Giving employees impossible assignments
- Deliberately changing work rosters to inconvenience particular individuals
- Suppression of ideas

- Deliberately withholding information that is vital for effective work performance
- Spreading rumours about an individual or group

A person who displays bullying often has controlling needs and focuses on select targets. On the surface, a perpetrator may be charming and intelligent. People who are being bullied are often not believed at first and may be labelled as weak or negative by co-workers. Others sometimes recognise the perpetrator's behaviour, but prefer to stay neutral to avoid the risk of being targeted themselves. Individual lives and organisations can be seriously damaged by inaction or passive responses.

In recent years, workplaces have become more aware of the need to assertively performance manage staff who repeatedly display unwanted behaviours. Bullies are often oblivious to their actions and may or may not be mortified when their behaviours are brought to their attention.

It is also important to note what bullying is not. It is not when someone expresses a different opinion, has a conflict or debate or is undergoing constructive and honest feedback in a performance review. It is not when someone is unintentionally uncivil or takes a bad mood out on someone on a rare occasion, when desperately tired or worried.

In these situations, sometimes it helps to say, 'I'm not sure if you realise this but sometimes you . . .'. Confronting someone like this does not always work, but entirely avoiding confrontation never works.

A common false myth assumes victims of bullying are oversensitive, weak individuals who are unable to stand up for themselves. Individual doctors cannot be expected to initiate and endure onerous complaint processes on their own. If you feel you are being bullied by someone, consider enlisting the following networks of support:

- Seek regular debriefing from a skilled general practitioner/family physician, psychologist or psychiatrist who understands the irrational nature of the bullying and your inability to 'fix' it on your own. It helps if your doctor is independent from your workplace to allow them to advocate effectively on your behalf, especially if you require stress leave or wish to make a complaint.
- Try to have no contact or avoid contact with the bully, but if this is not possible, remain brief and always professional.

- Try to enlist the support of trusted people at work, particularly other victims of the bully. Address 'splitting' promptly by communicating clearly with others.

- Do your work to your best ability, proactively seek out kind colleagues and stop trying to seek the approval of the bully – nothing will ever be good enough. Do not seek the understanding of the bully or share your vulnerabilities including your distress, as it will be used against you.

- For extreme stress at work, practise 'extreme' self-care outside of work – do what works best for you in terms of relaxation and rejuvenation. Stay connected with people you love outside of work.

- Do not internalise the irrational behaviours of the bully and do not waste your precious time ruminating or rehearsing how you will respond at your next meeting – there is no right way to 'play' irrational mind games. Instead, spend your time with people who support and energise you.

- Obtain a copy of the antibullying workplace policy and follow the correct procedure about making a formal written complaint if this is appropriate.

- An antibullying policy will usually recommend documenting the damaging conversations, emails, telephone calls, minutes of meetings or any other objective evidence of a repetitive pattern of destructive behaviours; and to make a formal confidential complaint in writing about the bully to the appropriate manager or senior doctor in the hospital, medical service or other health provider. As the support of witnesses and other victims is also important, try to maintain your relationships with these people through regular communication.

- During a complaints process, it is your right to have confidential meetings without the bully present, especially if you believe you will be bullied in a joint meeting or there is a power differential between you and the bully. If you have been subjected to bullying, you are entitled to a formal apology as well as reassurance that the bullying will stop and others will be protected.

- Also try to maintain a constructive relationship with your manager/senior doctor to whom you make the formal complaint. During any investigation, anticipate that the bully will deny your allegations and attack your integrity, competence and work ethic. For these reasons, attempts at mediation are often not appropriate. Avoid being defensive, but be ready to calmly counter these unfair attacks when they are brought to your attention. Stay focused on the main issues when you make a complaint, and always use facts and evidence, not hearsay or rumour.

- Remember that your emails, letters and social media posts may be scrutinised by others in an investigation, and used against you unless you are always polite and professional. Therefore, never write anything that could be later construed as defamatory or 'emotional'.
- If your manager/senior doctor is the bully or is also being targeted by the bully, it may be necessary to submit your complaint to a more senior human resources director, CEO, or chairman of the board, depending on the hierarchy of your workplace. Whistle-blowing procedures can be helpful and protective in this situation.
- Health service directors, CEOs and medical practice employers must ensure that effective occupational health and safety policies are in place, outlining non-compliance penalties and the use of just and fair disciplinary processes. People in leadership roles can be held liable if occupational health systems fail and they, therefore, should understand and fulfil their responsibilities, which include routinely monitoring staff turnover rates, incident reports, staff and patient complaints and outcomes of exit interviews to identify any problems. However, do not prematurely complain to senior levels unless you have exhausted the other avenues outlined in workplace policies.
- If patient care is at risk or is being compromised, seek medicolegal assistance and support from your medical indemnity organisation. You may also need to seek medicolegal advice as to whether a complaint should be made to a regulatory authority if patient care is at risk.

A common cause of bullying, narcissistic personality disorder (NPD), is explored in depth in Chapter 15.

Summary

All organisations, including health services, have a legal responsibility to ensure that their workplaces are safe and free of discrimination, racism, sexual harassment and bullying. Vicarious liability means that an employer may be found to be liable for the damaging behaviours of its employees. Robust health and safety policies and procedures must be complied with, and doctors must be aware of safe workplace policies and undergo routine occupational health and safety training.

Discrimination, racism, sexual harassment and bullying are unlawful. Too many people have been hurt by toxic, unacceptable behaviours in healthcare. It is up to all of us to call these destructive behaviours out and support victims.

15 Confronting narcissistic personality disorder

How doctors treat each other

I met a young doctor who used to work with me recently. I had just completed my night rounds in the hospital and I was leaving for home. And then I saw him. He was unkempt, exhausted and appeared famished. Worst of all, he looked like a man who has totally given up on being a doctor. He appeared hesitant when I asked him what was wrong, but I could not just leave him there.

After much persuasion and insistence on my part he agreed to join me for a late supper. While he ravaged through his first proper meal of the day, he finally opened up. He has started working for the past week in a new speciality. Though the hours are longer, it was not an issue. He was well aware of the sacrifices he was expected to make.

However, the degradation, humiliation and constant harassment have finally taken their toll. He was literally chased out of the ward just minutes before he met me because he could not remember the details of a patient he clerked. He was not allowed to refer to his notes and had to recite the lab results by heart like a trained poodle. The words were abusive, hurtful and condescending. And worst of all, it was said right in front of the patient.

He finished his meal and stood up to leave. And as he left he said this: 'Please don't worry about me. I will be fine'. I was not convinced. The shame of being publicly humiliated is not a stain that washes easily.

The doctor-patient relationship often takes centre stage, but the epitome of good clinical practice depends on how the doctors treat each other. The medical profession is filled with fragile and vulnerable egos that often have trouble working with each other in a genuine collaboration of trust and mutual respect.

We complain, argue, fight and obsess for the sake of our patients, but do we dare reflect for even an iota of moment our actions and attitude towards our fellow caregivers?

Dr Dharmaraj Karthikesan[1]

---

[1] Dr Dharmaraj Karthikesan is a Malaysian Interventional Cardiologist and blogger at https://dharmarajkarthikesan.com/.

DOI: 10.1201/9781003296829-18

Dr Dharmaraj Karthikesan tells a story that many doctors can relate to. The degradation, humiliation, harassment and abusive, hurtful and condescending words are sadly familiar. We know the devastating impact of these behaviours by senior doctors on early career doctors is real, but how many of us have recently stopped to ask young colleagues why they are 'exhausted or have given up on medicine'?

Why do toxic behaviours persist in medicine, when bullying, sexual harassment, discrimination and racism are unlawful? Why would any doctor risk their reputation or their career by displaying unprofessional behaviours towards colleagues or patients?

A major consideration is narcissistic personality disorder (NPD). This psychiatric condition occurs in about 6% of the general population, so of course it exists amongst health professionals, including the medical profession. Unfortunately, doctors with this disorder can wreak havoc in in the health system if the disorder is not identified and managed appropriately. Many people prefer not to confront others with NPD because there can be a disproportionate reaction which results in legal action or career destruction. The impact of toxic behaviours on patient care and junior doctors can be especially devastating because of the power differential involved.

Narcissistic personality disorder in medicine

Doctors with NPD may manifest dysfunctional behaviours in a number of ways. Fundamentally, a doctor with NPD is arrogant, feels entitled and believes others have a problem. In subtle or not so subtle ways, they let colleagues know they are 'special', exaggerating their exceptional skills in patient diagnosis and management.

A doctor with NPD may seem charming on the surface and have many admiring followers. Generous one day and dismissive or aloof the next, they justify their quick temper as necessary to keep colleagues on their toes and to uphold a high standard of patient care.

Some patients may adore them as they inflate their achievements in their consulting rooms, while making derogatory comments about the clinical management of other doctors. Others abhor them, particularly if patients have been on the receiving end of volatile and unprofessional behaviours.

It can take time to recognise the repetitive behavioural patterns of a doctors with NPD as they may slowly undermine their victims with repetitive nitpicking and sarcasm, drip feed low-grade abuse that is difficult to call out, avoid eye contact or roll their eyes with disdain when no one else is looking or give out backhanded jabs masqueraded as jokes. Intermittent stonewalling and private taunting can also be difficult for victims to prove.

It is not easy to call out an employer or clinical supervisor who has NPD because on the surface, they can appear to be trying to help their victim. In reality, they may be quietly investing their time into their subordinates for 'a return', exploiting them financially, expecting them to work unreasonable hours, taking credit for their achievements, performance managing them unfairly, focusing on their vulnerabilities with patronising concern, or making veiled threats about job or training security to keep their victims in a powerless position.

Nothing is ever good enough, which creates excessive fear in the workplace, paradoxically reducing the performance of other doctors and endangering patient safety. Others find it difficult to challenge the doctor with NPD as they twist words, misconstrue situations, or are easily slighted by routine peer review, constructive feedback or minor criticisms.

Doctors with NPD may create smear campaigns against others and engage in pathological lying. This often occurs without the knowledge of victims, who are unable to defend themselves against false rumours as they can be the last to find out. The falsehoods often focus on what hurts doctors most, for example, being accused of failing to pull one's weight, a lack of integrity or incompetence.

When confronted, a doctor with NPD usually lacks empathy or may pretend nothing has happened. To maintain their superior status, power and control, the perpetrator may also play the martyr or accuse a victim of being toxic, dishonest, mentally unstable or 'not up to it', which causes further harm. A doctor with NPD can be quick to threaten legal action for defamation while continuing to spray lies about others, which is a very effective way to split people. As a result, the complainant is sometimes wrongly accused of poor behaviour, rather than supported by others in the workplace.

Doctors with NPD often target high-achieving victims whom they envy. When the target lacks boundaries in relation to self-protection and self-care, they tend to try to appease and tolerate their tormentor for too long. The mind games are irrational and there is nothing the victim can do to 'win' or fix the situation when the rules keep changing. Any individual intervention only makes matters worse while the perpetrator continues to enjoy 'playing' with their victim.

In response, victims naturally become upset, hypervigilant and defensive, and when their stressed demeanour confirms the doubts of colleagues about their mental health, they may gradually lose their support network. Recommending self-care strategies, resilience training and cognitive behavioural techniques in this situation can be harmful because further responsibility is placed on the victim to change, without addressing the bully's destructive behaviour.

Change is difficult because doctors with NPD fail to recognise narcissistic traits as negative as they feel superior to other doctors – and often say so directly or indirectly. Witnesses fear getting involved for fear of becoming targets themselves, and remain silent when it appears 'there are always two sides to a story'. In some recent high-profile cases, hospitals, medical services and other health providers have turned a blind eye to bullying, particularly when doctors are senior, generate healthy incomes or have skills that are in high demand in an area of workforce shortage.

With all these challenges in mind, how can we hold doctors with NPD to account?

Greater awareness of damaging behaviours is important. Anyone can exhibit narcissism or narcissistic personality traits or types from time to time in different forms from mild to severe. When doctors are under stress, they can act out. The more we recognise the traits in ourselves and others, the less likely they become a problem. NPD is different and pathological. It is a diagnosis not to be taken lightly, requiring comprehensive consideration of diagnostic criteria and intensive management, including long-term psychotherapy by a specialist psychiatrist.

There are many reasons why doctors with NPD need our help to get help. They lack insight and seldom seek help themselves. The quality of patient care may be at risk, particularly if the doctor is impulsive, overconfident about their capabilities or ignores peer review. A doctor with NPD can also have an adverse impact on the health of their victims and patient safety by creating a negative workplace culture. They can be depressed and, in severe cases, may be at risk of harming themselves if they lose their professional standing or are ostracised by their colleagues when their negative behaviours are exposed.

Notwithstanding the challenges, the damaging behaviours of a doctor with NPD must be called out and monitored by a collective of respected senior doctors or a senior leadership team, rather than expecting individual victims to speak up. Bystanders must speak up.

If patients are placed at substantial risk of harm, a notification to the appropriate regulatory authority should be considered but only after expert legal advice, to ensure notifiers have statutory protection from legal action. Unfortunately, if all else fails, it may take an intervention by a regulator to ensure the doctor with NPD attends regular psychotherapy as part of restrictions on their medical practice.

None of this is easy. However, we should never allow the damaging behaviours of any doctor to reach this level. Collectively, good doctors must take responsibility for holding bullies to account and believing victims.

Summary

Why would any doctor risk their reputation or their career by displaying unprofessional behaviours towards patients and colleagues? A major consideration is narcissistic personality disorder (NPD), which occurs in about 6% of the general population and is prevalent in medicine.

Unfortunately, doctors with this psychiatric condition can wreak havoc unless the disorder is identified and managed appropriately. Confronting others with NPD can be difficult as there may be a disproportionate reaction which results in legal action or career destruction. The impact of toxic behaviours on patient care and junior doctors can be especially devastating because of the power differential involved. Patient care can be compromised.

Collectively, good doctors must take responsibility for holding bullies to account and believing victims. It can help victims to enlist the support of professionals inside and outside the workplace including experienced legal professionals and an independent general practitioner/family physician, psychologist or psychiatrist for regular mental health care.

Preventing and managing patient violence

After I was assaulted in my consulting room, I immediately told other staff what had happened. They replied 'Well you did keep him waiting – he was pacing up and down angrily in the waiting room before the consult. We get abused every day like that. Get used to it.'

> *General practitioner beginning at a new rural practice*

The above response to an incident of abuse or assault is clearly totally unacceptable – but unfortunately common in medical practice.

Increasing patient or carer violence in healthcare is a sad reflection of increasing community violence. Threats and incidents of violence are serious occupational health and safety issues, and should never be tolerated 'as part of the job' in health services because of duty of care issues. The effects are serious for doctors and other staff and include anxiety, depression, post-traumatic stress-related illness, diminished productivity due to poor concentration, social withdrawal and reduced participation in the medical workforce.

As doctors, we are quick to recognise that patient or carer anger is common and usually not directed at us personally (Chapter 11). However, if anger escalates, we must recognise the early point at which understandable emotion tips into unacceptable behaviour. In this critical moment, we may be able to enlist the support of others in the workplace to de-escalate the situation and prevent an assault.

The definition of assault is any act that intentionally or recklessly causes another person to fear or be subjected to physically or mentally harmful, offensive contact. Physical injury or contact does not always occur. Threats of exposing people to bodily fluids (e.g. blood, spitting), and verbal threats of harm including rape or sexual touching also constitute assault.

Verbal assaults can sometimes be more damaging than unintended or intended physical assaults. For example, consider this scenario: a threat by a patient to abduct a doctor's children from school is likely to be more harmful than an accidental lashing out by a patient in extreme pain.

DOI: 10.1201/9781003296829-19

We are all responsible

Governing bodies and management teams of health services, including hospitals and community clinics, have overarching responsibility for systems of occupational health and safety and can be held collectively or personally liable for harm caused in the workplace, including harm caused by patient or carer violence. It is therefore the responsibility of all employers to provide a comprehensive orientation to new staff and ongoing training about all occupational health and safety issues, including policies and procedures on the prevention and management of patient or carer violence.

Any threats or incidents of violence must be formally reported immediately through the correct and most senior channels to ensure an assault is optimally managed for the victim as well as the perpetrator. By routinely reviewing any occupational health and safety incidents, employers are able to identify ways of continually improving workplace systems to prevent future issues.

However, individuals, including doctors, working in a health service also have a responsibility to keep up to date with all safety policies and procedures to ensure that they respond early and appropriately to unacceptable behaviours of patients or carers as first responders at the front line. Any threat or incident of violence should be reviewed thoroughly at a timely clinical team meeting.

All incidents should be formally reviewed in a timely manner

Here are some simple questions to help the whole team debrief, learn from an incident, and tailor policies and procedures to prevent future incidents:

- **What happened?** Have we talked to all the victims and witnesses? What are the facts? Should the police or security be notified?
- **Are staff safe now?** Do staff including doctors require debriefing or employee assistance to manage any physical or psychological trauma? What was the advice of police or security?
- **Was the assault intentional or unintentional?** In assessing the severity of violence, or the risk of recurrence, we must examine the intention behind the threat. This distinction is important because intentional incidents are criminal assaults, which should be reported to the police. This distinction can also be difficult as patients who display violent behaviours may have

an underlying temporary or permanent cognitive impairment such as head injury or other brain disorder, severe psychiatric disorder or drug and alcohol abuse, all of which require assertive clinical management. In this situation, patients have little insight into the impact of their negative behaviours, and police or security are usually called early to allow the clinical team to provide essential medical or psychiatric treatment safely.

- **What factors may have triggered the violence?** There is no justifiable excuse to abuse or assault anyone, but it is important to identify the triggers. For example, keeping someone waiting while attending to other patients is of course never an acceptable excuse for abuse or assault. However, if waiting times are routinely excessive, it may help to improve workplace policies to manage work flow more efficiently or warn patients about waiting times in the future.

- **Could the incident have been prevented?** Are all staff aware of their responsibility to identify patients at risk of violence early? For example, any patients displaying problematic behaviours in waiting areas must not be allowed to enter a consulting room with a doctor or other clinician without support or security in place. Patients who are displaying irritability, agitation, or anger in a waiting room should be identified promptly and asked why they are upset. If they display any sign of cognitive impairment, they must be urgently and appropriately clinically managed with support, for the reasons stated above. If they have insight, they should be provided with a written code of conduct clearly outlining acceptable and unacceptable behaviours. Anyone who shows a lack of regard for a code of conduct should be asked to leave temporarily in order to calm down and to return only when they are able to comply with behavioural guidelines.

- **How should we manage this patient now?** If an abusive or violent patient refuses to calm down or leave a health service, clinical staff must keep themselves and other patients safe until police or security arrive, as a priority. After any incident and after a patient has left the health service, the patient must be followed up by telephone and formal letter to outline acceptable behaviours when visiting the health service again in the future. This follow-up may be undertaken by police, security or the management of the health service in consultation with the medical defence provider, whatever is most appropriate to the particular situation.

- **Should we flag the patient's file to warn other practitioners about the future risk of violent behaviour?** If a patient has displayed threats or unreasonable behaviours in a health service, the incidents should be documented in their clinical record and the front of their file clearly flagged to warn other staff at future consultations. Patients and carers who are at greatest risk of perpetrating assault on other staff are those who have past histories of having done so before.

- **Has the incident been formally reported to the governing body of the health service and have any systems of safety been changed in response?** What other safeguards or barriers can be put in place to minimise the risk of recurrence in the future? (see p 142 on preventing violence through the implementation of policies and procedures) Does the health service have a formal policy on when to terminate the doctor-patient relationship? (see page 145).

A team meeting to discuss the above issues not only assists a clinical and non-clinical team debrief after a specific incident and manage a particular patient, but helps to prevent future episodes of violence by improving systems of workplace safety.

Most of all, doctors and other staff must feel confident expressing anxieties regarding unacceptable patient behaviours and be reassured their concerns will be acted on. All health services, including hospitals, medical practices or clinics, have a responsibility to protect all employees and contractors and must not accept threatening behaviours from patient or their carers as a 'normal' way of working or 'just part of the job'.

Assertive management of mental illness and patient-initiated violence

The association between violence and mental illness is a sensitive issue. It must be emphasised that many people with mental health problems are more likely to be the victims rather than the perpetrators of violence. People with mental illness often experience very damaging stigma and discrimination in the community and no one wants to make this situation worse. Nevertheless, there are times when people with untreated disorders lose control of their ability to regulate their emotions. When these patients lack insight, doctors have a responsibility to manage threatening behaviours assertively and to ensure that their patients are not at risk of harm to themselves or to others.

Doctors of all specialities in addition to psychiatrists have an important role in the early identification and early access to optimal treatment of serious mental illness and drug and alcohol abuse, as this is more likely to result in a good prognosis and therefore prevention of any future behavioural issues. On the other hand, if abusive or violent behaviours are due to a lack of patient insight because they are part of a psychiatric condition, it is essential that the patient is monitored regularly for compliance with treatment to prevent future risks in a health service or in the community.

Unfortunately, people with mental illness and drug and alcohol problems are overrepresented in the criminal justice system. This is a human rights issue directly related to poor access to comprehensive mental health care in the community for people with:

- Severe personality disorder
- Alcohol and drug problems
- Untreated psychosis

Severe personality disorder

This disorder is a disorder of the regulation of emotions and affects about 2% of people, especially young women. The disorder is thought to be often related to neglect and physical and emotional abuse as children or negative stressful events in adolescence. People with a personality disorder are sensitive to rejection and may react with anger at mild disturbances. They are often seen by doctors as a result of being harmed through their destructive behaviours related to:

- Frantic efforts to avoid real or imagined abandonment
- Unstable and intense personal relationships
- Impulsivity in at least two self-destructive ways including excessive spending, gambling, sex, abuse of alcohol and other drugs, dangerous driving and road rage or binge eating
- Recurrent threats of self-harm, self-mutilation or suicidal behaviour
- Rapid mood changes and difficulty controlling anger, temper and violent behaviour
- Transient stress-related paranoia or dissociative symptoms

Specialist group and individual psychotherapy and pharmacological treatments can be very effective. A multidisciplinary mental health team including a psychiatrist, psychologist, mental health nurse and general practitioner or family physician can significantly help a person with a personality disorder who is displaying negative or destructive behaviours to set clear limits and prevent or manage any threats or incidents of violence.

Alcohol and drug intoxication

When patients present to us acutely intoxicated with drugs and alcohol, we must always be alert to the risk of physical violence because of their lack of insight. Drugs of addiction should not be prescribed to patients who are known addicts unless they are part of an evidence based multi-disciplinary treatment program. If our safety is ever threatened by a patient who appears to be affected by drugs and is seeking a prescription for a drug of addiction, we should consider giving the patient what they want to protect ourselves, ask them to leave or leave the environment ourselves immediately. If we do this, we must then report our actions to the police and our medical defence organisation. We must also be mindful that if a health service gains a reputation for prescribing drugs of addiction, word will get around to other patients seeking 'quick fixes', potentially putting other staff at risk of violent threats.

Where possible and appropriate, patients with histories of aggressive behaviours while intoxicated should be referred to inpatient or outpatient detoxification programs and/or specialist addiction medicine programs.

Untreated psychosis

It is a shameful fact that people with psychosis are also overrepresented in the criminal justice system. About 10% of people who commit murder or major crimes are acutely psychotic at the time of the incident. Tragically, many of these people have fallen through the gaps in our mental health systems and end up receiving mandatory treatment in the criminal justice system.

Patients who are at risk of harming themselves and/or others require emergency involuntary admission to hospital. Early intervention is essential which is why assertive clinical management of early psychosis is everyone's responsibility, not only the responsibility of the specialist mental health team.

Preventing violence through tailored policies and procedures

Here are some common approaches to policies and procedures on topics such as creating safe environments, home visit policies, responding to stalking and terminating doctor-patient relationships, which have been provided as examples only. There are many other standard occupational health and safety policies and procedures which can be tailored and regularly updated to respond to the unique needs of a health service.

Please do not wait until an incident of violence occurs before policies and procedures are put in place or read and implemented by all staff.

Safe physical environments

We all have a responsibility to both our patients and the members of our staff to ensure that the physical environments of our health services are safe for everybody. Here are some practical tips for creating safer physical environments:

- Create physical barriers between the waiting area and the consulting rooms to prevent unauthorised access by patients to working areas. Most modern businesses have a barrier to prevent clients entering consulting rooms without a staff member to protect the security of staff, cash, personal and practice property and confidential documents.
- Install security locks on all windows and access doorways, and lock the back doors and all consulting rooms whenever they are empty.
- Glass in all windows and doors should be shatter-proof, and consider removing any pictures in public areas with non-shatter-proof glass as the glass can be broken and used as a weapon.
- The chairs in consulting rooms can be arranged so that the doctor or other treating health professional is always sitting closest to the door. However, many professionals recognise that it may be better to give their patients easy access to the door to allow the patient to leave if they become agitated.
- Where appropriate, install duress alarms and ensure there is an agreed staff policy in place to respond when an alarm is activated and ensure that drills are held on a regular basis to test the adequacy of the response.
- Maintain a practice policy of never allowing a staff member to be alone on the premises at times when the practice is open to patients.
- Install effective lighting in corridors, car parks, walk ways and the external surrounds of buildings.
- Erect fencing to prevent the practice grounds and car park being used as a public thoroughfare.

Home visit policy

Home visits are an important part of the care of some patients, particularly the terminally ill or the frail and elderly. However, the safety of the attending doctor must always be considered.

Where possible, patient files should be flagged to ensure staff are warned if they are likely to be unwelcome at the home, or if the patient or other residents at the address have a known history of violence. Consider whether home visits without the use of an accompanying person for appropriate security are appropriate.

- Do not agree to home visits to patients threatening suicide or domestic violence or who are aggressive in their language without involving the police.
- Do not visit patients requesting specific pain relief medication or repeat prescriptions for drugs of addiction if they are not known to you.
- Keep a record at the practice of the registration, make, model and colour of all doctors' cars.
- Always walk on the best-lit side of the street, stay away from bushes and parks, and check the back seat before unlocking your car on return. Park your car so it is pointing in the direction of the exit, so you can leave quickly if you need to.
- If there is a lift, make sure to stand by the control panel to control the lift and have quick access to the alarm.
- Ensure procedures are in place and followed if staff cannot be contacted or do not return or check back in as expected.
- If you use a deputising service, it must be alerted regarding any patients who you think may be at high risk of being violent.

Stalking

Stalking is more common than we think. It is a pattern of repeated, unwanted attention, harassment and contact where the offender threatens physical harm or causes mental distress. Stalking should be recognised early so that it may be dealt with promptly and effectively. Every medical workplace should have a policy in place which informs all staff how to protect themselves from stalking. Here are some strategies for dealing with stalking:

- Document every contact with the stalker, including telephone calls, emails, letters and deliverables. Record all cases of being followed by car or on foot or being watched. Have a phone with a caller-identification screen. Log all calls from the stalker, recording time, date and nature of the call, for example, 'heavy breathing'.

- When a complaint about criminal conduct is made to the police, their assistance should be sought in taking out an intervention order and seeking further legal advice.
- Contact the police every time the stalker makes contact. The police should also maintain documentation. Request that the police assess the security of your home and practice.
- Advise the practice team, friends, family and neighbours of the situation. Ask people to watch for any unusual activity near your home, workplace or car.
- Never enter into a conversation with a stalker.
- Vary your routines. For example, go home by different routes at different times and arrive at work at different times.
- Keep your car locked when you are driving. If you travel by public transport, plan your trip to avoid excessive waiting times at bus or train stops. When stepping off a bus or train, ensure you are not being followed.
- Keep the outside of your practice and home well-lit and free of places where a stalker may hide. Install appropriate locks, deadlocks, window security, floodlights, security screens and door alarms in your practice and home.

Cyberstalking has been defined as the use of the Internet or other electronic means to stalk or harass an individual, a group or an organisation. It may include false accusations using monitoring, identity theft or threats. Any threats using digital media should be reported to the police.

Terminating patient–doctor relationships

There are going to be times when it is necessary to terminate the care of a patient. This may be related to violent or inappropriate behaviour by the patient or other occasions when the doctor is unable to continue to provide the best possible care.

As with all aspects of clinical care, a thoughtful and considered approach, including clear communication, will help minimise any potential harm to the patient. Taking a zero-tolerance stance and abruptly terminating a doctor-patient relationship after unacceptable patient behaviours, without a plan for future medical or psychiatric intervention or follow-up, will usually be ineffective as it may be met with further threats or it may deflect abusive or violent behaviour onto other colleagues or to the wider community.

It is often wise to seek medicolegal advice from a medical defence organisation when terminating a doctor–patient relationship. This advice will include appropriate instructions for when a patient requires ongoing medical care.

Summary

Prevention of patient-initiated violence is dependent on recognising potentially high-risk situations and different forms of assault. Patients known to have untreated personality disorders, drug and alcohol problems or psychosis can experience great difficulty regulating their emotions and navigating healthcare settings, which may predispose them to violent behaviour. However, patients with mental illness are much more likely to be the victims than the perpetrators of violence. Doctors of all specialities, not only psychiatrists, have a responsibility to help people with mental illness access early comprehensive assessment and treatment.

If an incident of violence does occur, we must be aware of how to immediately manage this by collaborating and supporting each other, sometimes terminating patient relationships if appropriate, notwithstanding our duty of care under such circumstances. The utmost importance of prevention and first feeling safe in the workplace by working together with colleagues is the paramount theme.[1]

---

[1] L. Rowe, B. Morris-Donovan, and I. Watts, *General Practice: A Safe Place*, RACGP, 2009.

Every doctor building strong relationships with colleagues by sharing challenges

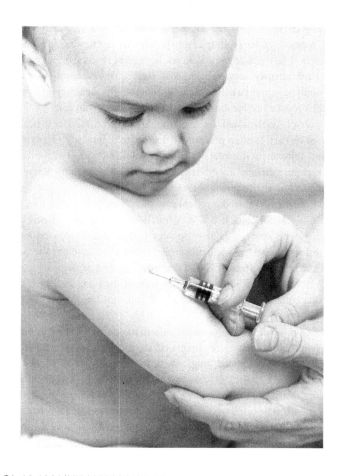

DOI: 10.1201/9781003296829-20

As doctors, we carry an enormous sense of obligation and commitment to our patients, which is admirable. Sometimes we are only preoccupied with getting through each day to care for our patients and families and to preserve ourselves. We may think we do not have time to build strong relationships with colleagues too. However, when we care for each other, we also help ourselves, because we create a positive culture in which we can all thrive.

Our life-long medical friendships are usually forged when we face shared challenges at work. Often these special bonds sustain us through other periods of adversity and have been critical to the maintenance of our mutual wellbeing. For all these reasons, it is important that we are generous with our support and mentorship of colleagues.

One of the most obvious indicators of a caring workplace culture is when clinical teams stand by a colleague who is suddenly unable work full time, must retire early or take sick or compassionate leave due to mental or physical health issues. Unfortunately, busy, overworked doctors can inadvertently overlook this opportunity to support a colleague, while others in the medical profession have unhealthy reputations for shunning doctors who are 'not up to it'.

As previously discussed, common human resources failures in healthcare (outlined in Part 2) often predispose doctors to mental injury, particularly burnout, adjustment disorders, depressive disorders, anxiety disorders, and post-traumatic distress disorders. We may correctly attribute blame to 'the system' but ignore the further harm the profession may inflict by failing to support colleagues in need, particularly when damage to physical or mental health is work inflicted. It is a very hurtful realisation for unwell doctors or doctors who are retiring after decades of service and self-sacrifice when they find themselves suddenly disposable after they have put the needs of others first all their lives. It is also demotivating and damaging for the rest of the clinical team, who take a mental note of the poor treatment of their departing colleague and justifiably ask 'is this how I will be treated in the future?'

Let's be more direct. Our medical culture has been described as uncaring, unforgiving, ego-driven, crisis-orientated, caustic, toxic, dysfunctional, dehumanising, money-orientated, fragmented, paternalistic, arrogant, aloof, hierarchical, belittling, fearful, mistake-averse, combative, resistant to change and power orientated. While we are often told that it's OK to talk about our vulnerabilities and to create healthy boundaries between our work and life, our medical culture is rarely conducive to doing so. In reality, medical workplaces can be harsh, cold environments, with very little understanding for doctors who are perceived to be not pulling their weight.

At first glance, this assessment could be regarded as overly critical. However, when we consider the ongoing high rates of mental illness and suicide in doctors, especially young doctors, can we really defend the status quo?

Unfortunately, the medical profession often perpetuates outdated and destructive myths about mental illness in doctors. For example, many doctors accept burnout like a badge of honour and regard help-seeking for mental illness as a sign of a weakness or incompetence. Consequently, mental illness is significantly under-recognised and under-treated in doctors as they tend to inaccurately self-diagnose and inadequately self-manage their condition. Not surprisingly, many doctors tend to battle on alone and seek help late during a crisis – burnt out and depressed, partially self-medicated, resistant to treatment, prone to relapse and at risk of suicide. It is the responsibility of doctors of all specialities (not only those with psychiatry training) to question why we allow unacceptable attitudes and myths about mental illness to continue in a profession that prides itself on being evidence based in its approach.

In Part 3, we call for doctors to recognise shared challenges at work as opportunities to build strong relationships with colleagues. Together, we can reduce the big burden of mental illness and suicidal thinking in the medical profession by recognising workplace mental injury and supporting each other through loss, grief and serious mental and physical illness. Doctors, like our patients with serious illness, do not always have full insight into their own problems when they are vulnerable, and may require appropriate assistance to get the right professional help.

We also call for senior doctors to take more responsibility for the training, supervision, mentoring and general care of earlier career colleagues in the current environment. The common 'worse in our day' mantra by senior doctors has to stop. Young doctors have faced extreme challenges, disconnection from colleagues and isolation from families during recent public health crises, but are often hesitant to complain for fear of damaging their careers. For this reason, there is a need for greater advocacy for work-life balance and flexibility in training programs for early career doctors by colleagues with established careers.

The good news is that every doctor has more influence than we realise to change our medical culture together. Through shared challenges and adversity, we develop enduring relationships with colleagues which can last a lifetime.

We can enlist these strong connections to collaborate and advocate for healthy medical workplaces by:

17. Mentoring every early career doctor
18. Preventing and identifying mental injury
19. Reducing mental illness stigma
20. Helping colleagues seek early mental health care
21. Improving every doctor's mental health literacy
22. Supporting colleagues with mental illness
23. Learning from loss, grief and serious physical illness

Mentoring every early career doctor

Dr Justin Coleman's refreshing reflections on the positive aspects of his medical career remind us about the benefits of seeking career advice from experienced doctors throughout our career transitions.

> *If you read the wrong kind of comments in the online medical media – as I do, religiously – you might conclude that retiring doctors are glad to be leaving the sinking ship. These disembarking medicos proclaim they would discourage their child from ever boarding the leaky vessel. Why commit to years of study, long hours, frustrating paperwork, little respect and crappy pay?*
>
> *After all, being a doctor is a tough gig these days. Especially if you stretch 'these days' to include one million days ago. Hippocrates noted in his opening line of the first ever book about the burden of being a doctor, 'Life is short, and art long, opportunity fleeting, experimentations perilous, and judgement difficult'.*
>
> *Life is less short since Hippocrates' day, but the rest still rings true. Today's graduates will face increasing bureaucracy and regulation. Recent reports highlight the threats of bullying from within the profession and of litigation from without – although I'd argue neither is escalating.*
>
> *Would I encourage my child to do medicine? You bet I would, and here are five reasons why.*

We help people

> *I'd never disparage someone slaving away frying burgers or selling insurance. Both can make the world a better place, especially if they care about their clients and colleagues.*
>
> *But at the end of a year doctoring, you can pretty safely say that a whole lot of folk have been grateful for what you do. In 15-minute increments (on a tough day, 45-minute), I plug away at trying to ease my patients' distress.*
>
> *Sometimes I can offer a cure, sometimes thoughtful advice and occasionally I fail to achieve either. But on balance, people walk out better than they walk in.*

We fix stuff. Actually fix stuff

> *Those yearning for the good old days should read* The Youngest Science *by Lewis Thomas. Thomas attended Harvard Medical School in 1933 and learned to, as he put it, 'comfort the incurable'; watching compassionately over patients as they died from syphilis, tuberculosis and heart failure.*

DOI: 10.1201/9781003296829-21

I'm as sceptical as anyone when it comes to curtailing medical hype, but you must admit, modern medicine spectacularly fixes a whole lot of problems. Sometimes by imaging, resecting and chemically pulverising a cancer, and at other times playing the long game, gently nurturing mind and body into a healthy old age.

Some doctors complain that Gen X seems happier to pay a homeopath than a general practitioner. But remember: in the long run, people actually want to be fixed.

The job pays well and is secure

Do you worry about oversupply, market instability and easier ways to earn a crust? Maybe – but name a university course where earning a reasonable living over a lifetime is substantially more secure.

Variety and flexibility

Many of my patients who are labourers or office workers spend the first half of their career going wherever work takes them, and the second half hanging on to a tedious, repetitive job.

I could probably be parachuted into any part of Australia and I'd find some sort of gainful employment. If there wasn't a general practitioner job immediately going, I'd hitchhike to the closest regional centre to work as a locum, surgical assistant or medical educator.

With a bit of planning, I could consider medical admin (briefly), overseas aid work, a medical specialty or even the ultimate in alternative careers – medical writing.

Things might not be so rosy if I were a new graduate, or overseas-trained, or a female doctor about to start a family. But I'd still have more choices than an accountant.

We hang around motivated, independent thinkers

Cynical as I am about the rare peer who wants little more than a flash car and European holidays, the fact is that most doctors I meet are good folk who think hard about their patients and have interesting opinions.

Rarely have I had a wasted conversation at a medical conference or an online doctors' forum. I don't always agree with the viewpoint, but enjoy the exchange.

If my child was to choose to study medicine, I bet his peers would be a delightful group of enthusiastic, motivated, intelligent young men and women; a fine bunch to accompany him through the next 40 years.

Which brings me to my conflict-of-interest statement: this article is not merely theoretical.

My middle son is about to begin studying medicine, and I'm delighted.
No reason he shouldn't enjoy his career as much as I have.

Dr Justin Coleman[1]

All doctors can benefit from having informal or formal mentors throughout their careers. In this chapter, we are especially advocating for senior doctors to provide more positive support to their early career colleagues. Unfortunately, too often, younger doctors are negatively influenced by cynical older doctors suffering from burnout; they are watching more experienced colleagues and absorbing their attitudes and behaviours, good and bad.

Early career doctors require special support and guidance to deal with all the challenges discussed in Parts 1 and 2 of *Every Doctor* as well as a balanced view of the short and long term, satisfying and worthwhile aspects of a medical career. For example, the following brief quotes from doctors of different specialities, as captured by Professor Philip Hébert, also remind us of the privilege of pursuing a career in medicine.

You talk and I will listen

We give patients as little as 12 seconds to tell their story before we start interrupting them. And then we keep on interrupting them. . . . You can understand why patients feel they can't get a word in edgewise. This can lead to all sorts of problems for doctors and patients alike: our hurriedness contributes, no doubt, to some of the dissatisfaction with modern medical care. What observations can be made about medical training that might counter this?

I canvassed the views of 50 colleagues: from family docs and surgeons, psychiatrists and critical care docs, to internists and paediatricians. I was, frankly, surprised by how quickly and enthusiastically most responded. Despite the negative things you may have heard about healthcare, a positive view of medicine is still alive and well. I received many excellent responses.

A family physician suggested: 'If there is one thing to learn, to do really well as a physician, it is to listen. In the midst of the intensity of medicine, the crises, the sadness and the everyday, and the wall of computer screens, always listen to your patient. The patient will give you a better history if they see you are listening'.

---

[1] Dr Justin Coleman is a General Practitioner, medical writer, editor and blogger: https://drjustincoleman.com/

An internist observed: 'Think of that patient as the only person you are seeing today, and you can achieve a connection that each patient will appreciate. Every patient is a person, an individual, and giving them each your full attention offers them the respect and connection they deserve'.

Another family physician had this to say: 'I used to draw inspiration from the heroes I met in literature and on the screen. Now, as a doctor, I have the great privilege of being in the presence of heroes. Regularly, in my office, at the bedside, and in living rooms across my community I am amazed by the courage, compassion, and tenacity shown to me by my patients who allow me to journey with them as we walk together on a path towards healing. They continue to be my greatest inspiration'.

A psychiatrist wrote: 'Most of us go into medicine because we want to help people – it is an honour and a privilege to be able to help people as their physician – if this remains your primary focus you will be happy in your work while making a positive difference in the lives of your patients. There is nothing more satisfying'.

A geriatrician wrote of the 'gratitude you feel that you have joined a long line historically of people like yourselves who have dedicated themselves often in many small ways to the betterment of their fellow beings'.

An intensive care unit doctor wrote: 'As a doctor, you will have the privilege to be present for ALL of the key moments in human life, far more than you would experience in one lifetime. Be humble. Be grateful. Be mindful. Art and science don't have to be in opposition. Let them be informed by AWE'.

An anaesthetist wrote: 'Be grateful for the opportunity and enjoy every day!'

A paediatric endocrinologist simply said: 'You're in for the most exciting time of your life! Buckle up!'

A critical care physician observed: 'This is the start of a journey. On this journey, you will be part of wonderful and terrible stories. You will have the power to effect positive change. You will also be powerless to prevent dreadful outcomes. You are more than just a witness, or a storyteller on this journey, you are an integral part of it, a player in the stories of the people you care for. Bring your best self. And always remember that although their stories become part of your own story, first and foremost you are there for them'.

An emergency medicine doctor observed: 'You are human. Do not think of yourself as bad or incompetent for making mistakes. Errors are the fountain of wisdom'. He emphasized: 'Every good thing I have done in my entire life has come from a mistake'.

A clinician scientist said: 'It's okay to say, "I don't know" and "I'm not sure". Your patients and colleagues will respect you more, and the job of being a doctor will be easier. This is where the resilience of the doctor-patient relationship comes in if you are honest and open with patients'.[2]

Professor Emeritus Philip C. Hébert

Transition from medical student to intern

In my first few months as an intern, I felt like I had to know everything. It was a huge mental burden. I quickly realised that the registrars and consultants I looked up to the most were the ones who constantly asked questions and knew their limitations; this is what made them intelligent doctors. Asking for help builds a stronger team, and developing a management plan in discussion with that team builds your confidence. Nobody expects you to know all the answers.

Dr Evelyn Daniel, general practitioner registrar

As an example of the additional support medical students may need when making the major step up to their first year as an early career doctor, here are some suggestions from doctors who have transitioned successfully.

It is normal to experience anticipatory anxiety in any major transition in your medical career. Despite all the advice and preparation, there will be days as an intern where you don't have time to exercise, you have to eat take away all week and you feel like you have no time for anything outside medicine. There may be times when you feel out of your depth and you have to call your supervising registrar three times with the same question. It happens to most new doctors and it gets better. You can do a few practical things to prepare for your first year and to make the transition easier for yourself.

When you are in your final year

- Establish a trusting relationship with a family physician/general practitioner close to where you live. Talk to them about starting your new role. Ensure you receive treatment for any common or chronic medical conditions such as anaemia, migraines, irritable bowel, dysmenorrhoea, depression or anxiety.

---

[2] Professor Emeritus Philip C. Hébert is a Canadian family physician, bioethicist and author of *Doing Right: A Practical Guide to Ethics for Physicians and Medical Trainees*, and *Good Medicine: The Art of Ethical Care in Canada*.

- Try to establish healthy patterns of sleep prior to commencing your long hours as a doctor by conditioning your brain with mindfulness, meditation, relaxation techniques and/or breathing exercises. Do whatever works for you – regularly.
- An online brief course in cognitive behavioural therapy techniques has been shown to reduce depressive symptoms in first-year doctors. Try it at: https://moodgym.com.au/
- Establish a regular exercise routine that is possible to continue when you are working. For example, attend a regular gym or dance session, use stairs instead of lifts, join a sporting team that does not mind if you miss a few games, walk to work if possible or get up earlier for a run or a bike ride.

During your first term as an intern

> If I could give one piece of advice to my intern self, it would be this – you are entitled to sick leave, you are entitled to support. When I first started working, I didn't feel like an important cog in the wheel that is the running of the hospital, and so I didn't feel deserving of sick leave. Then I realised that to be a functioning member of the patient care team – I needed to work in a way where my interests were protected too. I knew I would burn out if I didn't take sick leave when I needed to – and I see many colleagues do this.
>
> Dr Christopher Dowling, Psychiatry trainee

- Reassure yourself you are still learning and it is completely normal to feel out of your comfort zone. You will feel frightened and out of your depth – but this will alleviate with time.
- Always just ask – ask for help. You are not expected to have all the answers, and you do not have to make any decisions with which you feel uncomfortable or unsure. There will always be someone you can ask for help. Early career doctors are often called upon to make snap decisions, sometimes over the phone, by nursing staff who may not be aware of your workload, level of expertise or familiarity with the patient. You are allowed to defer these decisions if you are unsure. If a patient you are managing deteriorates, never feel ashamed to escalate – to a senior nurse, registrar, consultant, or by activating a medical emergency code.
- It is okay, and often safer, to say 'I don't know, but I will find out'. In fact you will hear doctors far more senior and experienced than you echo this sentiment. We are always still learning.
- Talk to your colleagues. You will often find that other new doctors are concerned about the same things. You are going through a challenging and life

changing year with your co-interns; debrief with them, listen to their stories, lean on them.

- Also ask for help from and refer to allied health and nursing staff. You can learn a lot from physiotherapists, occupational therapists and speech therapists. Ask the administrative staff about paperwork or the nurses to help with procedures. Pharmacists are a wealth of knowledge and can help with choosing and charting drugs, interactions and dosing.
- Routinely debrief with your clinical team and your own trusted family physician/general practitioner after any traumatic experiences. Many treating doctors offer after-hours or telehealth services.

Being on call seven days consecutively can be extremely stressful. Your nervous system is constantly firing and although humans are not inherently built to withstand that level of stress, it is frequently expected of early career doctors. When my phone rings at 3 AM, I never know what is going to be on the other end of that. You are making decisions when you are tired, and you often second guess yourself. But there is always someone to call for advice, for a debrief, for a laugh. Remembering you are not alone and reaching out to others is the most valuable tool in the junior doctor's kit.

Dr Amy Derrick, rural early career general practitioner

Senior doctors can be a great source of wisdom to younger colleagues but many underestimate the influence they have and the satisfaction gained in being a role model and a mentor. For this reason, early career doctors may need to be proactive in seeking a retired or senior doctor's career advice. Sometimes, early career doctors benefit most from being listened to by their senior colleagues about how medicine has changed. At other times, the words from senior doctors: 'It happened to me too and it felt awful, but I got through it – you will too' can be very validating and reassuring.

In the following piece, Dr Vicki Kotsirilos outlines the benefits of being mentored throughout her career.

Mentoring changes lives

Now nearing 60 years of age, still working in a busy general practice, continuing to be a strong voice within the medical and wider community through teaching and writing, I feel it is my turn to help support and nurture younger people's aspirations.

I believe I am still learning, growing, and evolving, and open to new mentors as my life journey continues. I reflect upon my own mentors in the past who have helped shape me as a strong woman and how they influenced my path and journey in life.

*I am **immensely grateful** to my mentors. I believe I chose my mentors as required for my own purposes during my informative years, education and working days – from primary and high school, university days, during the five years of hospital training, in teaching environments and in general practice to this day.*

I was privileged to have great (and bad) teachers and medical supervisors who recognised my inner strengths. Fortunately, my instincts picked what was right for me and ignored what was not. I allowed myself to be guided by my own intuition and trusted my mentors to support the journey and path I was driven by.

My choice of mentors was based on those who inspired and fulfilled my needs at the time. They taught me well, and I modelled them to adapt to the work I was involved with. My mentors included older women and men; the choice was not gender-based.

Women I valued more as friends and emotionally supportive. Most of my mentors were men. As I moved to different roles and positions, I was blessed to work with very kind supervisors. I, too, want to be a good mentor to younger people and convey similar features as I had the greatest teachers to teach me. My mentors shared similar characteristics and features that I admired and resonated with.

They were:

- *Loved by the wider community and held with great respect*
- *Leaders and respected in their own fields*
- *Kind and gently spoken*
- *Fun to be with, yet intelligent and wise*
- *Relaxed and willing to learn from their students, including myself*
- *Humble and kind – if I thanked them, they thanked me back*
- *Grateful and conveyed a sense of importance in me*
- *Actively listening and recognised my strengths, goodness and well intentions*
- *Guiding me and carved a pathway to allow me to grow*
- *Seeing power and greatness in me and*
- *Providing me opportunities for further growth!*

These are the features I resonated with, passively and subconsciously learnt from, adopted and reflected. I was constantly in awe and grateful to my mentors. I held them with utmost respect.

My pearls of wisdom

So, if I was to share any wisdom from experience to younger people, I would suggest the following points may be of help but, it is up to you to choose which of those points you resonate with and yearn to learn from:

- *Find a mentor who inspires you and respect in your life and/or work*
- *Share the passion you hold, inspiring others to share your vision and goals*
- *Seek support with like-minded people within your community*
- *Always use respectful and kind dialogue – people are more likely to read respectful emails than harsh ones*
- *Have fun in your journey through life*
- *Allow yourself to be inspired and heartened by the littlest acts of goodness that take place in your life – receive compliments with gratitude*
- *If your vision and actions uphold something good and worthy, that vision will be shared by others too*
- *Nurture your passion – be relentless and persevere*
- *Never focus on negative knockbacks or diverse opinions; just learn from them and divert your course and find other solutions*
- *Don't measure your goals and success in time – major goals can occur later in life unexpectedly.*
- *Practice gratefulness and mindfulness with every kind act – including when people open doors for you*
- *Simplify life, look after yourself with a healthy lifestyle (e.g. diet, exercise, reduce stress, sleep restoration, rest) and conserve your energies to do what you really want to do!*

Believe in yourself

Truly believe your goals, vision, and passion. Persevere, develop resilience, forgive, let go and don't get caught up in the negatives. Find common ground with people you need to work with. Find a mentor that you admire and seek the qualities in them that you choose to adopt. First do good for yourself, before your family and friends and the wider community. Take good care of yourself. Doctors have a powerful and respectful voice in the community and can help create change for a better world, but it is important not to experience feelings of burnout.

Self-care where the journey starts

Ensure that you nurture yourself physically, spiritually, and emotionally by being with family and friends who are kind, caring and supportive of you. Find fulfilling work and if you are not happy and can't change your situation, consider it a good learning lesson, and move on to another role. There is a lesson in every experience – good or bad.

Follow your passion and heart

As a doctor you have a powerful respectful voice; the community value you and any contributions you can offer. If you have a passion for something good, be open to learning and become the expert. We are intelligent. Find and speak to a mentor for guidance. Follow your passion!

Associate Professor Vicki Kotsirilos[3]

Summary

It is refreshing to read the stories of senior doctors who continue to love what they do. They have much to share about what they have learnt through extensive clinical experience (often the hard way) to make the path easier. Every early career doctor will benefit from informal and formal mentoring and debriefing with a senior doctor.

---

[3] A/Professor Vicki Kotsirilos AM is an Australian general practitioner with a professorial position with NICM Western Sydney University. She is the lead co-author of the popular textbook *A Guide to Evidence-based Integrative and Complementary Medicine*.

Preventing and identifying mental injury

Historically, many myths and misunderstandings have existed with regards to mental health issues. Literature over the centuries is filled with stereotypes and fears about people with mental illness. Indeed, for many cultures, a mental illness in the family is a source of great shame. In fact, for people with no experience of mental health problems, there is often the incorrect belief that mental illness is a choice and that if the individual were simply stronger or more motivated, they could magically 'snap out of it' and get themselves better.

Mental health conditions are extremely common in the community and have a major impact on people's day-to-day lives, as anyone who has been through the experience will tell you. For many people one of the hardest things is the uncertainty about recovery, and indeed, it is often a person's very sense of hope that is diminished. For people experiencing mental distress there often is a powerful sense of hopelessness combined with a sense of despair that they will never recover. As a general practitioner, I can tell you, never underestimate the ability of the mind, and the capacity of human beings to recuperate and mend themselves.

Dr Grant Blashki[1]

Dr Grant Blashki outlines some of the myths and misunderstandings about mental illness in the community that deter help-seeking with a powerful message about recovery. Unfortunately these myths and misunderstandings also persist in many workplaces of health services, where there is often little understanding of how to promote mentally healthy environments for staff including doctors. Healthcare workplaces usually offer debriefing and employee assistance programs including professional counselling to health workers. However, doctors are sometimes unintentionally excluded from mental health promotion and employee assistance programs.

---

[1] Dr Grant Blashki is Lead Clinical Advisor for Beyond Blue, Associate Professor at the University of Melbourne and a practising general practitioner. *Fragility and Hope in a World of Uncertainty Future Health Leaders* 2018.

DOI: 10.1201/9781003296829-22

Doctors rarely take time off work when mentally unwell and we rarely make work-related claims for stress or mental illness. This means there is very little data or literature on workplace mental injury in the medical profession, which in part is the reason that the heavy burden of mental illness and suicidal thinking persists in medicine.

Mentally unhealthy medical workplaces

In the preceding chapters, we have highlighted ways to address some major medical workplace issues which can result in mentally unhealthy environments – unsafe hours with no time for breaks to eat or take a bathroom break, flaws in occupational health and safety standards, poor communication, patient anger and violence, discrimination, racism, bullying, harassment, and lack of support for career transitions, clinical incidents/errors, traumatic incidents and grief to name a few.

Many of these common stressors in our workplaces have been exacerbated by recent public health crises, including restricted patient access to healthcare, lack of health funding, health workforce shortages and highly anxious and frequently angry patients and families.

While the stressors noted above can exacerbate pre-existing mental illness, more often, a previously very healthy doctor will first develop a mental health problem because of the failure of a medical workplace to respond adequately to acute traumatic experiences, chronic mental fatigue, stress and burnout, which predispose them to developing anxiety and depression. Additionally, medical staff rosters often contain little redundancy or flexibility, making taking time off or advance leave requests near impossible.

Vicarious traumatisation, where doctors become distressed after repeatedly being exposed to traumatic patient histories, is also commonly unrecognised. Doctors who have had past histories of exposure to child abuse or domestic violence when younger are at particular risk of being re-traumatised at work.

Not only do many medical workplaces continue to predispose doctors to mental injury, they can stigmatise mental illness as a weakness. In this situation, doctors are deterred from seeking help for fear of career and reputational damage. This common lack of acknowledgement of mental health issues among the medical workforce leaves many doctors to struggle alone without treatment and without the capacity to reach out to other colleagues when feeling vulnerable.

When a mental illness is unrecognised and untreated or undertreated, a doctor may be pushed into crisis, resulting in an abrupt departure from work and no support from workplace colleagues to return to work. Loss of employment and identity can then be devastating for a doctor, particularly when they have cared for others for a lifetime, only to be abandoned in their time of need. This is not only damaging for the doctor affected but for those remaining in the workplace who take note not to divulge their vulnerabilities or mental health problems at work.

When a doctor admits the need for time off due to mental health concerns, the medical workplace can be unsupportive because 'everyone is burnt out and depressed' – or worse, discriminatory. When a doctor returns to work following time off for a mental illness, there are often no light duties – patient care demands a fully functioning doctor and there is little understanding for doctors unable to pull their weight. A doctor in this situation will justifiably feel a sense of injustice when their mental health condition is ignored or not validated, and they have to prove that they are or have been unwell.

Sadly, many medical workplaces do not recognise the clear benefits of helping doctors to stay at or return to work, both for the individual doctor and the medical workplace, particularly at a time of medical workplace shortage. A mental illness will inevitably relapse when an unwell doctor returns to the same mentally unhealthy environment, there are unrealistic expectations on return to work or the employer does not acknowledge the ongoing sources of stress or trauma.

Suicide among medical practitioners is much higher than in the general population. To our shame, these monumental losses may have been preventable if their workplaces had been approachable, supportive and mentally healthy environments.

Mentally healthy medical workplaces

We can change this by supporting each other with humanity and compassion. We can all work together to create a mentally healthy medical workplace where we promote a kind, caring culture in simple ways such as treating each other with respect in team meetings and taking time to debrief. Saying thank you and acknowledging clinicians for their work means more than we know.

This is not to remove the onus of drastic change from medical workplaces and organisational leaders, but to highlight how everyday kindness can make a difference too. We must also cooperate to ensure doctors work safe hours and under optimal occupational health and safety standards, as well as raise awareness to contemporary policies to prevent and promptly address any discrimination, racism, bullying or sexual harassment (Chapters 14 and 15).

Prevention is the key word here. Every doctor can be proactive in supporting colleagues in their clinical teams and developing practice policies on self-care. This involves an acceptance by the team that it is 'normal' for every doctor to have annual comprehensive preventive health assessments, including mental health screenings, regular debriefing, early intervention for excessive stress, regular appointments with a psychologist or psychiatrist, best practice management of mental illness and postvention with an independent family physician/general practitioner after trauma or a crisis.

Prevention: Every doctor can benefit from an annual comprehensive preventive health assessment for routine screening of their physical and mental health.

Early intervention: Every doctor could consider attending their own doctor at least every six months for routine debriefing for common negative experiences to prevent burnout and manage inevitable stress.

Intervention: Every doctor must have their own trusted independent doctor for evidence-based treatment of mental illness, including major depression, adjustment disorders, eating disorders, obsessive-compulsive disorders, anxiety disorders or psychosis.

Postvention: Every doctor should have a trusted doctor in case of crisis or for acute debriefing after exposure to trauma, especially following the suicide of a patient or colleague.

Doctors of all specialities must have their own trusted family physician or general practitioner (Chapter 9). Doctors should not treat colleagues in their close clinical teams or doctors who are members of their families, because they cannot provide proper objectivity and review. They must establish confidential crisis management pathways for their staff and refrain from instilling guilt when doctors are too unwell to work.

Each of us must do more than send the occasional SMS or ask the clichéd 'Are you OK?' If we suspect a colleague is quietly suffering, we should look behind the 'emotional shield' and make time to listen carefully as a trusted friend and facilitate the right professional intervention. When we suspect our colleagues and friends are at risk, it may help to ask, 'I need to know you are being looked after and you are safe – what can I do to support you through this difficult time?'

Most other first responders have formal training and post-incident interventions to try to minimise the negative impact of repetitive trauma. Doctors tend to go from one crisis to the next, from one day to another, bouncing back from adversity to care for the next patient and console the next anxious relative. All of us can withstand a bad day, a tragic loss or a temporary excessive workload, but when this becomes chronic, we inevitably become triggered. This is why formal postvention after any traumatic experience must become accepted as an essential part of workplace support for doctors as well as other clinicians and non-clinicians.

For all these reasons, it is important for every doctor (especially non-psychiatrists) to recognise the signs of two common mental health disorders that may originate in the workplace, as these conditions may be prevented or treated early, resulting in a good prognosis and early recovery – adjustment disorder and post-traumatic stress disorder.

The following sections are deliberately brief because it is important that the assessment of whether **adjustment disorder or post-traumatic stress disorder** have arisen as a result of work should be made on the basis of comprehensive psychiatric assessment by a clinician with specialist mental health skills. There must be a thorough consideration of the onset of symptoms and related workplace circumstances, not self-diagnosis or diagnosis by a work colleague.

Adjustment disorder

The ICD 11 classification of mental disorders classifies adjustment disorder as:

> *a maladaptive reaction to an identifiable psychosocial stressor or multiple stressors (e.g. divorce, illness or disability, socio-economic problems, conflicts at home or work) that usually emerges within a month of the stressor. The disorder is characterised by preoccupation with the stressor or its consequences, including excessive worry, recurrent and distressing thoughts about the stressor, or constant rumination about its implications, as well as by failure to adapt to the stressor that causes significant impairment in personal, family, social, educational, occupational or other important areas of functioning.*

Adjustment disorder may manifest as chronic concentration or sleep problems or increase in alcohol use. Common symptoms include sadness, excessive worry, difficulty concentrating, feeling hopeless, nervous and overwhelmed, not enjoying life, food or social connection, crying, insomnia and suicidal thoughts or behaviours.

It often resolves within six months unless the stressor persists. There are different types of adjustment disorder, with a prominence of depressed mood, anxiety or mixed anxiety and depressed mood, or disturbance of conduct (e.g. reckless driving, taking unnecessary clinical risks).

Although adjustment disorder is milder and more self-limiting than many other psychiatric disorders, it is important to treat this condition with workplace interventions such as time off or reductions in work stressors and psychological therapies such as cognitive behavioural therapy. Unrecognised and untreated, it can interfere with a doctor's ability to function optimally and may be a precursor to major depression and generalised anxiety disorder.

Post-traumatic stress disorder

Acute stress is defined as a short-term justified reaction to a stressful event. It can last between two days and four weeks. After experiencing an episode of trauma, it is a normal reaction to have cycling of strong emotions, usually for about ten days. The cycling may involve memories of the event and avoidance behaviour, sometimes with associated feelings of numbness and denial.

According to the ICD11, post-traumatic stress disorder (PTSD) '*may develop following exposure to an extremely threatening or horrific event or series of events. It is characterised by all of the following:*

- *Re-experiencing the traumatic event or events in the present in the form of vivid intrusive memories, flashbacks, or nightmares. Re-experiencing may occur via one or multiple sensory modalities and is typically accompanied by strong or overwhelming emotions, particularly fear or horror, and strong physical sensations;*
- *Avoidance of thoughts and memories of the event or events, or avoidance of activities, situations, or people reminiscent of the event(s); and*
- *Persistent perceptions of heightened current threat, for example as indicated by hypervigilance or an enhanced startle reaction to stimuli such as unexpected noises. The symptoms persist for at least several weeks and cause significant impairment in personal, family, social, educational, occupational or other important areas of functioning.*

Post-traumatic stress disorder is characterised by feelings of intense fear, helplessness or horror following a traumatic event. This disorder can develop in the months after witnessing traumatic deaths or suicides as first responders (including doctors), being involved in major motor vehicle accidents, medical emergencies, natural disasters, homicide, family violence, physical or sexual assault, stalking, threats, home invasion or property damage. It can also occur after unexpected deaths of medical or surgical patients as described in this quote:

> *I feel I should have sought crisis debriefing after my first patient death on the operating table. I spent months feeling that it was my fault (which it wasn't) and being terrified that every patient was going to lose blood and die. Compounding the problem was my junior status, my rural location and lack of consultant support. When the death occurred, the consultant left the hospital immediately after telling me to close the abdomen and 'sort it out' with the family. I suspect mentoring, a supportive network and appropriate crisis debriefing would all have been helpful to me.*

> *Anonymous General Surgical Registrar*

According to ICD-11, complex post-traumatic stress disorder (Complex PTSD) is a '*disorder that most commonly occurs after prolonged or repetitive events from which escape is difficult or impossible. All diagnostic requirements for PTSD are met. In addition, Complex PTSD is characterised by severe and persistent:*

- *Problems in affect regulation;*
- *Beliefs about oneself as diminished, defeated or worthless, accompanied by feelings of shame, guilt or failure related to the traumatic event; and*
- *Difficulties in sustaining relationships and in feeling close to others.*'

Complex PTSD can occur after repeated severe stressors over a prolonged period of time, such as being recurrently exposed to traumatic, lonely deaths as a doctor during a pandemic.

Doctors, of course, are vulnerable to these disorders by being repetitively exposed to trauma, death or unexpected negative outcomes. Doctors may also be at risk of repetitive vicarious traumatisation after listening to the stories of patients who have experienced traumatic events. Here is a description of how complex PTSD commonly manifests:

> *It started with a vague sense of emptiness when I was not distracted or preoccupied. I felt terrible and I didn't know why. Then there was an overwhelming sadness, loneliness and inertia. I felt at war with myself and always on guard. I was constantly looking for threats but strangely numb. When I was triggered with loss at work, I felt like a dark cloud was descending on me and like I was falling into a bottomless abyss. I couldn't stop thoughts about past traumas from my childhood, which were being replayed over and over again in my mind. I woke frequently because of vivid nightmares about exams. Even after a few days of rest, I still felt helpless.*
>
> *When I asked for help and no one responded, it became much worse. I will never get over this.*
>
> *Anonymous Doctor*

Common features of PTSD include the following:

- Repeatedly reliving the traumatic event through unwanted and recurring memories, often with nightmares
- Being overly wound up with insomnia, irritability, lack of concentration and constantly on the lookout for signs of danger
- Avoiding activities, places, people, thoughts or feelings associated with the traumatic event to avoid painful memories
- Feeling emotionally numb or cut off and detached

When we help our patients work through traumatic experiences, we encourage them to carefully confront the memories of trauma, allow them to re-experience the thoughts, talk about the event, and cry, with our support. We encourage our patients to seek support from family and friends as this can help our patients find meaning in the trauma and facilitate recovery. Our patients usually require reassurance that there is likely to be a period of adjustment before a sense of equilibrium and resilience is restored.

We need to be open to doing this for ourselves after witnessing a traumatic event by seeking debriefing, and if appropriate, professional counselling. However, there are many reasons why doctors do not seek help. We regard traumatic events and delivering bad news as a normal part of our job. Often, we do not have the ability to confide in family and friends about our personal reactions to a traumatic event as patient confidentiality is involved. We may not take the time to attend debriefing or counselling, and instead of resting and taking time out after a traumatic event, we often have to respond to our patient, their family and sometimes the whole community fallout following an incident. In order to deal with an emergency at hand, we learn to put our feelings on hold and delay our own reaction to a traumatic incident.

Doctors working in rural and remote areas may experience even greater stress when responding to significant incidents or catastrophes. This is because they are often working in isolation, and sometimes with inadequate or poorly maintained equipment and facilities. Rural doctors often know the victims of traumatic events personally or socially, and may suffer greater self-recrimination and an excessive burden of responsibility. They may be exposed to possible sanctions from community members of rural towns when resuscitation attempts have not been successful. Despite these special challenges, it can be particularly difficult for rural doctors to take time away from busy practices to attend to personal distress and grief.

As doctors, we can underestimate the seriousness of post-traumatic stress disorder. It is essential to seek incident debriefing, and professional help with a family physician or general practitioner, grief counsellor, psychologist or psychiatrist in a timely manner. Psychotropic medication may be required.

Summary

Everyone, including doctors, deserves a healthy workplace where they feel encouraged, supported and appreciated, to allow them to do their best work. Everyone therefore has a role, both in protecting their own mental health and creating a mentally healthy workplace for all their colleagues.

Because of the challenges of our work, the whole health service team including clinicians and non-clinicians require ongoing proactive support across mental health promotion, prevention, early and optimal intervention and postvention.

The features of adjustment disorder and post-traumatic stress disorder are described briefly to help raise more awareness of workplace mental injury amongst doctors of all specialities, especially non-psychiatrists. These common mental health disorders can be prevented or treated, resulting in a good prognosis and early recovery. Mental injury is not a weakness, and we all deserve support from our colleagues and our workplaces.

19 Reducing mental illness stigma

Learn from me

I discovered the global CrazySocks4Docs Day – held annually on 1 June – only in 2018. The day aims to 'encourage conversations about mental health and help reduce the stigma for doctors experiencing mental illness'. When I discovered the day thanks to my burgeoning Twitter obsession, I experienced an incredible and overwhelming reaction.

Almost exactly 30 years before, as an intern in the central Queensland city of Rockhampton, I had tried to kill myself. Three decades later, I am now President of a specialist college, but I had kept the entire episode to myself and tried to forget it. I am deeply ashamed of not learning from my own experience and using it to help others.

I hope it isn't too late.

Perhaps by fate I was introduced to Australian cardiologist Dr Geoff Toogood, the incredible and inspiring founder of CrazySocks4Docs, at a College meeting a couple of weeks ago. The meeting was so unexpected and so overwhelming I choked and could barely speak, but it made me determined to take something positive from my own experience all those years ago. Hence this article.

I have a strong feeling that my own experience mirrors that of many doctors around the country, but it is worth explaining. I hope it will help others understand why I have been silent and have not taken the actions I should have. When I heard that a junior doctor I knew had taken his own life on New Year's Day this year, I could not bring myself to read any of the details. The tragic outcome could easily have befallen me.

My internship was a very bad year. I had found medical school difficult – I was not a natural academic like so many others in my year – but hoped that my intern year might prove better. I was wrong.

Halfway through 1988, it seemed clear to me that I was making even more of a hash of internship than I had of many subjects back at university. To make matters worse, regional Rockhampton was a long way from my family and my junior doctor colleagues all seemed to be more capable and were thriving.

As I reached the halfway point in my internship, I felt overwhelmed with inadequacy. I had a patient die and felt responsible. My ward work was

DOI: 10.1201/9781003296829-23

just barely adequate. My consultants and registrars were not exactly glowing in their feedback. I had an all-pervasive sense of failure, that so many years of struggle at medical school had been a complete waste and that I was little short of dangerous. I could see no way out.

So, one night, I made careful plans to kill myself. I won't go into detail but suffice to say that I wanted the end to be painless and clean. I stole some supplies from the wards – standards of drug security were much slacker 30 years ago – and set about writing letters. Luckily, I had few personal affairs to put in order.

Incredibly, a work colleague arrived unexpectedly and began knocking on the door of my small hospital unit. That person – I won't reveal the gender – knew I was in because my car was parked just outside. There were knocks and calls, 'I know you're in there . . .'

It was completely distracting. I had inserted a cannula in my left hand, so took it back out and threw the tubing and bag of intravenous fluid in the bedroom. When I answered the door, I must have looked very flustered and suspicious.

I will never know what made this person visit me unexpectedly. Perhaps my emotional state wasn't as well disguised as I thought. Perhaps it was just plain good luck. Perhaps it was something else.

I spent quite a while talking to the person, though not about my plans for the night. Enough, however, to make me take a step back from the brink. To reconsider. To think about other options. Looking back, that person probably had an inkling that I was about to do something dramatic. That impromptu visit saved my life.

I won't pretend that I had an epiphany or that I suddenly was better. I did seek help, although I didn't completely disclose just how close I was to suicide.

Rather than put my career, for what it was worth then, further in jeopardy by talking to one of my hospital colleagues, I made an appointment with a general practitioner in town. I started in a roundabout way, and ultimately confessed that I had made elaborate plans to kill myself.

To this day, I can remember the general practitioner's advice. Under no circumstances tell anybody or see a psychiatrist (I only knew of one in the town at the time, and was about to become his intern for a three-month term!). If I had a record of suicidality or mental illness, I would never be able to buy income protection or life insurance, and I would probably never get a good job. Indeed, don't tell anyone . . .

I was bonded to the Royal Australian Navy, with the hope of spending time as a seagoing medical officer. The advice I had received was startling – what if I was rejected from serving and had to pay back my return-of-service instead? I couldn't afford it. There was no way I was going to risk my Navy job – what if they were so worried about me jumping overboard that I was banned from the fleet?

I elected to try antidepressant treatment, but I remember it being very unpleasant. The options were more limited 30 years ago. The general practitioner warned me that if anyone found out about prescriptions for antidepressants, I might be in trouble with the Queensland Medical Board, perhaps struck off until I could prove myself.

The episode left me with two key messages, both of them very wrong. This first was that not thriving as an intern (or being 'a-copic', as one of my registrars disparagingly put it) meant I would never be appointed to a training program. The second was that seeking help was a sign of weakness, something to be ashamed of and hidden.

Today, I am President of my College. I have had a good career and, on balance, have done more good than harm to the patients I care for. In the end, there was some light at the end of the long, dark tunnel. I just couldn't see it at the time.

Why shine a light on my own past, 30 years later? Why speak about this so publicly? I have had a good career and achieved most of the things I had hoped to. Why rake up the past? Why not stay silent as I have for three decades?

If a person who has reached the highest point in their specialty still feels ashamed of events 30 years ago, and is reluctant to admit it, how must those who are going through things and feeling disempowered now feel? I am determined to use my own example to point out that mental health problems are nothing to be ashamed of.

Today, I am not ashamed of how I felt or what I did 30 years ago. I am ashamed and disappointed in myself that I have not used my position to advocate more strongly for colleagues in difficult emotional circumstances. I am ashamed that I was embarrassed and ashamed.

Doctors commonly are under pressure, are more prone to mental health problems, and often have access to the means of killing themselves. These are occupational hazards. In the same way that pilots are exposed to simulated decompression and hypoxia so they recognise the warning signs, we should recognise the warning signs and the debilitating and potentially lethal effects of psychological decompression.

When trainees of the College of which I am President took their own lives, I stayed silent.

When a junior doctor took his life while working at the same hospital that I did when I tried the same thing, I stayed silent. When I met Geoff Toogood, I stayed silent. Even after the shock realisation that CrazySocks4Docs *day was almost exactly 30 years after I tried to kill myself as an intern, I stayed silent.*

Enough silence.

It is absolutely vital that each and every one of us is honest and acknowledges the pressures and strains of our profession; that we see mental health issues not as sources of shame, but as potential occupational hazards that put not only ourselves at risk, but the patients we care for. I should have spoken up sooner.

For every doctor, especially our juniors, it is important to understand that mental health and emotional issues are nothing to be embarrassed about or ashamed of. They are important and need acknowledgement and treatment. We need to support each other and make this message abundantly clear.

If I had not been interrupted, I would have died 30 years ago. Luckily for me, that didn't happen. Now I find myself a College President. If you feel now the way I did 30 years ago, seek help and support as soon as you can. Speak out. Who knows where you might end up.

Professor Steve Robson[1]

Better awareness, recognition and treatment of mental illness in doctors

Professor Steve Robson's life was saved by his colleagues who took the courageous step to intervene – their 'unexpected interruption' was in fact in response to their growing concerns that he was at risk of suicide. In publishing his story, which has been read by many tens of thousands of doctors, Professor Robson has dramatically reduced the stigma of mental illness and suicide in the medical profession across the world. We applaud his courage in openly speaking about a topic that has previously been unspeakable.

In the decades since Professor Robson's experience, the assessment and management of mental illness has changed significantly. General practitioners/family physicians, psychiatrists and psychologists have also advanced significantly in their treatment of depression, anxiety and trauma. There are a wide range of online and face-to-face mental health professional training options, with an emphasis on evidence-based psychological therapies and appropriate

---

[1] Professor Steve Robson is former President of the Royal Australian and New Zealand College of Obstetricians and Gynaecologists, and the current President of the Australian Medical Association. First published in *MJA Insight Plus*, Issue 28, 22 July 2019.

prescribing of effective psychotropic medications. There is now a greater respect for patient privacy and there are severe penalties if treating clinicians breach patient confidentiality.

There is also a greater awareness by medical regulators that a punitive approach to doctors with mental illness is counterproductive. For this reason, medical boards encourage doctors to seek help for mental health care early. Mandatory reporting only applies if a doctor is at serious risk of harming patients, which is rarely the case.

Special barriers and challenges for doctors with mental health problems

Not surprisingly, doctors suffer from the same mental illnesses as the general population. Like the rest of the community, doctors fear the stigma of admitting to symptoms of mental illness and often receive late or suboptimal treatment, which can result in a poor prognosis or increased likelihood of future relapse. Many doctors do not recognise mental illness in themselves, despite their knowledge of the symptoms and signs. Doctors commonly say, 'I'm just run down' or 'It couldn't happen to me'. In addition, many members of doctors' families, friends and work colleagues fail to recognise or support a doctor with a mental illness because they stereotype the doctor as 'the strong one'.

One of the most common signs of mental illness can be a failure to thrive in work or study, secondary to poor concentration and difficulty with decision-making. Doctors have a tendency not to take sick leave and are experts at wearing emotional disguises, often continuing to provide a high standard of patient care at the expense of their own health.

Unfortunately, when doctors do admit to difficulty cope with work demands, they can often be viewed critically by other colleagues for 'letting the team down'.

We must recognise these unique barriers, stigmas and challenges doctors with mental illness face. It is often necessary for doctors to gently approach a colleague struggling with mental illness at work and assist them in seeking professional help, preferably early.

Many psychologists, psychiatrists and other mental health workers routinely seek supervision and debriefing to work through the vicarious effects of consulting clients with mental health problems. Doctors of other specialities are also affected by patient suffering, but tend not to reach out for support, debriefing or professional help for mental health issues because of the negative stigma attached to mental illness. This requires an attitudinal change.

Summary

Medical workplaces can be harsh environments where there is little compassion for doctors with mental health problems, which creates a stigma surrounding mental illness in the medical profession.

The impact of mental health disorders amongst doctors is underestimated. For those in medicine, daily exposure to distress, grief, trauma and uncertainty is normal, as are burnout and sleep disturbances. These experiences can leave us highly susceptible to mental illness in a workforce where seeking help has unique barriers and acknowledging human fallibility is discouraged. The medical profession has a responsibility to dispel the negative stigma of mental illness and encourage all patients to access optimal mental health care, including every doctor.

Helping colleagues seek early mental health care

Wilful forgetfulness

A doctor's best debriefing tool after a hard day is wilful forgetfulness. I recently invited two friends, a neurosurgeon and an anaesthetist, to dinner. My husband is a general practitioner and I am an oncologist – due to our schedules, it took us weeks to find a convenient date. Our friends arrived many hours late. The surgeon had been operating on a brand-new mum whose headaches revealed a brain tumour. He inserted a life-saving shunt that night, but her prognosis was grim. The anaesthetist had been monitoring another precarious situation where the patient's life still hung in balance. Earlier that day, my husband's elderly patient had suffered a near cardiac arrest while chatting to him. The waiting room was evacuated and sirens rang out. That same evening, I had received a tearful call from a terminally ill patient. He was in excruciating pain, the hospice was full, there was a long wait in emergency and he was frightened of dying. Could I help?

These were the accounts of our day as we greeted each other. Then the oven beeped, reminding us of a dinner many times reheated. In the course of just one day, we had been witness to serious and tragic life events; yet, as if observing a silent code of conduct, we never once mentioned those misfortunes as we ate. One such event once in a life might have ruined most people's appetite for food and company, but not ours. We were different.

That night, I didn't sleep. My thoughts turned to the young mother who would not see her baby grow up. And I fretted over my sick patient. I suspect we all had a disturbed night, our equanimity fractured by the fate of our patients. But I also knew that the next morning we would return to work, our facade repaired. For in that small space between sleep and wake, we would have consoled ourselves that bad things happen and our job as doctors is to not let ourselves feel too bad about them lest we fail our future patients.

A doctor's best debriefing tool after a hard day therefore turns out to be wilful forgetfulness. If you can minimise or better still, normalise catastrophe, you can keep going. Except, as a recent Australian survey of more than 14,000 doctors and medical students shows, this attitude comes at a great cost. One in 10 doctors entertained suicidal thoughts in the past year, compared to one in 45 in the community. More than a quarter of doctors are highly likely to suffer from mental illness. Oncologists like me, who routinely deal with death, face an especially high risk, as do young women and international doctors. This laudable study has caused a collective gasp in the community, but for most doctors, it has simply put sobering numbers to a problem we are all too familiar with. Far too many of us have lost a dear friend and able colleague to drugs, alcohol, crippling mental illness or suicide. Many more feel like helpless bystanders as we watch good doctors slowly self-destruct.

Every doctor knows that the very problems we counsel our patients for are those that beset us in far greater measure. So, you might ask why intelligent, driven, capable doctors would ignore the warning signs that they know by rote. Again, the survey identifies what every doctor either knows or suspects: the stigma attached to mental illness is magnified within the medical profession. Doctors regard their mentally ill peers with uncertainty and fear. They consider them less capable and are less willing to hire them or work with them. It therefore makes sense to keep problems under wraps in an unsupportive environment.

For me, watching the journey of some of my mentally ill friends has been in turns frightening, unsettling and sad. It's a tightrope to envelope a colleague in understanding while protecting their patients from harm as a result of inattention. As a sympathetic observer, it is tempting to become impatient with at-risk doctors who don't or won't seek help, even though they have access to it. But it is also difficult to convince doctors to appreciate the extent of their problem, because we have been shaped to believe in our infallibility. Diseases afflict our patients, they don't touch us. Our patients are defined by their illness, while we are defined by our ability to cure their malady. Medical education shies away from discussing our vulnerabilities. Students and young doctors are rarely reminded that despite their hallowed place in society, they are prone to the same vicissitudes of life as everyone else. It is no wonder that when faced by personal catastrophe, a doctor's first response is to deny the problem exists.

Doctors have a long tradition of being considered different from the rest of society. But when it comes to mental illness, our serious differences are jeopardizing our own health and that of our patients. The culture of medicine demands a change. To do any less would be to short change doctors and patients.

Dr Ranjana Srivastava[1]

---

[1] Dr Ranjana Srivastava is an Australian Oncologist, a Fulbright Scholar and the award-winning author of *After Cancer: A Guide to Living Well*. Article first published in the *Guardian*, reprinted with permission.

When a colleague says 'I'm depressed'

Our first response to a colleague who says 'I am depressed' is critical for a number of reasons. As Dr Ranjana Srivastava emphasises in her story, doctors can have tough emotional masks and it is difficult for our colleagues to trust someone and disclose their vulnerability. Due to the enormous stigma surrounding mental illness in the medical profession, doctors, when they do reach out, may have suffered quietly for a long time, are probably sleep deprived and could be at risk, perhaps self-medicating with antidepressants, benzodiazepines or alcohol. Simple reassurance is not enough.

We must listen intently. If this doctor is a friend, we can help them get the right treatment from a general practitioner/family physician with mental health training and experience. As doctors, we are in a better position than most patients to use our networks to find the right help, including accessing independent general practitioners/family physicians outside our geographical area of practice to protect our confidentiality, doctors' health advisory services or telehealth support for those of us who are working remotely or doing shift work.

When we are the treating doctor

When we are the treating doctor, listening is also our most powerful skill because the presenting problem is usually not the main reason for the consultation. Often a doctor patient will cry when we ask them how they feel, because very few people ask doctors this question or take time to listen to the answer fully. Many doctors rarely disclose their stories of grief, trauma and injustice, and it is a relief for them to do so.

It is important for treating doctors to offer the same high standard of care they would offer their other patients, which includes taking a comprehensive mental health history and checking for psychotic symptoms, substance misuse, cognitive decline and suicide risk.

Take a comprehensive mental health history

Optimal mental health assessment involves asking these questions in a sensitive manner in a confidential environment:

- What is the nature of the presenting problem?
- What are the specific symptoms?

- What events led to this presentation?
- Are there any symptoms or signs of underlying physical illness, which may have predisposed this person to mental illness such as an endocrine disorder, infection, neurological disorder, cardiovascular disease, collagen disorder, malignancy or metabolic disorder?
- Is there relevant past history? What past and current medications has this person been taking, including drugs that may be associated with depressive symptoms such as analgesics, anti-inflammatory agents, antihypertensive, antineoplastic, neurological agents, steroids or hormones?
- What is the developmental history as a child, adolescent and young adult?
- What is the education and work history?
- What is the family history?
- What is the quality of relationships with partners, children and significant others?
- What is the suicide risk?

To obtain a full history, we must earn trust by reassuring our doctor patients about confidentiality and dispelling the myths surrounding mandatory reporting to regulatory authorities. Most of us have never had to report a doctor with mental illness to a regulatory authority, as colleagues usually comply with treatment and take time off work if needed.

Here is a framework to ensure we have covered all aspects of a comprehensive mental health assessment over a few consultations.

Address common risk factors

Only by fully exploring common risk factors can we be proactive in addressing them.

Of course, doctors have the same risk factors for mental illness as the general population. Unsurprisingly, our doctor patients may have family histories of mental illness and alcohol and substance misuse, chronic illness or pain, negative life experiences and relationships, fractured family structures, family of origin histories of violence or suicide, and histories of child abuse. These histories can be triggered repetitively when our doctor patients are caring for their own patients with these common problems.

In addition, we often have perfectionist, self-critical, hypervigilant and task-oriented personality styles that make us great doctors, but put us at risk of failing our own impossible expectations. When doctors become aware that their personality strengths can also be vulnerabilities, they allow themselves to set healthy boundaries and become even stronger than before. Patients need doctors who are caring, dedicated and healthy – not selfless. We are trained to 'first do no harm' to our patients, and we also need to adopt this principle for ourselves.

Recognise a mixed pattern of atypical symptoms

Doctor patients may present with a mixed pattern of symptoms related to depressive disorder, anxiety disorder and post-traumatic stress disorder due to acute and chronic exposure to patient trauma, violence, abuse and death, including suicide.

They often present with atypical symptoms, such as uncharacteristic irritability or anger, difficulty concentrating or making decisions because of excessive worry, lack of empathy, social withdrawal and/or fatigue or low energy due to insomnia. Diagnosis and treatment can therefore be complex.

Ask the hard questions

To work through all the issues, it is important to cover the other aspects of a comprehensive mental health history in detail – past history, family history, past/current medication, developmental history, education, work history, social history, suicide risk and past and current suicidal thinking.

As suicide is more common among doctors than in the general population, doctors are frequently traumatised by a colleague's death and then placed at risk of suicide themselves. It's not easy to ask doctor patients this question: 'Many people who are under extreme pressure feel like harming themselves. Have you ever felt this way?' but it is essential. Doctors have easy access to means, and ongoing suicide risk assessment is critical.

Overcome the special pitfalls of management

Most doctors are experienced with adjusting their approach to patients with different levels of health literacy, including colleagues with high health literacy. However, doctors treating other doctors may need to keep in mind that a doctor patient may present late with serious and complex medical or psychiatric issues. They have often tried self-investigation and self-medication before seeking external help.

Optimal management of mental illness requires diagnosis, formal treatment with structured psychological therapies and/or appropriate doses of medication, regular review and relapse prevention strategies.

It's easy to fall into the trap of providing brief telephone follow-up or repeat prescriptions for doctor patients too busy to attend in person. Follow-up long consultations are required to prevent a relapse of mental health problems in any patient.

Formal psychological treatments such as behavioural therapy, interpersonal therapy, acceptance therapy, and cognitive behavioural therapy may be evidence-based in the general population. However, these therapies can have limitations in doctors because we are trained to 'overthink' and have well-developed negative mental filters and negative cognitive biases. Being risk-averse is part of being a good doctor. It is not easy to overcome these ingrained traits by challenging negative thinking with the usual cognitive behavioural therapy techniques. Structured formal mindfulness-based cognitive behavioural therapy has been found to be an effective treatment for depression. Antidepressant medication may also be required.

Many general practitioners/family physicians with mental health training are capable of providing these treatments, but it's important to recognise that colleagues may prefer to be referred appropriately to a psychologist or psychiatrist.

Although doctors tend to take very little sick leave, many medical workplaces fail to support doctors when they request a lower patient load or time off work. Sometimes, doctor patients require their treating doctor's support to take sick leave because of their fears for their career if they disclose mental health problems.

Unfortunately, these fears are often justified. In this scenario and with the doctor patient's permission, the necessary certificate can be supplied directly to the workplace by the treating doctor, without divulging the medical reasons and without the need for the doctor patient to personally justify their temporary absence. This, of course, is the right of any employee.

Summary

When a doctor says, 'I am depressed', simple reassurance is not enough, but a willingness to listen fully can be a powerful skill. We can help colleagues access the right professional help. It is important for doctors to develop a relationship with a trusted independent general practitioner/family physician early in their career whom they can reach out to for early mental health care or in times of crisis.

As doctors, we are skilled at adjusting our consultation styles to the level of health literacy of our diverse patients. For our doctor patients, we can appropriately adjust our approach to their high level of mental health literacy. We must also undertake a comprehensive mental health history and overcome the special pitfalls of treating doctors as patients.

21 Improving every doctor's mental health literacy

Put faith in 'repaired' colleagues

Recently, I was speaking with a Japanese artist who specialises in kintsugi – 'the art of precious scars'.

Kintsugi artists restore broken pottery. The philosophy is to treat breakage and repair as part of the history of the piece rather than disguise it. The repairs are illuminated by the nature of the repair, which are often done in gold. She showed me photos of her exhibitions and the art was indeed beautiful. Its true meaning was a little lost to me at the time, but was greatly reinforced when I read a book by Tomas Navarro about kintsugi's potential connection to mental health.

The craft takes many years to master, and indeed each piece takes many hours to complete. It is both a work of art and love, with each piece beautifully restored.

The repaired pottery of kintsugi is not viewed as defective because it is damaged and has been repaired. It is proudly displayed, not hidden away.

Recovery from a mental health condition requires expert medical artistry from the counsellors and can indeed take a long time. The repair may also leave scars, often invisible, but as with the pottery, the repaired person can still function. Indeed, just as the repaired pottery is viewed as a thing of beauty, so we should view those that bear the scars of mental illness. They are testament to their own resilience and strength. We should exhibit them in the same way.

It is not clear that we do that in the medical profession.

I have many scars. Most are invisible, but it is who I am, and it is my history. I can function equally well now in my job and in my everyday life. Like all who have been through mental health struggles and recovery, it's our vulnerabilities and our responses to them that should be embraced. We should feel able to proudly display them.

Far too often we who have had mental health issues have been viewed as not being made in the correct way – not blasted in the furnace or shaped on the pottery wheel for strength. We are seen as not resilient enough – not made of the right stuff.

Just like a pot, if we are dropped from a great height or hit in the correct spot, we will break and maybe even shatter. But don't we have the right to repair? Shouldn't our recovery be valued?

DOI: 10.1201/9781003296829-25

We have gained awareness – pots break, and so do humans. We know this now, but it's in the normalisation and respecting of the repair that we are still lacking.

In kintsugi, often the pottery is shattered and requires complex repair, which can take time and money. Just as this ancient art requires the skill of the artist, the time and space in which to weave the magic and the appropriate tools and support, mental health recovery requires time, money, personnel and respect for the 'repaired pot'.

We have become very aware of the shattered people much like the shattered pots. But a repaired pot is just lying idle, waiting, not performing its role, until someone has faith that it can do its job, just as before. We need to urgently provide the resources and skills to repair our 'broken' colleagues. Give them the time to recover or get support. And then we must allow them to display their scars and perform their roles. Otherwise, unlike the repaired pots, they will remain shattered.

Dr Geoffrey Toogood[1]

Dr Toogood's story is a reminder to us all to *'provide the resources and skills to repair our "broken" colleagues. . . . Give them the time to recover or get support . . .'*

In this chapter, we summarise brief information about common mental health conditions, with an emphasis on seeking independent, individualised but evidence-based assessment and treatment rather than self-diagnosis. It is important that every doctor from every speciality has a high level of mental health literacy, not only for their patients, but to assist colleagues to access the right help. In the words of psychiatrist, Dr Vikram Patel:[2]

Mental health is too precious to be left to psychiatrists alone. We believe that mental health is everybody's business. And there is no health without mental health.

---

[1] Dr Geoffrey Toogood is a Cardiologist and a long-time advocate for mental health. He has swum the English Channel. He came up with the idea of CrazySocks4Docs day, which is now an international initiative to recognise doctors' mental health. This piece was first published in *MJA Insight Plus*, Issue 30, 6 August 2018.

[2] Dr Vikram Patel is an Indian Psychiatrist and researcher, Co-Founder and former Director of the Centre for Global Mental Health at the London School of Hygiene and Tropical Medicine (LSHTM) and one of the world's 100 most influential people by *TIME* magazine.

Why are there continuing high levels of mental health problems in the medical profession?

Although mental illnesses can be treated successfully, there are a number of reasons why doctors are continuing to report high rates of depressive disorder, anxiety and other fear-related disorders, post-traumatic stress disorder and suicidal ideation.

In addition to the common risk factors in the general population such as chronic exposure to stressful events, physical health conditions, substance abuse, uncaring relationships, isolation and loneliness and family history of mental illness, we are surrounded by misery, grief and trauma at work. Doctors may be more at risk of mental illness because of common personality traits including the tendency to worry a lot, overthink, have low self-esteem and be perfectionist, sensitive to personal criticism, self-critical and overly negative or risk averse.

As previously discussed, doctors tend to work long hours and suffer from chronic sleep deprivation. For these reasons, it can be difficult to recognise or assess our own mental health issues or those of a work colleague because low-grade depressive or anxiety symptoms in doctors are sometimes perceived as 'normal'.

Unfortunately, doctors do not tend to take sick leave to consult their own doctor, nor do they like to spend their precious time off waiting in other doctors' waiting rooms. Rather than seeking formal support and management, doctors sometimes self-medicate (although all doctors know they should never self-prescribe drug treatment for their own mental illness) or seek ad hoc treatment from a medical friend, which is clearly inadequate.

For all these reasons, many doctors may mask their depressed or anxious mood, and usually continue to provide a high standard of care to patients at great expense to themselves.

It is imperative that doctors seek formal counselling and optimal management from an experienced, independent treating doctor or psychologist. The treating professional must appreciate that for all the wrong reasons, doctor patients often present late with atypical or partially self-treated symptoms of mental illness, and may continue to function normally at work.

Atypical symptoms are sometimes described as feelings of general unease, quiet desperation and numbness rather than sadness. Other symptoms include loss of interest in anything outside work, withdrawal from people, excessive guilt, taking too much personal responsibility for things going wrong, being easily offended or defensive and uncharacteristic anger, frustration or excessive cynicism.

When they present to another doctor, many doctor patients will present with a tough emotional shield. In this situation, it takes time for the treating doctor to develop trust by listening fully and to get beneath the shield to build an effective therapeutic relationship.

Most doctors will be aware of the latest formal classifications and descriptions of mental illness from the ICD-11 and DSM-5 manuals. In the next section is a summary of the main symptoms and management of only a few common mental illnesses such as depressive disorder, anxiety and other fear-related disorders including panic disorder. We have deliberately kept this section brief as our main message in this book is for doctors to seek evidence-based professional help for mental health problems, not to self-diagnose or self-treat.

Depressive disorder

According to the ICD-11, a depressive episode is '*characterised by a period of depressed mood or diminished interest in activities occurring most of the day, nearly every day during a period lasting at least two weeks accompanied by other symptoms such as difficulty concentrating, feelings of worthlessness or excessive or inappropriate guilt, hopelessness, recurrent thoughts of death or suicide, changes in appetite or sleep, psychomotor agitation or retardation, and reduced energy or fatigue*'.

Dysthymia tends to be less recognised than depression as the symptoms are not as severe or present every day. According to ICD-11, '*Dysthymic disorder is characterised by a persistent depressive mood (i.e., lasting 2 years or more), for most of the day, for more days than not. In children and adolescents depressed mood can manifest as pervasive irritability. The depressed mood is accompanied by additional symptoms such as markedly diminished interest or pleasure in activities, reduced concentration and attention or indecisiveness, low self-worth or excessive or inappropriate guilt, hopelessness about the future, disturbed sleep or increased sleep, diminished or increased appetite, or low energy or fatigue. During the first 2 years of the disorder, there has never been a 2-week period during which the number and duration of symptoms were sufficient to meet the diagnostic requirements for a Depressive Episode*'.

Seasonal affective disorder (SAD) is a mood disorder that has a seasonal pattern related to the variation in light exposure in different seasons over a few years. It is usually found in countries with shorter days and longer periods of darkness, such as in the cold climate areas of the Northern Hemisphere. However, doctors who are not exposed to much sunlight, such as radiologists or those working night shifts, may also be at risk of SAD. Light therapy can be an effective treatment for this form of depression.

Antenatal and postnatal depression in women during pregnancy and in the year following childbirth often result from a combination of factors and affect not only the mother but her relationship with her baby and partner, as well as the child's development.

Formal early optimal treatment is preferable for all types of depression as it results in a better prognosis. The following are examples of effective formal psychological therapies:

- **Cognitive behaviour therapy (CBT)** is a psychological treatment that recognises thinking patterns (cognition) and behaviour patterns that affect the way we feel. By thinking more rationally about common difficulties, it helps to shift negative or unhelpful thought patterns and reactions to a more positive and solution-orientated approach.
- **Interpersonal therapy (IPT)** is a psychological therapy that focuses on skills to strengthen personal relationships and overcome relationship and other problems.
- **Behaviour therapy/Behavioural activation** is a major part of cognitive behaviour therapy, but it focuses on planning activities that are pleasant and enjoyable to help overcome social withdrawal and inactivity.
- **Mindfulness-based cognitive therapy** (MBCT) is different to the treatments above as it helps change our process of thinking, not only the content of our thoughts. It helps us to let go of unhelpful thoughts and emotions, as well as realising that we do not have to respond to every thought or emotion. It is about learning to develop a new relationship to our thoughts and emotions. Mindfulness encourages us to notice when automatic thoughts are occurring and to alter our reaction. It encourages our attention to our attention, without making any judgements about whether thoughts are positive or negative.

In offering formal psychological therapies, it is important to recognise that doctors may find it difficult to reduce critical self-talk, overthinking, over-checking or negative cognitive bias. These common thought habits are part of the risk-averse nature of everyday medical practice. Juggling excessive demands through multi-skilling is a common way to successfully attend to hundreds of patients and thousands of important decisions each week. In response to being challenged to change their thinking patterns, it is common for doctors to become frustrated that they cannot stop 'faulty' thinking patterns or intrusive worrying.

Individual psychological therapies may also be counterproductive when doctors are working in toxic cultures, where bullying, harassment or discrimination are being tolerated. For example, helping doctors with anger management skills may not be helpful when anger as a response to injustice, inequity and poor quality of patient care is justified. Some challenging experiences in medicine cannot be solved with 'rational thinking'. Sometimes it is better to sit with sadness, fear, pain and uncertainty for a while. At other times, it is more effective to challenge a negative workplace culture than to focus on strengthening individual skills.

It can take time for psychological therapies to work because brain habits and conditioning do not change easily. It can help to rest, accept overthinking without judging it as good or bad, and practice muscular relaxation regularly. Seeking out supportive family and friends, planning simple pleasant experiences, and creating worthwhile goals outside of medicine can also help.

If formal psychological therapies do not improve symptoms, it may be beneficial to seek a second opinion. More often, antidepressant treatment may be required after a thorough assessment by an experienced treating family physician/general practitioner and/or psychiatrist.

Selective serotonin reuptake inhibitors (SSRIs) are the preferred drugs in most people for the treatment of depression, including postnatal depression, because of the lower side effect profile and safety in overdose compared with older classes of antidepressants. There can be a delay of one to two weeks before any benefit is experienced and the full effect may not be apparent for four to eight weeks.

Well-known side effects of SSRIs may include increased appetite, weight gain, nausea, constipation, postural dizziness, drowsiness, dry mouth, sexual dysfunction and increased sensitivity to sun exposure, but these symptoms are usually minor. To increase compliance, these side effects may be managed appropriately by simple techniques such as increasing exercise, adjusting diet, increasing fluid intake and dividing doses.

Common warning signs of a depression relapse include changes in sleep pattern, decreased concentration, withdrawal and isolation, lack of energy, irritability, loss of interest in usual activities and lowered mood. To prevent the likelihood of a relapse or recurrence of depression, a number of psychological strategies are used including structured problem-solving, mindfulness and sleep techniques (Chapter 7), relaxation training and assertiveness and communication training. Long-term maintenance antidepressant medication may be recommended to prevent relapse in people at risk, including those with chronic exposure to stress.

The explanation for the increased prevalence of suicide in doctors compared with the general population is multi-factorial. As already discussed, doctors face barriers in accessing mental health care and work in stressful and often unsupportive environments with easy access to lethal drugs. Recurrent thoughts about death, suicide or self-harm are a medical emergency in anyone. Anyone in this situation must seek urgent psychiatric support and advice.

Anxiety and other fear-related disorders

Feeling anxious is often a normal reaction. Intermittent high levels of anxiety may be an appropriate response to dealing with excessive demands. Temporary levels of anxiety can improve performance and be protective.

Anxiety disorders are different. They are characterised by prolonged distress and tension out of proportion with life stressors, which impairs functioning.

According to the ICD-11, '*Anxiety and fear-related disorders are characterised by excessive fear and anxiety and related behavioural disturbances, with symptoms that are severe enough to result in significant distress or significant impairment in personal, family, social, educational, occupational, or other important areas of functioning. Fear and anxiety are closely related phenomena; fear represents a reaction to perceived imminent threat in the present, whereas anxiety is more future-oriented, referring to perceived anticipated threat. A key differentiating feature among the Anxiety and fear-related disorders are disorder-specific foci of apprehension, that is, the stimulus or situation that triggers the fear or anxiety. The clinical presentation of Anxiety and fear-related disorders typically includes specific associated cognitions that can assist in differentiating among the disorders by clarifying the focus of apprehension*'.

Anxiety disorders are usually caused by a combination of factors, which may include personality factors, difficult life experiences, family history, substance abuse and physical health problems such as thyroid disorders. Stressful events may predispose one to the development of anxiety disorders, including frequent job changes, change in geography, relationship problems, exposure to trauma or verbal, sexual, physical or emotional abuse and/or death or loss of a loved one.

Symptoms of anxiety disorders may include feeling nervous or restless, muscle tension, increased heart rate or palpitations, rapid breathing and sometimes acute hyperventilation, sweating, trembling, feeling weak or tired and difficulty concentrating or thinking about anything other than worrying issues. It is common for people with anxiety disorders to present with other somatic symptoms such as difficulty breathing, gastrointestinal disorders, sensations of choking or a lump in the throat, chest pain and feeling faint or dizzy.

Types of anxiety and other fear-related disorders include:

- Persistent excessive or unrealistic worries which interfere with life, work or activities (generalised anxiety disorder)
- Uncontrollable compulsions or obsessions, including over-checking, fear of germs, overcleaning, overcounting and repeating routine activities and actions (obsessive-compulsive disorder)
- Intense excessive worry related to social situations (social anxiety disorder)
- An intensely irrational fear of everyday objects and situations (phobia)
- Recurrent panic attacks (panic disorder)

According to ICD-11, '*Panic disorder is characterised by recurrent unexpected panic attacks that are not restricted to particular stimuli or situations. Panic attacks are discrete episodes of intense fear or apprehension accompanied by the rapid and concurrent onset of several characteristic symptoms (e.g. palpitations or increased heart rate, sweating, trembling, shortness of breath, chest pain, dizziness or light headedness, chills, hot flushes, fear of imminent death). In addition, panic disorder is characterised by persistent concern about the recurrence or significance of panic attacks, or behaviours intended to avoid their recurrence, that results in significant impairment in personal, family, social, educational, occupational, or other important areas of functioning*'.

Symptoms of a panic attack can include:

- Heightened vigilance for danger and physical symptoms
- Anxious and irrational thinking
- A strong feeling of dread, danger or foreboding

- Fear of going mad, losing control or dying
- Feeling lightheaded and dizzy
- Tingling and chills, particularly in the arms and hands
- Trembling, shaking or sweating
- Feelings of unreality and detachment from the environment
- Fear of losing control, of going 'crazy' or of dying are also common

People may start avoiding activities or certain situations to minimise or avoid the possibility of a future attack.

Suggestions on how to cope with a panic attack include:

- Avoid 'self-talk' that focuses your attention on your symptoms. Telling yourself to 'Stop panicking!' or 'Relax!' is usually counterproductive.
- Remind yourself that the symptoms of a panic attack are uncomfortable, but not life-threatening and when you experienced this before, nothing bad happened to you.
- Try to focus your attention on something else. For example, slow your breathing by inhaling in for the count of four, holding your breath for two and exhaling on the count of six. Or try to recall the words from a favourite song.
- Try not to leave the situation; if you allow the symptoms to pass, you will restore confidence in your ability to cope next time.

Formal psychological therapies, relaxation therapy and online mental health resources used in depression are also very effective in managing anxiety disorders.

In addition, cognitive bias modification is a simple technique to break the habits of anxious thinking and reduce subconscious attention to negative stimuli, risks and threats. We can always find something to worry about and this can cause a feeling of general unease or mild irritability. For example, we may be watching for anything that may go wrong, unconsciously and constantly scanning the world for risks and threats, and assuming the worst-case scenario without evidence. This can take a lot of energy. It is possible to retrain the mind to consciously reduce excessive hypervigilance, but this can take time.

By becoming aware of our negative biases, we can try to consciously shift our attention to trying to scan the environment for positive images and sensations. We can also use healthy cognitive disassociation as a technique to help separate ourselves from negative or unpleasant thoughts. For example, sometimes it helps to try visual distancing where we can try to imagine viewing an event or our thoughts from a distance. In addition, it can help to try self-reassurance and kindness with self-talk like 'This is painful and part of being human'.

SSRIs are also very effective in the treatment of anxiety disorders, but as previously discussed, psychotropic medication must never be self-prescribed.

Benzodiazepines are not recommended in anxiety disorders as they can reduce alertness, compromise coordination and be addictive. They may occasionally be useful intermittently for a very short period of time (up to two or three weeks) as part of a comprehensive treatment plan, but never as the first or only treatment. It is also important to note that alcohol is harmful when used to treat mental health problems (Chapter 22).

Summary

Our summaries of common mental health conditions such as depressive disorder, anxiety and other fear disorders are deliberately brief because we wish to discourage readers from self-diagnosis and self-treatment. If experiencing mental health problems, doctors must seek out and consult a trusted family physician or general practitioner, psychologist and/or psychiatrist early to prevent the many negative consequences of mental illness.

Supporting colleagues with mental illness

Please stay

The only career advice my father ever gave me was not to follow in his footsteps and become a doctor. I had no plans to – I already knew I wanted to be a journalist – and never asked him more about it.

Within a year he had died by suicide, in the grip of depression. I was 16 when I found him in our yard, his stethoscope nearby. It seems that, a practitioner to the last, he had listened as his own signs of life began to fade.

It's been 25 years since our family was blindsided by my father's suicide.

Always the taciturn type, he had told my mother of his depression without revealing its depths. She assured him of our love, that we would all get through it together.

He took his life less than a week later, at 48. It still pains me that he died alone. Had he been able to speak openly about his darkest thoughts, and given all of us who loved him every chance to help, he might be here now – a part of our lives, and still living his.

But I know myself how suffocating stigma can be. It was years before I discussed Dad's suicide outside our family, for fear that he – that we – would be judged. My grief was complicated by feelings of guilt, shame, anger and abandonment, and I grappled with them largely on my own.

Eventually I came to understand that Dad had not made a choice to leave us. It wasn't death he wanted, but relief. With more time and treatment, he could have found it. There were far better paths than the one he took; lost in his despair, he just couldn't see them.

There are so many things I wish I had said to him. If I had my time again, I'd keep it simple:

You will get better.
Don't give up hope.
We love you.
We need you.
Please stay.

Ms Kim Arlington, journalist

DOI: 10.1201/9781003296829-26

Unfortunately, there are too many stories of suicide in doctors, where in retrospect it was noted that they had uncharacteristically withdrawn from others. Ms Kim Arlington's memories surrounding the tragic death of her father remind us of our responsibility to check in with colleagues showing any signs of mental illness.

Doctors are in a position to recognise and compassionately respond to their colleagues' early symptoms and uncharacteristic behaviours, which often first manifest at work. Whatever our speciality, we must identify potentially catastrophic mental disorders which compromise our colleague's insight or put the care of patients at risk. Disorders such as untreated psychosis (bipolar disorder, schizophrenia), intoxication and substance abuse disorders and cognitive decline may cause temporary or permanent impairment and require assertive early intervention.

Clearly, this is about helping colleagues take time off work to receive independent comprehensive psychiatric and neurological assessment and treatment as soon as possible. In many countries, doctors are mandated to report seriously impaired colleagues to the medical practitioners' board or regulator, which sometimes deters doctors from seeking help. It should not be left this late before there is an intervention.

Responding to suicidal thinking in doctors

For our distressed patients, we have been trained to respond, 'Many people who are under extreme pressure feel like harming themselves. Have you ever felt this way?' However, many of us would feel uncomfortable saying this to a colleague in distress, because we understand the special barriers deterring doctors from disclosing suicidal thinking. But not doing so can be fatal.

Community suicide prevention and intervention strategies usually address general risk factors including mental illness, alcohol and substance abuse, chronic illness and pain, previous non-fatal suicidal behaviour, genetic and biological factors, negative life experiences and relationships, fractured family structures, family of origin history of violence or suicide, work stress and social isolation. It is essential that we also identify these risk factors in our doctor patients, as they are as prevalent in doctors as in the rest of the population.

Doctors have additional risks for suicide, including high rates of self-medication, access to lethal means and our exposure to traumatic death and suicide in patients, often without routine debriefing or postvention, which also need to be identified.

One of the many dimensions that requires more research is the significantly higher rate of burnout, mental illness, suicidal thinking and death by suicide of female doctors and female medical students compared with the general population (about two and a half times higher). These gender differences may relate to additional risk factors in women doctors and students including an increased prevalence of stress, depression, anxiety, eating disorders, post-traumatic stress responses, postnatal depression, intimate partner violence, domestic violence and patient violence, childhood sexual abuse and exposure to workplace bullying, harassment and discrimination, all requiring special care.

Fears around confidentiality of clinical consultations and mandatory reporting to medical boards are often broadcast widely, but this concern is frequently misplaced. Mandatory reporting is usually only relevant if doctors are placing the public at risk of 'substantial harm' because of a health issue, which is rarely the case. The confidentiality of doctors' health information, like that of other patients, is protected by strict privacy laws in many nations, and we know how to make an effective complaint in the unlikely scenario of a breach.

In the general community, there is an evidence base underpinning effective suicide prevention programs, which usually involve initiatives across prevention, early intervention, optimal treatment and postvention. Unfortunately, we have not invested in the same evidenced-based solutions for the medical profession, and we have failed to address the scale of our problem. Of course, the topic of doctor suicide is complex and distressing, but we must confront the uncomfortable fact that we can prevent doctor suicide if we implement evidence based comprehensive suicide prevention programs.

How can we prevent doctor suicide? As we have discussed in Parts 1–3, we can:

- Prevent and manage our burnout
- Destigmatise mental illness
- Encourage all doctors to have their own trusted treating doctor
- Provide early, evidence-based management of mental injury
- Change our medical culture to be kinder and more supportive to everyone
- Build strong relationships with colleagues by sharing challenges

Part 4 on saving lives through medical co-leadership advocates for health system change to not only save patient lives, but also to save doctors' lives by preventing suicide.

Doctors' health programs must also be tailored to address the special needs of groups of doctors more at risk, including young doctors, women doctors, Indigenous doctors and doctors who have migrated from other countries. What we 'are doing' or 'have done' for doctors' health is not enough. While we have many competing priorities in medicine, the poor mental health of doctors and medical students, which reflects global trends, deserves ongoing urgent action by the whole medical profession and all medical organisations. None of this is easy, but we can prevent the tragedy of doctor suicide – together.

In the following sections, we discuss the symptoms and signs of bipolar disorder, schizophrenia, substance use disorders and cognitive decline; because these illnesses may result in mental impairment that places patient safety and doctors' lives at risk. As there is usually an inherent lack of insight and heightened risk of suicide in doctors with these conditions, there is a need to be proactive in assisting a colleague to get the right professional help – early. Major depression, anxiety disorder and post-traumatic disorder, which are also risk factors for suicide, have been discussed in Chapter 21.

Bipolar disorder

Bipolar disorder 1 and 2 are forms of psychotic illness. People with bipolar disorder may experience extreme highs and lows of mood and may behave in an irrational or risky manner. The cycles of highs and lows vary from individual to individual.

According to the ICD-11, '*Bipolar type I disorder is an episodic mood disorder defined by the occurrence of one or more manic or mixed episodes. A manic episode is an extreme mood state lasting at least one week unless shortened by a treatment intervention characterised by euphoria, irritability, or expansiveness, and by increased activity or a subjective experience of increased energy, accompanied by other characteristic symptoms such as rapid or pressured speech, flight of ideas, increased self-esteem or grandiosity, decreased need for sleep, distractibility, impulsive or reckless behaviour, and rapid changes among different mood states (i.e., mood lability). A mixed episode is characterised by the presence of several prominent manic and several prominent depressive symptoms consistent with those observed in manic episodes and depressive episodes, which either occur simultaneously or alternate very rapidly (from day to day or within the same day). Symptoms must include an altered mood state consistent with a manic and/or depressive episode (i.e., depressed, dysphoric, euphoric or expansive mood), and be present most of the day, nearly every day, during a period of at least 2 weeks, unless shortened by a treatment intervention. Although the diagnosis can be made based on evidence of a single manic or mixed episode, typically manic or mixed episodes alternate with depressive episodes over the course of the disorder'.*

'Bipolar type II disorder is an episodic mood disorder defined by the occurrence of one or more hypomanic episodes and at least one depressive episode. A hypomanic episode is a persistent mood state lasting for at least several days characterised by persistent elevation of mood or increased irritability as well as increased activity or a subjective experience of increased energy, accompanied by other characteristic symptoms such as increased talkativeness, rapid or racing thoughts, increased self-esteem, decreased need for sleep, distractibility, and impulsive or reckless behavior. The symptoms represent a change from the individual's typical mood, energy level, and behavior but are not severe enough to cause marked impairment in functioning. A depressive episode is characterised by a period of depressed mood or diminished interest in activities occurring most of the day, nearly every day during a period lasting at least two weeks accompanied by other symptoms such as changes in appetite or sleep, psychomotor agitation or retardation, fatigue, feelings of worthless or excessive or inappropriate guilt, feelings or hopelessness, difficulty concentrating, and suicidality. There is no history of manic or mixed episodes'.

Doctors with untreated bipolar disorder may present with difficulty making decisions and concentrating, or may become uncharacteristically reckless. Grandiose ideas, inflated self-esteem, increased energy, enhanced libido, impaired judgement and impulsive behaviour along with impaired insight may put a doctor at risk of ruining their reputation and place their patients at serious risk of harm.

As with other serious mental illness, the sufferer requires a lot of support from their colleagues at work and their family and friends. Most of all, it is essential that a doctor with a sudden onset or relapse of bipolar disorder is actively assisted to seek help from their treating doctor early.

Mood-stabilising medication such as lithium is used to treat depressive and manic symptoms. An antidepressant may be added to treat depressive symptoms, but must be ceased if there are manic symptoms. Manic symptoms may also require a benzodiazepine or an antipsychotic.

To reduce the likelihood of recurrence, a prophylactic mood stabiliser is used. Doctors as patients must be educated about the risk factors and the early signs of relapse of a bipolar disorder. It must be emphasised that anyone with bipolar disorder must attend routine reviews by an experienced independent family physician/general practitioner or psychiatrist, and comply strictly with their medication.

Schizophrenia

Schizophrenia is another form of psychotic illness which also interferes with a person's ability to think, feel and behave.

According to the ICD-11, '*Schizophrenia and other primary psychotic disorders are characterised by significant impairments in reality testing and alterations in behaviour manifest in positive symptoms such as persistent delusions, persistent hallucinations, disorganised thinking (typically manifest as disorganised speech), grossly disorganised behaviour, and experiences of passivity and control, negative symptoms such as blunted or flat affect and avolition, and psychomotor disturbances. The symptoms occur with sufficient frequency and intensity to deviate from expected cultural or subcultural norms. These symptoms do not arise as a feature of another mental and behavioural disorder (e.g., a mood disorder, delirium, or a disorder due to substance use). The categories in this grouping should not be used to classify the expression of ideas, beliefs, or behaviours that are culturally sanctioned*'.

Acute psychosis, especially first-onset schizophrenia, should be treated as a medical emergency. Schizophrenia, which often emerges in young adulthood has a better lifetime prognosis if treated with antipsychotic medication early, usually within one week of the development of acute symptoms. If a psychiatrist is not immediately available, any doctor may initiate treatment with antipsychotic medication for acute psychosis. Failure to do so may result in lifelong disability or death by suicide or occasionally by police.

It is important for people with psychosis to establish a strong relationship with their treating doctor and other supporting healthcare providers. Education and support of the patient and their family and friends are essential for a good outcome. The focus is on early intervention but the sufferer often lacks insight and requires the support of others to seek treatment. Early recognition by colleagues at work is usually essential because facilitation of early treatment of schizophrenia by an experienced independent psychiatrist is associated with a good prognosis. As with all mental illnesses, most people who receive optimal treatment lead happy and fulfilling lives. However, late treatment is often associated with poor prognosis and lifelong disability.

Again, the importance of assisting colleagues to get the right independent psychiatric assessment and management early cannot be overestimated.

Substance abuse disorders including alcohol dependence

A substance use disorder is generally characterised by a strong desire to take alcohol or drugs or prescribed medication, with harmful physical and psychological consequences which may include reduced work performance, negative impact on relationships, depression or physical illness including liver damage.

The use of any substances must be assessed within the context of the individual's life and their readiness for change. A comprehensive psychiatric history is important to identify possible comorbidity including depression, anxiety, psychosis, post-traumatic stress disorder, eating disorders and bipolar disorder. The severity of dependence, the physical health consequences, and any risk-taking behaviour associated with substance use must be explored by the treating doctor. The treatment and management plan must be adjusted according to the history and the motivation of the individual. It is essential that a doctor with a substance use disorder is monitored and reviewed regularly by an independent, experienced treating doctor.

It is important to remember that anxiety, depressed mood and sleep disturbance can be symptoms of withdrawal from alcohol dependence. The use of alcohol temporarily relieves the withdrawal symptoms. Over time, higher levels of drinking are required to achieve the same effect and a tolerance is evident. Use of substances including alcohol at work should always be reported to regulatory authorities.

According to ICD-11, *'Alcohol dependence is a disorder of regulation of alcohol use arising from repeated or continuous use of alcohol. The characteristic feature is a strong internal drive to use alcohol, which is manifested by impaired ability to control use, increasing priority given to use over other activities and persistence of use despite harm or negative consequences. These experiences are often accompanied by a subjective sensation of urge or craving to use alcohol. Physiological features of dependence may also be present, including tolerance to the effects of alcohol, withdrawal symptoms following cessation or reduction in use of alcohol, or repeated use of alcohol or pharmacologically similar substances to prevent or alleviate withdrawal symptoms. The features of dependence are usually evident over a period of at least 12 months but the diagnosis may be made if alcohol use is continuous (daily or almost daily) for at least 3 months'.*

Cognitive decline

Worldwide workforce shortages are placing greater demand on doctors to remain in clinical practice, and many doctors continue to work beyond the age when peers in other professions retire. Other doctors feel under pressure to continue to work full-time in order to meet financial commitments and the desire to provide for their families.

Our retirement should be a personal choice and age discrimination has no place in medicine.

However, because it is common for us to have driven natures, many of us fail to seek or heed the advice that we might give to our own patients about slowing down, engaging in other worthwhile pursuits outside work, and enjoying the many joys of the later years of life. Some doctors continue to work even if they are experiencing the effects of chronic disease, chronic pain or mental health concerns.

Knowing when to retire is an important decision and a critical challenge for some. Many doctors choose to retire before their health affects their clinical practice. For example, some surgeons choose to retire by the age of 65 years, despite their skill and experience. Other doctors, who have suffered from mental illness, choose to have well-planned career breaks and attend their own doctor regularly for objective reviews of their situation.

Senior doctors should not be discriminated against for their commitment and dedication to their patients. Many doctors continue to work effectively and contribute enormously to the health and wellbeing of the people of their local communities in the later years of their lives.

However, we must encourage each other to plan for career breaks and eventual retirement from practice. We must also ensure we take heed of our colleagues' concerns if they gently broach the subject. It is our responsibility when we notice a colleague in difficulty to say, 'I can see you are having some problems. How can I support you?'

Cognitive decline is another cause of mental impairment and is associated with very serious implications for public safety. It can be very difficult to approach this subject with a colleague, but we must do so. Medical practitioners are required to report an impaired colleague at substantial risk of harming patients to the relevant medical board or similar organisation. This action usually results in formal peer review and appropriate intervention, which may include temporary or permanent deregistration. However, if colleagues intervene early in cases of mental dysfunction, the dignity of the doctor may be protected and intervention by a medical board may become unnecessary.

All doctors have a responsibility to respond early and appropriately under these circumstances in the interests of patient safety, but this can be a harrowing outcome for a doctor after a long and dedicated career.

Summary

Doctors must proactively care for themselves and colleagues throughout experiences of stress and mental illness by encouraging everyone in the medical workplace to have their own trusted family physician/general practitioner who can provide regular health screening, early intervention, debriefing, postvention and acute care in times of a crisis.

Unfortunately, there are cultural barriers in medicine that deter many doctors from seeking help early, and as a result doctors may present late or with partially self-treated mental illnesses and impairment including bipolar disorder, schizophrenia, substance use disorders and cognitive decline. Early recognition and intervention are the key factors in effectively managing these potentially debilitating conditions.

As doctors, we need to care for each other in meaningful ways and know the right questions to ask a colleague who is in distress, lacking insight or impaired. We must all do better with responding to our colleagues when they need our assistance.

Learning from loss, grief and serious physical illness

Even doctors – or perhaps especially doctors – need to be touched by something personally to understand the suffering of others. We've been taught about the enormous power over life and death that is invested in us; we can be deluded into thinking we are almighty. Almost instinctively we view death, incurable disease and disability as challenging our power. We forget that this is all part of life. I guess that we have to defend ourselves against the human suffering that confronts us every day, otherwise we'd quickly go under. Medical jargon helps keep us remote, yet seeing colleagues suffer is hard. If we think too much, we realise that we – and our loved ones – are just as vulnerable as the rest of humanity.

Dr Jane Wilson-Howarth[1]

Loss

Loss is not only felt with death, disability and loss of independence. Other life changes such as relationship breakdowns, job changes particularly due to unemployment or retirement and role changes when children are born or leave home can leave a profound sense of loss too. Grief and anger are of course normal reactions in these circumstances. When we react with an unhealthy avoidance of these feelings and don't debrief about them, they can paradoxically become entrenched or have a long-term impact on wellbeing and predispose us to depression.

As Dr Jane Wilson-Howarth points out, while dealing with a major loss or personal crisis can be devastating, many doctors have also used the lessons learned through such an event to become even more effective clinicians, healers and mentors.

Grief

Despite our frequent exposure to loss in our line of work, we are not immune from experiencing acute or prolonged grief. Doctors, like the rest of the

---

[1] Dr Jane Wilson-Howarth is a British Physician, lecturer and the author of *A Glimpse of Eternal Snows: A Journey of Love and Loss in the Himalayas*.

DOI: 10.1201/9781003296829-27   **205**

population, can experience intense emotional reactions during bereavement, including sadness, irritability, worry, anger, guilt, insomnia, bad dreams, loss of interest in usual activities, depression and anxiety. Grief can be more debilitating if there is a history of mental illness, a lack of social support from family or colleagues, or an unexpected or violent death of a loved one, especially a spouse or a child.

Many doctors also experience loss vicariously for their patients. Every doctor has had a patient they will never forget, a time when they thought '*this patient could be me, or my loved one*'. Every doctor can recall a patient whose devastating circumstances forever changed the way they practise medicine or the way they view the world. Our job can be marred with sadness and tragedy, and as inherent empaths, we can carry the burden of this cumulative grief.

Everyone reacts differently to grief. While some people are unable to concentrate on normal activities, others will wish to continue burying themselves in working. Each person's reaction is normal and should not be judged as pathological just because it differs from the expected. However, it is only when we make time for deep reflection that we will work through grief and emerge stronger.

At a time of bereavement, it is OK to allow ourselves to cry and to talk about our feelings, especially with our family or friends who share or understand our grief. When we experience grief at work, it is important to engage in debriefing and reflection, either with colleagues or a trained professional, to ensure we do not crumble under the weight of cumulative grief. We must avoid the temptation of self-prescribing psychoactive drugs, and should consult with our own doctor if we feel we need assistance.

It's important to remember that although grief is a normal reaction, prolonged grief can become a disorder that requires treatment with formal psychotherapy and antidepressant medication. According to the ICD-11, '*prolonged grief disorder is a disturbance in which, following the death of a partner, parent, child, or other person close to the bereaved, there is persistent and pervasive grief response characterised by longing for the deceased or persistent preoccupation with the deceased accompanied by intense emotional pain (e.g. sadness, guilt, anger, denial, blame, difficulty accepting the death, feeling one has lost a part of one's self, an inability to experience positive mood, emotional numbness, difficulty in engaging with social or other activities). The grief response has persisted for an atypically long period of time following the loss (more than 6 months at a minimum) and clearly exceeds expected social, cultural or religious norms for the individual's culture and context. Grief reactions that have persisted for longer periods that are within a normative period of grieving given the person's cultural and religious context are viewed as normal bereavement responses and are not assigned a diagnosis. The disturbance causes significant impairment in personal, family, social, educational, occupational or other important areas of functioning'.*

Serious physical illness

Many of us remember thinking we might have the symptoms of various serious illnesses we learned about during our early years as medical students. Over the years, we tend to develop a healthy level of denial of personal illness, which may be one of the reasons we tend not to seek help from other doctors.

But when doctors are actually diagnosed with a serious or life-threatening illness, many of us experience those old feelings of heightened anxiety because we know too much about options, possibilities and risks. We can gain access to our investigation results before our own doctor, which has its pros and cons. Patient brochures only give us limited information and we may spend our time on searching medical literature and treatment options, rather than seeking the support of friends and family.

Our medical friends tend to ask us about the technical details of our disorder, rather than providing an opportunity to explore our feelings. Our colleagues who fully understand the reality of our answers may find it difficult to discuss the reality of our situation.

On the other hand, our non-medical friends may tell us just to think positively; perhaps they know many people with similar illnesses who have survived. This oversimplified response reflects a lack of understanding and unwillingness of others to confront serious illness. Unfortunately, doctors who are patients can recount many stories of their own patients who have not survived their illness.

These unhelpful responses to doctors experiencing serious physical illness can be damaging. We need to listen more to the experiences of our colleagues in these situations, not only to provide better support, but to learn more constructive ways to communicate to our seriously ill patients. For example, we can all learn from Dr Peter Goldsworthy's experience of being diagnosed with multiple myeloma during the pandemic – and emerging with patience and hope.

Honey sandwiches

When asked about his plans for Christmas Day, one of my patients, an elderly bloke living alone, told me he would do what he did every year:

make himself a honey sandwich, catch the tram down to Glenelg, and eat it sitting on the jetty. I invited him to join my family for some turkey instead; he said no. Thanks anyway. He had the beach to himself, he enjoyed it, he'd done it that way for years.

John Donne notwithstanding, some people are content to be islands, entirely of themselves. Not many, judging from the number of lonely, isolated patients who have been ringing me lately, for reassurance and comfort, and for whom a honey sandwich, solo, is nowhere near enough nourishment. They, like me, like most of us, are not made to be hermits. Our separate clods belong to Donne's larger continent, or at least, if we are lucky, to a family-sized chunk of it.

Luis Bunuel put it another way: solitude is a wonderful thing – as long as you can talk about it with someone afterwards. A good joke with a long tail: it doubles as good advice. Even John the Baptist, living in the wilderness on a diet of locusts and (yes) wild honey came out to talk about it with someone eventually.

I'm talking about it here, today, sentenced to my second term of medical home detention, although this time along with a million other high-risk people: the elderly, mostly, and those a little younger, like me, who have drunk too deeply from the Elixir of Age (generic name: chemotherapy) and been left with prematurely senile immune systems.

At least I know what I'm in for. And while cancer might have added a little pepper to my medical confinement last year, we are all in danger now. Does any of this make me an expert? Can I recommend any survival strategies – as against survivalist strategies, like joining a queue at a gun shop? I can only speak for myself, for what worked for me. Which of course includes all the strategies that are common knowledge anyway, or fast becoming so: exercise, music, poetry, meditation, chocolate, Skyping children and grandchildren, Zoom-supervised meals with friends, chocolate. Social media, antisocial media. Chocolate. Jokes, of course – especially the black jokes and comic routines doing the internet rounds that keep us sane. Can a viral joke stem a viral epidemic? No chance, but they are an effective antidote to the panic epidemic. More common knowledge: these various nourishments are best fitted into a daily schedule, as into a Webster pack. I'd put jokes into my own Webster, and my patients', taken three times a day after meals and at bedtime, if the email inbox wasn't an even more reliable source.

So: regular small sandwich bites. But not too many. The spacious days must be left largely empty, allowing time for thinking, for self-stock-taking, for new adventures and discoveries. Human nature, mine at least, abhors a vacuum, and will opportunistically book out any blank calendar. It took practice, but I learnt to love the open spaces, the slower time zones, of quarantine. I even learnt to love my insomnia, to lie contentedly in the darkness as the bits and pieces of a poem, say, came together, slowly. A visit to Bunnings (an Australian hardware chain) was out of the question, even for a single 5mm torx-head screw, which once upon a time was sufficient excuse for a sizzled sausage-and-sauce sandwich, but a poem can be fitted together on the workbench of the mind in much the same way as a piece of furniture in the shed: turning it this way and that, jointing bits on, shaving bits off, polishing it up – all without spare parts or tools.

Another thing I learnt was to encourage any latent stoicism I could find inside myself, as I also try to do with my patients. Stoicism, like eating alone on jetties on Christmas Day, is easier said than done. Not all temperaments are capable of it, and for those who have endured more than any human should have to endure, it can be impossible – but most of us can aspire to it. I have a soothing meditation app on my phone, but I prefer dipping into Marcus Aurelius, who begins his Meditations by thanking his parents and teachers for the life lessons they taught. I often think of the example of my grandmother, widowed in the Depression, raising four children in penury. My 94-year-old dad reminded me recently of her words to him, at age 11, when his father died: 'We will get through this,' she said, 'with strength and will.' She did. They did. With the help of her stern Methodist faith. Dad's stoicism came from her, although he preferred Seneca to the Bible. In isolation himself now, along with Mum, and increasingly frail, he allows himself a bottle of Chivas Regal every few days, but he's earnt it. Seneca should have lived so long.

I'm more of a part-time stoic, which suits a part-time sort of cancer, but when undergoing a stem-cell transplant last year I tried to follow Dad's example whenever I felt especially claustrophobic: read some Seneca, or Marcus Aurelius. Or go back to the source and read Epictetus. And if, after a few days, their stern advice tasted more like a shit sandwich, there was always the easier-to-digest stoicism that folk wisdom trails through our everyday speech. No use crying over spilt milk. It is what it is. There are people worse off than you, princess.

Clichés, yes. But that's the thing about clichés: some clichés, however shop-worn or hollow-sounding they become, they can rise to the occasion. They are always, at some level, still true – or perhaps more accurately, waiting to be true again, however briefly. That's how they get to be clichés. Democratically elected truth.

This applies especially to the cliches about love. Because another thing I learnt last year: many more people loved me than I thought, or at least thought I deserved. I know I am lucky in this. I've been lucky to have someone sharing my solitary confinement, which is probably an oxymoron.

At times I felt like a honey sandwich myself, to flog the metaphor through another furlong, although my family were the honey, my close-pressed cerebral hemispheres soaking it up like two thick, highly absorbent slices of greying white bread.

I thought about luck a lot, especially about the first luck we ever have. Genetic luck, geographical luck, familial luck. The big birth-right lottery, the biggest you can ever win – or lose. Human inequality begins there, as we leave the messy starting-gate, often with immensely heavy handicaps. You might as well be born with a terminal disease in some parts of the world, or even those parts of Australia where life expectancy is so much lower. Through no virtue of my own, I happened to be born in a country where enormously expensive life-saving treatments such as stem cell transplants are universally and freely available – and not, say, in the US, where two-thirds of individual bankruptcies are due to medical expenses.

The most important lesson I learnt last year, personally, perhaps for the first time in my life, was patience. Home from hospital, bald-headed and toddling around the house in nothing but pull-up diapers, I felt I had been born again. Proper attention to cooking was my first baby-step: slow, immersive cooking of the kind that is so nourishing you don't need to eat afterwards; slow, immersive eating afterwards anyway (still a work in progress): slow, immersive everything.

I've never been good at immersing myself in anything for long periods except writing. Days when I get nothing down leave me decidedly unstoical. Keeping a journal of your quarantine seems worth recommending, and is at least a good way of talking about it with someone, even if it's only yourself. In any event, writing is the best way I know of thinking about things. Slow, immersive thinking, in which you are often talking with your even slower, and more deeply immersed, unconscious, who is patient enough to nut things out even when you are asleep, or preoccupied with other stuff.

Reading also requires patience. Between working too hard at medicine, and compulsively scribbling, I'd read very little in recent years. I'd reached an Elle MacPherson end-point: 'I'd only read a book I wrote myself.' Apocryphal in her case perhaps, but not in mine: the only book I was ever currently reading was the one I was currently writing.

Slow, immersive reading was a joyous discovery. A rediscovery: when had I stopped? I can't list an entire nineteenth century's worth of novels, one will do. I tried reading The Mill on the Floss in bed when I was at high school, but it bored me to sleep and I didn't pick it up again. Last year I picked up Middlemarch, my wife's favourite novel, and had to take a sleeping pill at 3am to get away from it. And that was just the first night.

My last bit of advice is: hope. In this I am an expert. I have seen hope, and it works. Yes, I'm an optimist, and perhaps optimism is only best practice if you talk about it with a pessimist afterwards – but the restraints are easing, a little, and although winter might be another hurdle, with a pinch of luck, my and your confinement will be over sooner than expected. You might get a bit edgy and impatient as the final release date looms, a mix of 'will I make it?', and 'is it safe to go outside yet?' Feeling more secure in hospital than at home at times last year, I remembered the 'gate-fever' of a long-termer I examined in a prison sick parade prior to his release some decades back. 'Make them lock me up again', he begged, overcome by anxiety. 'In my safe world, with my safe routines'.

I hope he walked out the door as I did last year, as we all will soon enough. It was, and will be, thrilling – like stepping out on a first date, a first date with the world.

And everything will be a honey sandwich. But shared.

Dr Peter Goldsworthy[2]

Being a doctor patient can be an advantage. We know how to access evidence-based health information, navigate the health system assertively and seek the best specialist care promptly. We gain a new understanding of the fear and powerlessness experienced by our patients. We gain a new understanding of the value of good communication and simple questions like 'How are you feeling?' and 'How can I support you?'

Facing a personal crisis is challenging for anyone, but personal pain can be a teacher. For doctors, it is associated with unique challenges that require special care from close family, friends, colleagues, and a doctor we trust. It is never easy to allow others to see us when we are vulnerable and to ask for support. When we do, we open ourselves to experiencing the profound love and kindness of others. We may then ask ourselves, why we waited for a crisis to happen before we did so. Healing is not just about recovering what has been lost or repairing what has been broken, as Professor Helen Milroy writes:

Healing is part of life and continues through death and into life again. It occurs throughout a person's life journey as well as across generations. It can be experienced in many forms such as mending a wound or recovery from an illness. Mostly, however, it is about renewal. Leaving behind those things that have

---

[2] Dr Peter Goldsworthy combines writing with the practice of medicine. His numerous literary awards include the Commonwealth Poetry Prize, the FAW Christina Stead Award for fiction, and, together with composer Richard Mills, the inaugural Helpmann Award for Best New Work for the opera *Batavia*. His most recent book is a novel, *Minotaur*.

wounded us and caused us pain. Moving forward in our journey with hope for the future, with renewed energy, strength and enthusiasm for life. Healing gives us back to ourselves. Not to hide or fight anymore. But to sit still, calm our minds, listen to the universe and allow our spirits to dance on the wind. It lets us enjoy the sunshine and be bathed by the golden glow of the moon as we drift into our dreamtime. Healing ultimately gives us back to our country. To stand again on our rightful place, eternal and generational. Healing is not just about recovering what has been lost or repairing what has been broken. It is about embracing our life force to create a new and vibrant fabric that keeps us grounded and connected, wraps us in warmth and love and gives us the joy of seeing what we have created. Healing keeps us strong and gentle at the same time. It gives us balance and harmony, a place of triumph and sanctuary for evermore.

Professor Helen Milroy[3]

Summary

Doctors are exposed to different facets of human suffering in their professional and personal lives. We are just as susceptible to personal crises as our patients, and we may often feel vulnerable like our patients.

We may have intense emotional experiences when dealing with serious personal illnesses, and it is important to have our own trusted doctor and supportive relationships with friends and family. It is not just okay, but essential, to let ourselves grieve for our patients' losses and for our own personal losses, and accept care from our loved ones and our treating doctors in times of grief and illness.

---

[3] Professor Helen Milroy is a descendant of the Palyku people of the Pilbara region of Western Australia, and was born and educated in Perth. Australia's first Indigenous Doctor, she studied medicine at the University of Western Australia and is currently Professor of Child and Adolescent Psychiatry at UWA.

Every doctor can save lives through medical co-leadership

DOI: 10.1201/9781003296829-28

213

Inevitably, in a crisis, the leaders who have the biggest impact on the most people are rarely the 'official' leaders at the top. Rather, people like Dr. Anthony Fauci or a nurse pleading on camera for more supplies start to become the de facto leaders of the moment. They may have leadership positions with titles, but their influence extends beyond their official capacity to become the face of courage for many people – because they reveal an authenticity and urgency that reflects what people are feeling.

Leadership in an uncertain, fast-moving crisis means making oneself available to feel what it is like to be in another's shoes – to lead with empathy. Perhaps in the coming weeks, the unfortunate scale of this pandemic will make empathy easier for many leaders. But the awful scale can also have a numbing effect. It will be incumbent on leaders to put themselves in another's suffering, to feel with empathy and think with intelligence, and then to use their position of authority to make a path forward for us all. Crises of historical proportion can make for leaders of historical distinction, but that is far from guaranteed.

Drs Vivek Kaul,[1] Vijay H Shah,[2] Hashem El-Serag[3]

We wish to return to the first sentence in the introduction of this book. Medicine is a fantastic career. If we are experiencing deep satisfaction at work, and feel supported by a diverse group of colleagues, committed to collaborating to continually improve patient care through innovative new models, medical and surgical advances and new technologies, we know what great medical co-leadership looks like. If we have not personally experienced the challenges described in Parts 1–3 of this book, chances are we have been supported by the exemplary leadership of other doctors.

There is a vast array of medical literature, books and courses on health leadership, which we do not intend to summarise here. Part 4 of *Every Doctor* seeks to do something very different by focusing on leadership practice and experience rather than theory. Rather than speaking to doctors who are already in

---

[1] Source: Vivek Kaul, Vijay H. Shah, and Hashem El-Serag, Leadership during Crisis: Lessons and Applications from the COVID-19 Pandemic. *Gastroenterology*, September 2020;159(3):809–812. doi: 10.1053/j.gastro.2020.04.076. Epub 18 May 2020.

Dr Vivek Kaul is from the Division of Gastroenterology & Hepatology, University of Rochester Medical Center, Rochester, New York.

[2] Dr Vijay H. Shah is from the Division of Gastroenterology and Hepatology, Mayo Clinic, Rochester, Minnesota.

[3] Dr Hashem El-Serag is from the Section of Gastroenterology and Hepatology, Department of Medicine, Baylor College of Medicine, Houston, Texas.

positions of leadership or aspiring to be managers or medical administrators, we are reaching out to clinicians who do not currently recognise themselves as leaders or who have been discouraged from taking on official leadership roles after negative interactions with 'out of touch' health and medical bureaucracies.

Every doctor is already a medical leader in the everyday practice of medicine, by continuing to provide the highest standard of quality patient care and acting as an agent of change in fragmented, underfunded, overwhelmed health and aged care systems with chronic medical and nursing workforce shortages. Whether we are a general practitioner or family physician working in a remote Indigenous community, a subspecialist in a major tertiary teaching hospital, an educator, a medical director or a chief medical officer in a global health organisation, our contribution to patient care can be profound.

What is medical co-leadership? Medical co-leadership is about building relationships and trust with other like-minded colleagues, together co-creating a culture where people put aside personal politics and egos to work constructively together to make a difference to others' lives – our patients, our countries, our communities and our colleagues. It is a collective mindset at all levels of a workplace, recognising that every challenge is an opportunity to learn, listen with empathy and respond to feedback. Co-leadership is a practice not a title or an individual quest. The superhero myth has been dispelled during recent global and national disasters, and co-leadership is within everyone's reach.

Recently, we have witnessed many shining examples of where clinicians working in challenging environments have stepped outside their individual consulting rooms and banded together to respond to the impacts of the pandemic crisis, wars and natural disasters. In doing so, many doctors have discovered that co-leadership really matters – it can transform and save lives.

Some of our medical organisations have demonstrated the great leadership of their doctor members. For example, the Ukraine Medical Help Fund has been set up by a coalition of the European Forum of Medical Associations (EFMA), the Standing Committee of European Doctors (CPME), and the World Medical Association (WMA) to provide medical supplies to Ukraine. The World Organisation of Family Doctors (WONCA) has continually distributed up-to-date resources on COVID-19 throughout the pandemic through its 'Family Doctors on the Front Line' initiative. These initiatives demonstrate how many thousands of doctors can unite to make a profound difference by advocating on critical issues such as vaccine equity, quality and access of patient care, education and training and the impact of climate change on planetary health.

Unfortunately, there are other examples, where fragmented, bureaucratic and ineffective medical organisations have let us and our communities down. Recent global and local public health crises have also exposed deep flaws in our health systems, worsened health disparities and compromised the mental health of our populations. Consequently, many doctors and other health professionals are witnessing the distressing impact of the failure of leadership on people's lives, and doctors are bearing the brunt of justifiable patient angst and anger under these extreme circumstances.

These challenges should be used as a catalyst for health system transformation, and yet, many of our leaders are not listening and appear to be squandering the opportunity to reinvent healthcare to better protect against future health threats. As we are swept up in this chaotic environment, it can feel as if our work at the coal face is undervalued and futile. It can be common for doctors to feel like helpless pawns in someone else's chess game.

Moral injury has been described as a form of distress which may arise when doctors and other healthcare workers are repetitively exposed to patient suffering and loss of life due to systemic health inequities, forced to make difficult ethical choices about patient treatment because of lack of health access or funding, or oppressed by out of touch bureaucratic health hierarchies. Over time, moral injury can be collectively soul crushing for even the most resilient doctors.

In this environment, why would doctors take on the additional responsibilities and frustrations of leadership when many of us are only just surviving every day to do the best for each patient in front of us?

This question is the key to why medical co-leadership is so important. We have more influence than we think to collectively change the health system – to save patient lives, address the challenging conditions under which we work and prevent moral injury and distress. By recognising our united ability to influence the health system, we can also shift our mindset of the medical profession from surviving to thriving.

Of course, like most things in medicine, none of this is easy – but it's essential if we wish to improve our personal and professional lives – and our patients' lives.

Unfortunately, there are many barriers deterring doctors from taking on medical co-leadership. During our medical training, we learn about many aspects of our craft beyond our clinical and technical skills, including ethics and values, professionalism and communication, but few of us are taught about effective leadership in chaotic and complex health systems. Many doctors are discouraged from taking on formal leadership roles because of the personal politics and power plays of others, the tendency for doctors to cut down their tall poppies and bureaucratic frustrations such as time-wasting meetings. It can also be a career-limiting step to speak against the status quo or to disagree with groupthink in dysfunctional medical workplaces. Then there is the lack of time.

With all these challenges in mind, Part 4 of *Every Doctor* focuses on practical ways every doctor can co-lead change and make a difference by highlighting and honouring the stories of our exemplary medical role models, exploring ways to make our medical organisations work for us through strong advocacy, and encouraging doctors to gain leadership experience when it is appropriate to do so in their careers.

Every Doctor is a leader every day by:

- Continuing to provide the highest standard of patient care, particularly in challenging circumstances.
- Directly or indirectly contributing to global, national and local medical membership organisations.
- Practising leadership values and ethics to achieve better patient outcomes.
- Advocating through publishing and public speaking about issues that matter most to us.
- Honouring inspirational stories of medical co-leadership.

Making medical organisations work for us

Reflections on leadership during the COVID-19 pandemic

A crisis such as COVID-19 demands an agility and speed of response that public bodies, with their layers of scrutiny, are generally not designed to deliver. Add to this, decisions have to be taken on the basis of imperfect information, in an emotionally charged context, by exhausted individuals who are well aware they are dealing with matters of life and death. Add to this, remote working, social distancing, shortages of staff due to shielding, infection or isolating and lack of basic equipment – it is surprising more have not struggled.

. . . It is not just those who work in the so-called 'front line' who have suffered from the consequences of their work. Medical leaders in non-clinical roles have often found themselves in the invidious position of being seen simultaneously as scapegoat and savior: hero and villain. Having to position themselves in the conflicting position of needing to implement on-high orders whilst being attacked by their 'troops' as they felt they were being put into dangerous situations – exemplified by asking staff to work without appropriate Personal Protective Equipment or more recently insisting health staff work ahead of receiving their second COVID vaccine. For many this has been the first time they felt compromised by serving two conflicting masters. It was not the first time they faced the challenge of not knowing – after all, medicine is full of uncertainties and ambiguities, but for these leaders this was different as constant change and fear dominated their daily landscape, leading to anxiety.

Fatigue exacerbated psychological distress as taking any time out became impossible, compounded by lack of normal spaces and times for relaxation and recuperation. Good leaders, however, must take time out, model self-care to those they lead, recuperate and recover for the next stage, though even for the best ones, this is difficult, and they need to be given permission to rest and recharge their psychological batteries.

Across the world we are learning about the strengths and weaknesses of those tasked with leading us through this crisis. It is fair to say that all have struggled in different ways, some more than others. However, leaders

DOI: 10.1201/9781003296829-29

who have excelled are those who have shown compassion, empathy, connectedness and even vulnerability. They have been honest about the challenges and shared with us their uncertainties. Overwhelmingly, they have offered us hope, tempered with realism. In time, we all need to learn the leadership lessons emerging from this pandemic.

Dame Clare Gerada[1]

Change only happens if doctors unite and make it happen

We are currently working in health systems in turmoil, where we are witnessing the direct and indirect impacts of a global and local health crises, including a pandemic, new wars, natural disasters, serious health inequities, major ethical dilemmas and social injustice. At the same time, we are watching an exponential growth in transformational advances in medical, surgical and eHealth technologies. In the next decade, further subspecialisation of medicine and disruption of our unsustainable health systems are inevitable.

There are therefore a myriad of diverse issues confronting the medical profession, which our medical organisations must take leadership on. As an individual doctor, it is difficult to step outside the isolation of the consultation room and influence systems change. However, we can embrace a new definition of medical co-leadership, where every doctor recognises the strength of a united medical voice. When working with our medical organisations, we have considerable power and influence to fulfil our role as an advocate for improving patient care and our own working conditions.

There are stages in our lives and careers when we can participate in co-leadership directly, and other stages when we can only do this indirectly. At certain times, we may have the opportunity to co-lead health system change by directly contributing our clinical expertise, experience, insights and passion through office bearing roles in our work places and medical organisations. If we are working long shifts, responding to public health crises at times of acute

---

[1] Dame Clare Gerada is a London-based General Practitioner who is President of the Royal College of General Practitioners (RCGP) and a former Chairperson of the RCGP Council (2010–2013). She has professional interests in mental health and substance misuse. The above excerpt is from Clare Gerada, Reflections on Leadership during the COVID Pandemic. *Postgraduate Medicine*, 2021;133(7): 717–720. doi: 10.1080/00325481.2021.1903218.

medical workforce shortages, studying while working, sitting exams or caught up with family and other personal matters, we can co-lead indirectly through our membership of medical associations or colleges. The voices of all doctors must be heard, and we would particularly encourage doctors in the early stages of their careers who may be consumed with day-to-day responsibilities to ensure their views are represented by other medical colleagues and opinion leaders in our medical colleges, associations and other medical organisations.

Whatever our level of involvement, our medical organisations give doctors a powerful collective voice. As a united profession, doctors have considerable power and influence, especially when working with consumer advocacy organisations and bodies representing other healthcare professionals.

Our medical organisations need our help

While the diversity of the medical profession is one of our strengths, there are weaknesses associated with being represented by a complex and often-fragmented and bureaucratic system of medical organisations. Sometimes different medical organisations are in conflict with each other, which reduces the effectiveness of their advocacy to government and other health funders.

Unfortunately, many doctors give up trying to influence change in our medical organisations as they become disillusioned with time-wasting meetings, red tape, bureaucracy and personal politics. It is common for doctors to be critical of medical leaders and reluctant to engage with medical organisations, but we must understand that the leaders of our medical organisations are frequently under fire externally and internally, and tend to hold their positions for relatively short periods, which makes it difficult for them to achieve lasting or significant change.

Medical organisations are only as strong as the support of doctor members. We can make them work if we engage in constructive debate internally. We need to learn to disagree well, but present our consensus to the external world on important matters.

Like-minded doctors can co-lead change

We recommend that all doctors consider taking a leadership role by making a contribution to a group or committee of at least one medical organisation at an appropriate point in their career. By being involved even in a limited way we gain peer support and mentoring, have the opportunity to explore an area of special interest, diversify our professional activity, and learn how our organisations work and how we can access support in the future when we need it. For example, by offering to join a clinical committee on an area of special interest, we seek support and can often find friendship with other doctors with similar passions.

Chairing and participating in meetings

Unfortunately, time-wasting meetings are a common feature of medical organisations, perhaps because doctors usually do not receive training on how to chair and participate in meetings to achieve outcomes. As 'boring meetings' deter many doctors from contributing to their medical organisations, we have devoted a special section in this chapter to running effective, solution-focused meetings.

A well-chaired meeting usually has a clearly prioritised agenda in which everyone is encouraged to participate, and where it is recognised that the collective voice of consensus after a full debate is more effective than the voice of a few noisy, self-interested individuals.

Practical tips for effective chairing of medical meetings:

- A meeting chair is a facilitator of the meeting discussion not the dominator.
- Understand the terms of reference for the group meeting and the overarching strategic priorities, which determine the content of the meeting agendas.
- Standing items on each meeting agenda should reflect the strategic priorities and big-picture items for discussion. It helps to develop a calendar of agenda items to ensure that all items are covered within the following year.
- Develop realistic performance measures for each strategic priority and monitor progress on achieving outcomes within realistic time frames to help stay focused on outcomes and solutions.
- Meeting agendas should have invited input from all committee members and agenda papers should be circulated in a timely manner to allow everyone time to read them.
- Start each meeting on time and finish on time, but arrive early and stay late to engage informally with the other members of the committee.

- Ensure that every voice is heard but keep the discussion focused on the agenda.
- Encourage constructive debate and mediate differences of opinion.
- Foster consensus based on reasoning and evidence, not ego or the loudest voice.
- Ensure there are clear outcomes of every discussion documented in the meeting minutes with timelines, actions and accountabilities noted. A competent secretariat is essential.
- Ahead of each meeting, follow up the actions determined at the previous meeting to ensure they are completed.
- Review the board or committee strategy and charter at least annually to ensure they remain relevant and appropriate.
- Maintain confidentiality of formal meeting discussions but communicate your main messages effectively to your members or stakeholders where appropriate after each meeting.
- Review the performance of your board or committee at the end of each meeting while everyone is present, and also do this in a more detailed way on an annual basis.

When holding a virtual meeting, consider ways to encourage interaction and maintain the momentum of the meeting. Try to sign into the meeting early to connect informally with others, begin the meeting on time and remain focused on the agenda to keep on time and finish on time. Ensure all attendees are included in discussions appropriately and pause after each meeting topic to ask people to offer their thoughts, as this will keep everyone engaged.

Participating in meetings with medical colleagues can sometimes be initially daunting and you may feel intimidated, but your point of view is important and can help to shape the future directions of your organisation.

Any committee or practice meeting should have a purpose and clear expected outcomes:

- The meeting agenda should be distributed well before the meeting, and should list the people to attend, state the expected time of commencement and duration, and include well prepared background papers.
- Any meeting should result in agreed outcomes with documented minutes and resolutions.

- At the end of every meeting, all participants should feel as if their views and opinions are valued; if this is not the case on a repeated basis, you may wish to reconsider your involvement.

Practical tips for participating in meetings and influencing meeting outcomes:

- Read the papers for the meeting and always be prepared with at least **three points** you plan to make.
- Turn up early and sit in a prominent chair or position.
- Introduce yourself and engage with each of the other participants as they arrive.
- Before speaking, it can be helpful to note down the points you wish to make so you get your thoughts in order.
- Remember some participants may be hard of hearing so speak loudly and clearly.
- During the meeting, state your points of view with conviction and back them up with evidence.
- Be succinct and articulate the outcomes you are seeking.
- If interrupted, state clearly, 'would you mind if I finish?'
- When the meeting ends, leave only after you have engaged with other people to build networks and goodwill.

These principles also apply to virtual meetings, which require a mastery of technology and internet connections. It is particularly important during virtual meetings to give your full attention to all participants to ensure they remain engaged and to avoid multitasking during meetings. Ask that all participants leave their cameras on.

Try this exercise
When making decisions as a member of a committee, ask yourself:

Is this in the best interests of my organisation?
Is this in the best interests of our members?
Is this in the best interests of our discipline?
Not 'is this in my best interest'?

Leadership training

Our medical organisations also have a role in providing formal and informal opportunities for leadership training.

What is the best way to learn about medical co-leadership?

Many medical leaders will often admit that they discovered their leadership role by accident, through pursuing a cause they felt strongly about or by managing public health crises locally. Most often, we learn most about leadership by the way our inspirational role models make a difference to our patients and communities at a local, national or global level. We often realise that we can apply the same principles to our own work and in turn, grow into leadership.

There is vast medical literature on health leadership, formal courses and many different approaches to leadership training and experience, which are frequently promoted to us through our medical organisations and social media platforms. We recommend the following books about leadership journeys:

- Lalit Johri, Katherine Corich, Gay Haskins, *Mastering the Power of You: Empowered by Leader Insights.*
- John Bell, *Some Achieve Greatness: Lessons on leadership and character from Shakespeare and one of his greatest admirers.*
- Lord Nigel Crisp, *Turning the World Upside Down Again: Global health in a time of pandemics, climate change and political turmoil.*
- Dame Clare Gerada, *Beneath the White Coat: Doctors, Their Minds and Mental Health.*
- Dr Catherine Hamlin, *The Hospital by the River: A Story of Hope.*

While it may be difficult for doctors in active clinical practice to take time out for formal training, we recommend that every doctor considers putting a toe in the water by reading about inspirational leaders, supporting other leaders, seeking mentorship from an accomplished leader or participating in university or medical college leadership training programmes. Try to think of a medical leader who has inspired you or you admire. Chances are they are someone who has inspired you as a compassionate doctor, perhaps a colleague in your practice, one of your teachers or a leader of one of your medical organisations.

Here are some practical leadership tips for aspiring medical leaders:

- Give a leadership position a go in your medical college, association or workplace to see if you enjoy it.
- Preparation is the key to being an effective leader.
- Develop a clear understanding of roles and responsibilities of the leadership role, and what is expected in what time frame.
- Have a clear vision for what you wish to achieve, and articulate it frequently to others.
- Develop a detailed plan of action – with documented strategies, tactics and expected outcomes.
- Understand the time and energy commitment required.
- Be visible to people, make visits, give presentations and connect with your people.
- Communicate clearly and always be professional, constructive and courteous.
- Deflect praise to others, and routinely thank those who make a contribution.
- Shoulder any inevitable criticism yourself.
- Stand up for principle, even in the face of defeat.
- Do not countenance gossip.
- Debate issues and attitudes rather than criticising individuals.
- Meet potential adversaries afterwards and in private.
- Call out and stand up to bullies.
- Identify and manage risks.
- Listen and do not stop learning.
- Do not become arrogant.
- Nurture your supports and value your mentors.
- Allow time for yourself to recharge.
- Focus on the big picture and keep in mind how you wish to be remembered when you have finished in this role.

Summary

We can be proud of our profession. Each of us has the potential to be a role model for future doctors and contribute our own lasting legacy through the examples that we set in the way we live our lives and practise medicine.

Mostly, we demonstrate co-leadership by providing the very best care to our patients and their families. Sometimes, we seek other leadership roles to influence change in the environment in which we work including our clinics, health services, hospitals, medical organisations or in our local communities.

Our medical organisations can provide opportunities for leadership training to support our roles in advocating for our communities and our patients. By becoming involved in our membership organisations, even in a limited way, we not only support this effort, but also receive peer support and mentoring, as well as have the opportunity to develop areas of special interest and learn how our organisations work.

By experiencing the challenges of co-leadership first-hand, we develop a deeper awareness of the need to collaborate effectively and to support other leaders. Few of us will take on national and international medical and other leadership positions, although most of us are more than capable of doing so.

We believe that one of the most important roles of our medical organisations is to foster and train the next generation of medical leaders. Young doctors are the future of our profession and need to be welcomed by member organisations and given leadership opportunities when they have the time and willingness to take them on.

Practising leadership values and ethics to achieve better patient outcomes

In the following story, Dr Dhruv Khullar describes the complex task of leadership in managing a cardiac arrest and why physician leadership is critical for better patient outcomes, clinical performance and professional satisfaction.

Good leaders make good doctors

During our final year of medical training, I would take turns with the other senior residents responding to cardiac arrests in the hospital. We'd spend weeks camped out in the doctor's lounge, our hearts racing at the prospect of a patient's heart stopping, bracing for the moment a shrill pager or overhead speaker would signal an emergency. When the signal came, two dozen clinicians of different ranks and specialties would descend on the patient's room. It was then the on-call senior's job to conduct an efficient, morbid, sometimes miraculous symphony to revive a patient whose heart had stopped beating. The clinical aspects of running a code are straightforward, requiring little more than a handful of medications and a stopwatch. But the leadership task is exceedingly complex. Within seconds, the doctor in charge needs to impose order on a chaotic room rife with alarms, shouts, needles and tears. Who's performing chest compressions? Intubating the patient? Checking lab work that might unearth a clue? Who would be alerting the I.C.U. that a patient will – hopefully – be transferred within minutes? Most people think of doctors as scientists, caregivers or educators. But we must also understand doctors as leaders. Physician leadership is critical for better patient outcomes, clinical performance and professional satisfaction. That's true not only during emergencies, but also for managing chronic diseases or improving hospital efficiency.

Today, talk of leadership is so pervasive it can sometimes feel empty – the stuff of resume-padding and political advertising. But in medicine, effective leadership has tangible benefits. As our health system continues to struggle to devise ways to improve quality and reduce costs, it's increasingly

DOI: 10.1201/9781003296829-30

clear that a healthy culture can lead to better medical care. For their patients and their colleagues, doctors must be leaders.

Dr Dhruv Khullar[1]

Leadership values and ethics

Every doctor displays great leadership when they live and embrace strong values, ethics and professionalism in their everyday work. Professionalism in medicine is reflected in professional values, behaviours and relationships that promote public trust in doctors. Key professional principles include integrity, compassion, commitment to excellence, effective communication, continuous improvement and teamwork.

From day one of starting medical school, we have been reminded of the values articulated in the Hippocratic Oath. This version was revised in 1964 by Louis Lasagna, Academic Dean of the School of Medicine at Tufts University in the United States:

I swear to fulfil, to the best of my ability and judgment, this covenant:

I will respect the hard-won scientific gains of those physicians in whose steps I walk, and gladly share such knowledge as is mine with those who are to follow.

I will apply, for the benefit of the sick, all measures which are required, avoiding those twin traps of overtreatment and therapeutic nihilism.

I will remember that there is art to medicine as well as science, and that warmth, sympathy, and understanding may outweigh the surgeon's knife or the chemist's drug.

I will not be ashamed to say, 'I know not,' nor will I fail to call in my colleagues when the skills of another are needed for a patient's recovery.

I will respect the privacy of my patients, for their problems are not disclosed to me that the world may know. Most especially must I tread with care in matters of life and death. Above all, I must not play at God.

I will remember that I do not treat a fever chart, a cancerous growth, but a sick human being, whose illness may affect the person's family and economic stability. My responsibility includes these related problems if I am to care adequately for the sick.

I will prevent disease whenever I can but I will always look for a path to a cure for all diseases.

---

[1] Dhruv Khullar, M.D., M.P.P. (@DhruvKhullar) is a Physician and Assistant Professor of Medicine and Health Care Policy at Weill Cornell, and Director of Policy Dissemination at the Physicians Foundation Center for Physician Practice and Leadership.

I will remember that I remain a member of society, with special obligations to all my fellow human beings, those sound of mind and body as well as the infirm.

If I do not violate this oath, may I enjoy life and art, respected while I live and remembered with affection thereafter. May I always act so as to preserve the finest traditions of my calling and may I long experience the joy of healing those who seek my help.

Which are the most important values of a great medical leader?

What are your values?

In the following opinion piece, Professor Leon Piterman brings values and ethics to life during the COVID-19 pandemic:

Ethics in general, and medical ethics in particular, is about deciding what might be the right and just course of action in a particular situation. What might be right for an individual might not be right for the population and vice versa.

Ethics is underpinned by certain principles, so it may be useful to examine these principles in the COVID-19 era. These include: rights and duties, autonomy and paternalism, allocation of limited resources and individualism versus collectivism.

Health workers have a right to work in a safe and protected environment. We now have thousands of health workers around the world affected by COVID-19 and many are dying. When there is a shortage of personal protective equipment then health professionals are placed in an unsafe environment in breach of occupational health and safety legislation and legal action against their employer may ensue.

As health professionals, we have a duty to offer patients the best available quality of care to ensure survival. However, if the demand for care is so great, as it has been in many parts of the world, the supply of ventilators and ICU beds cannot meet demand, we have the ethical problem of 'allocation of limited resources'. This then poses a nightmare ethical dilemma for medical professionals, almost always doctors.

Who gets the best available treatment and who does not? Who might live and who will almost certainly die? What are the criteria that will be applied to resolve this dilemma and make a decision that is right and just? Is the life of a 70-year-old virologist and Nobel Prize laureate with diabetes and emphysema worth more or less than the life of a 40-year-old criminal serving a life sentence? What if the Nobel Prize laureate also had dementia?

Ethical debate and discussion on these sorts of issues are often conducted in the abstract with utilitarians taking one view and deontologists taking another view. But professional ethicists rarely have to make life-or-death decisions themselves. Fortunately, neither do most doctors. However, COVID-19 has changed all this especially for those doctors working on the frontline. These decisions are being made rapidly due to lack of available resources and quite possibly without much knowledge of whether the patient has had a good life and in the absence of any advanced-care directive.

If we are experiencing shortages of life-saving equipment in wealthy western economies, imagine the plight of poor African countries, our Pacific Island neighbours and India, and the decisions that doctors will be making in those places. Will we share our current excess stock of ventilators?

COVID-19 has raised the stakes on ethical debates to the here and now and away from the 'what if?' Globalisation has made COVID-19 transmission possible. There is now no place for individualism.

We must seek global, collaborative and collective decisions to ethically manage this crisis as we go forward.

Dr Leon Piterman[2]

A world away from Professor Leon Piterman in Australia, Dr Cynthia Haq at the University of California, Irvine, Family Medicine faculty in the United States reflects on how her team navigated the pandemic through a values and ethics-based approach to co-leadership.

I can't breathe: Pause, listen, reflect, add value

While serving as Family Medicine Chair at the University of California, Irvine in early 2020, we received an urgent call. 'We are overwhelmed! We need support. Can you help?' As a family physician with decades of experience, my response came naturally. 'What can I/we do to help? Where are the needs greatest?'

Within days, a resident and I were donning gowns, gloves, and masks to assess our first patient suspected with COVID-19 at our after-hours clinic, 'How can we help you today?' Beatrice (not her real name), a 35-year-old woman responded, 'I'm terrified. I feel like I can't breathe. I lost my job after the restaurant closed where I worked. I'm exhausted, can't pay rent, and don't know how I will buy food. Can you help me?'

---

[2] Dr Leon Piterman is Professor of General Practice at Monash University and has been in clinical practice for 40 years.

We did our best and wondered, could we offer more besides addressing her biomedical concerns?

As the pandemic continued, we confronted additional crises. The brutal murder of George Floyd, a Black man, by a White police officer who kneeled on his neck for more than 9 minutes while he pleaded 'I can't breathe', was captured on video and broadcast to the world. Blacks, Hispanics, Native Americans, and other people of color contracted COVID-19 and died at much higher rates than Whites. These images and figures illustrated the horrors and persistent damages from racism and discrimination in healthcare and in our society.

Concurrently, California experienced raging wildfires. The sky became dark; ashes rained down like snow as millions of acres burned. We couldn't go outdoors due to dangerous air pollution, yet we couldn't remain safe indoors with others due to the risk of contracting COVID-19. The deleterious impacts of global warming, drought, flooding, fires, and climate anxieties continue to threaten more people and communities, with the greatest harms falling on the most vulnerable.

In these crises, physicians are called to address chronic, complex and emerging health challenges *and to:*

- *Protect ourselves, clinicians, staff members, and patients.*
- *Carefully listen and examine to understand, and then effectively respond to the changing circumstances and needs of our patients, communities, and times.*
- *Expand our capacity to care for greater numbers of patients.*
- *Sift through mountains of emerging information to determine safe, innovative practices to transform patient care, medical education, research, and community engagement.*
- *Enable the vulnerable to work and/or receive care remotely.*
- *Reduce harms from the damaging effects of racism and climate change.*
- *Remain calm and provide reassurance and clear guidance despite uncertainties.*

The enormity of these challenges compels us to remember our values and select priorities. *At the University of California, Irvine, Family Medicine faculty, residents and staff draw on the following* *core values that emerged through many hours of reflection, retreats and discussions:*

- *__Excellence__: Deliver high-quality clinical services and education through continuous improvement, innovation, and scholarship.*
- *__Professionalism__: Demonstrate respect, integrity, humility, and compassion.*
- *__Diversity and inclusion__: Value the unique contributions of every department member. Foster interdisciplinary team-based collaborations.*
- *__Advocacy__: Promote health equity and social justice.*
- *__Sustainability__: Ensure careful planning, organization, accountability, and efficient use of resources.*
- *__Salutogenesis__: Cultivate nurturing environments for patients, trainees, staff, and faculty.*

How do we apply these values to guide our actions?

Returning to Beatrice, we paused, listened, examined, and found she was afebrile with normal respirations and blood oxygen, no cough, and few symptoms of COVID-19. We provided medical reassurance, yet also confirmed she was anxious, fearful, overwhelmed, and uncertain. We knew she needed more and offered breathing exercises and referral to social work for counseling, housing, and emergency food assistance. She trusted us enough to return later for COVID-19 vaccines.

We need many more effective, compassionate physician leaders to address the complex challenges of our profession and our times. I invite you, dear reader, to connect with and share with colleagues the values that guide your priorities, to pause and listen for when you can add value, and to be sustained by remembering that each of us is a brilliant thread in the rich tapestry of life.

Dr Cynthia Haq[3]

[3] Cynthia Haq is Professor and Chair of Family Medicine at the University of California, Irvine. She practices and teaches in the UCI Family Health Center, a federally qualified health center in Santa Ana, California. She wishes to acknowledge Alexandra Adams, MD, PhD, and Virginia Whitelaw, PhD, for their invaluable support, review and suggestions.

Summary

The opinion pieces from Dr Dhruv Khullar, Dr Leon Piterman and Dr Cynthia Haq bring to life the accepted ethics and values by which we practise medicine through their stories about everyday leadership and professionalism in medicine. Professionalism in medicine is reflected in professional values, behaviours, and relationships that promote public trust in doctors. Key professional principles include integrity, compassion, commitment to excellence, effective communication, continuous improvement and teamwork.

Whether we recognise it or not, every doctor is a medical leader, every day, in the way we uphold our ethics and the highest standard of patient care under challenging circumstances in underfunded and dysfunctional health systems.

Advocating through publishing and public speaking

Medical writing

'You will never be a writer.' As she dismissively tossed my mid-year exam result of an E at me, Miss Orr's remarks were loud enough to be heard by the whole year 12 class.

Two decades later, I discovered I could write. My 'sabbatical' working in Aboriginal health in Far North Queensland as a general practitioner changed my life.

Writing about tragedies, social injustice and health inequities gave me an unexpected release from my burnout from repeated exposure to trauma at work. I found a meaningful life purpose by advocating for my patients outside my consulting room.

Here is my first published article entitled *The stench of racism*:

At the Aboriginal health service in far North Queensland in Australia, I was given what seemed to be the simple task of helping to set up a 'well kids' clinic in an isolated settlement on the outskirts of a rural town. I noted that many babies and children were undernourished. Women did not breast-feed; families could not afford formula and they commonly fed their babies adult powdered milk or cordial. Most children of all ages had never been immunised and many were covered in scabies and impetigo, including a three-week-old baby.

A five-month-old baby presenting for routine immunisation at our clinic was delirious with meningitis. His 20-year-old mother and her aggressive partner refused to take him to hospital because their other two children had died there of cot death and during labour. I saw another two-year-old child with previous rheumatic fever and heart disease. She died in hospital one week later. I had known that Aboriginal babies were twice as likely to die as non-Aboriginal babies, but I could not believe that their general health could be so appalling.

In the first few weeks, the mothers replied to my questions with one-word answers and downcast eyes, sometimes just walking away to spit filthy phlegm through broken fly screens or to slap their toddlers. The children played with blue marbles in their mouths while running about wildly with my medical equipment and chasing dogs out of the clinic.

DOI: 10.1201/9781003296829-31

Aunties and grandmothers laughed riotously as each child cried as they received their needles. Amidst the chaos and the dancing of eyes, I found it difficult to work out which child belonged to which parent. They all seemed to belong to everyone. Although it would have been easy to assume that this represented a situation of gross child neglect, it seemed that it was actually a sad acceptance that illness and postnatal depression were a normal part of everyday Aboriginal life experience.

Although many of the women were unwell, they hesitated to talk about themselves, always putting the needs of the children before their own. As she held her sick granddaughter, one 40-year-old grandmother apologized for taking up my time as she mentioned 24 hours of right-sided weakness. Due to undiagnosed high blood pressure, she had suffered a recent stroke. She had been too busy looking after her children and grandchildren to walk an hour to the town doctor.

As the weeks went by, the women seemed to engage me with their eyes and discussed their problems spontaneously. I felt the importance of developing a trusting relationship. The more I saw of how people lived in such difficult circumstances the more I admired their strength.

As I drove to work, I often saw homeless Aboriginal people living in the parks, arguing and drinking alcohol. The 'park people' sometimes featured on the front page of the local newspaper because of concerns their presence was affecting the tourist dollar, and this reflected the hardened non-Aboriginal reaction to the problem.

It was difficult to answer my children when they asked why these people lived in public toilet blocks. One rainy night I found my seven-year-old son crying and when I asked him why he was upset he said, 'Because the park people will be getting wet'.

I feel a great need to talk about what I have seen, but few people seem to want to listen. While many people with little knowledge of Aboriginal health don't particularly care about my experiences, others ask the same questions: 'Why did you leave your comfortable practice to work in a low-status job?' 'Why have millions of dollars been poured into Aboriginal health when it is hopeless due to their lack of motivation and alcoholism?' 'How did you stand the smell?'

I can only answer that I have learnt a great deal and that my social conscience has been wakened. Stereotyping and generalisations are unjust, extremely damaging, and a barrier to Aboriginal people accessing available health services. For example, many Aboriginal people were insulted that the first question they were asked when they attended the local hospital was about their alcohol intake (although evidence suggests that 40 % of Aboriginal people are tee-totalers compared to less than 30% of non-Aboriginal *people). This attitude deterred many Aboriginal people from attending the hospital which meant they presented late with serious illness.*

I asked all of my Aboriginal patients where they found the strength to carry on through such difficult circumstances and their answer was always the same – and the same for me – their hope for their children's future. The only smell I have experienced is the stench of racism.

Dr Leanne Rowe

Every doctor is a potential writer because every doctor can recount inspirational and devastating patient stories such as the story told above. Doctors often only fully realise the power of their pen by default when they receive an unexpected reaction after publishing an opinion piece or story on a clinical issue they care or are concerned about.

Here are some tips for writing medical opinion pieces:

- Keep a notebook for recording thoughts and filing news items or research.
- Start with an issue you feel strongly about, a gap in understanding, a controversy or a difference of opinion.
- Formulate the main message(s) you wish your readers to take away from the opinion piece.
- Ask yourself, 'Why will my opinion piece be original/different/timely? Why am I the right person to write this?'
- Choose a special place to write – an outdoor table, pleasant veranda or café – to allow your brain space to think deeply without interruption.
- Recognise mood matters. Some people write freely when they are feeling down, frustrated, or angry about injustice and inequity. It can help to recognise that writing can be a constructive outlet when we feel this way.
- Structure the opinion piece well. For example:
  - Begin with a strong first sentence but also the end in mind.
  - Catch the reader's attention in the first paragraph. If you use clinical cases, de-identify and protect privacy.
  - Describe why the reader should care about the topic.
  - Outline the main issues (e.g. challenges, controversies and solutions).
  - Refer to the medical literature and others' opinions on the topic.
  - Create debate by pre-empting an inevitable critical response and including the counter-argument in the opinion piece.
  - Finish with a call to action. What change would you like to see?

- Tailor your piece to your audience and to where it is likely to be published.
- Allow an idea to evolve or develop into something else as you develop your piece.
- Review is critical:
  - Read your opinion piece out loud to your imaginary helpful editor and to your imaginary critical readers.
  - Edit it to about half the number of words by simplifying sentences and omitting duplication and unnecessary words.
  - Ask yourself, 'what is each paragraph trying to convey?'
  - Put the opinion piece aside for one to two weeks and then return to it with a fresh approach.
  - Ask a critical friend to provide feedback – even if you disagree with their opinion, it helps to strengthen your argument.
  - Take on board the suggestions from the editor as their changes will usually shift the opinion piece from good to great.
- When self-doubt strikes, reassure yourself that your clinical perspectives, insights and observations matter. You can have more influence on attitudes than you think.
- After the opinion piece is published, anticipate negative comments, which you may or may not choose to respond to. Expect that others will disagree with you. You have created change if you challenge robust debate or begin a conversation about an issue that matters.
- The proof of your success is ultimately your enjoyment in the process and challenge of writing.

Working with the media

Doctors are often cold called by news desks seeking opinions or a few sentences on 'hot' health topics of the day. Responding without preparation can be a trap as a few sentences may be taken out of context and distributed through local, national or global social media platforms. For these reasons, many doctors understandably feel anxious about being interviewed by the media and concerned that their words will be taken out of context or that they will be made to look unprofessional.

Formal media training can help doctors avoid media traps and work effectively with the media to advocate on important issues, but this is often expensive and not available to most doctors. However, there are some simple 'dos and don'ts' that most doctors can use to ensure their messages are delivered effectively.

For example, if you are contacted by a journalist, and you wish to speak on an important health topic within your expertise, pre-prepare three messages you want to get across and also the three things you will not say. Practice what you will say before calling back within the agreed time frame. It can be helpful to practice saying your response out loud, or call a friend to prepare your response.

Never feel pressured to give an instant response. Ask if they can email you the background details to the request so that you can give the issue some thought before responding. Ask about the journalist's deadline and commit to call back within an agreed time frame. Beware of the beat up – journalists can sometimes seek to set up conflict between interviewees from different organisations without you realising. Always have a strategy to hang up if you do not wish to be interviewed on this topic or feel you are being harassed.

Public speaking

Great public speakers resonate with diverse audiences and facilitate attitudinal changes. Many doctors are nervous about public speaking, but this is a skill we all can learn. There are many good training courses and books on the topic, which often suggest speakers tell stories to illustrate their points and be authentic, authoritative and brief. Medical TED Talks can be an effective way of brushing up public speaking skills, and here are some of our favourites:

- How Do We Heal Medicine? by Atul Gawande
- A Doctor's Touch, by Abraham Verghese
- Fake It till You Make It, by Amy Cuddy
- How Racism Makes Us Sick, by David R Williams
- On the Art of Medicine, by Ranjana Srivastava

Practical tips for public speaking:

- Admit to yourself how speaking in public makes you feel, and ask yourself why.
- Practice as much as you can and gain experience in front of big and small audiences.
- Know your material so well that you can speak without notes.

- Practice delivering your speech in front of a mirror or a small safe audience at home.
- Turn up early so that you know your room and how the audio visual equipment works.
- Make sure that you know who will make up your audience.
- When you speak, remember that you are the expert.
- Relax while speaking, turn your nervousness into positive energy and enjoy yourself.

Here is a powerful example of effective public speaking to a general practitioner audience at the Royal College of General Practitioners in the UK by Michael Kidd in 2022:

I dedicate this lecture, named in memory of one of the founders of the Royal College of General Practitioners (RCGP), Dr John Hunt, later Baron Hunt of Fawley, to the general practitioners of the UK and the world, in recognition of your dedication, compassion, and courage shown throughout the COVID-19 pandemic. You have demonstrated that general practitioners are a fundamental component of public health responses to health challenges, and that each of us has deep knowledge and insight into the healthcare needs and beliefs of the population of people we serve.

Born in 1905, John Hunt was a general practitioner who lived through the great pandemic of the first half of the 20th century, the Spanish flu, and through the early years of the great pandemic of the second half of the century, HIV/AIDS. In 1951, John Hunt wrote about the establishment of the RCGP: 'I had far rather start with a big idea in a small way, than a small idea in a big way.'

The RCGP has continued that tradition of big ideas, with the recommendations of the leadership and membership on the contributions general practice could make, and subsequently has made, in response to COVID-19. What big ideas need to be considered as we recover, rebuild, and renew our healthcare systems?

How general practice can support everybody including the most at-risk community members

At the outset of the pandemic, it was recognised that people most at risk of the effects of COVID-19 are those normally being cared for in general practice. Ongoing transmission of COVID-19 around the world continues to shine a spotlight on at-risk populations, including people who are often overlooked by healthcare planners, especially those who are socially disadvantaged. We need to continue to work with at-risk communities, and with the general practitioners who serve those communities, because the solutions to healthcare challenges are to be found within each community.

How people working in general practice are supported to receive the same level of protection as those working in hospitals

The disruptive consequences of the pandemic have been profound on everyone including general practitioners. Many are grieving the loss of loved ones, periods of separation from family and friends, the postponement of plans and hopes and dreams. Many have been working harder and longer than ever before and are feeling exhausted. Many have lived with the risk, and often the consequences, of infection, and the risk of transmission to loved ones.

How general practice can care for those with COVID-19 without compromising the care of others

As the majority of people infected with COVID-19, especially among the vaccinated, continue to be asymptomatic or with mild-to-moderate symptoms not requiring hospitalisation, ongoing medical care is being provided by general practitioners and other community-based health providers. Models of care have been developed to support safe provision of care for those being managed at home, with appropriate escalation if deterioration occurs. As we continue to live with COVID-19, as vaccination rates rise, and as we continue to provide home-based care to many of our patients, these models will continue to evolve.

How general practice can ensure continuity of regular healthcare provision and address the burden of missed or delayed care

We knew from past pandemics that there would be added risk when people stopped attending general practice because of concerns about the risk of infection. Many people have delayed preventive care interventions, including cancer screening, while others have delayed presentation for new symptoms or management of existing health conditions. It has been essential to retain the functional capacity of general practices to ensure continued provision of regular healthcare services. Telehealth has been adapted in many parts of the world to support continuity of care. There will be continuing challenges from long COVID and its impact on many people, as well as a long shadow of increased morbidity and mortality due to delays in diagnosis and treatment of medical conditions that would have been managed earlier under pre-pandemic conditions.

How general practice can continue to support mental health

The provision of mental health services is a critical component of general practice and need has been exacerbated during the pandemic by the impact of loss and grief, unemployment and business closures, and isolation and quarantine measures imposed on many people. The mental health impact on healthcare workers, including general practitioners, has also been significant. We knew from past pandemics that there would also be a long shadow of mental health concerns, especially among young people, with many people experiencing continuing distress and anxiety and depression, and the risk of increased rates of self-harm and suicide.

How general practice can be supported to continue to lead COVID-19 vaccination programmes

The substantial contributions of UK general practice to the national vaccination programme have demonstrated the importance of strong general practice with many preferring to receive vaccinations from their trusted general practitioners and nurses. While we can expect to be involved in future booster programmes, we also need to continue to focus on those who have not yet been vaccinated.

How to ensure the ongoing capacity of general practice to be prepared to meet future challenges

This pandemic has highlighted not only the extraordinary contributions of general practice, the fundamental importance of relationship-based healthcare, and the value the population places on general practice, but also the challenges of an ageing workforce, the burden of ever increasing workload demands, and the need to address resourcing shortfalls.

There will be inquiries into responses to the pandemic, and the recommendations, and the associated public debates and expectations, will shape future developments of public health and healthcare services, including general practice. There will be future health workforce challenges, with many general practitioners and others having delayed retirement due to the needs of the pandemic, and others who decide to move on to do something else with their lives. Societal changes continue to ripple around us over coming years; as general practitioners we will support our patients with challenges and transitions, as we always do.

John Hunt passed away on 28 December 1987 at the age of 82. I expect he would be very proud of the work during this pandemic carried out by

*the membership and leadership of the college that he helped found almost
70 years ago.*

Dr Michael Kidd[1]

Summary

Next time you feel strongly about an issue of injustice in medicine, try writing a considered story or opinion piece about it. Your pen can make a difference in changing attitudes and helping you connect and debate issues with like-minded people or hear opposing views. The process of writing will also help you work through your personal frustrations and find solutions.

Your clinical experience and observations matter and you will find it easier to get your piece published than you think. It may then be used as a platform to speak publicly at conferences or in the media about issues you care deeply about to create positive change.

---

[1] Michael R. Kidd, *RCGP John Hunt Lecture 2021: General Practice During a Pandemic: Seven Big Ideas*, RCGP. PMID: 34972806 PMCID: PMC8714518 (available on 2023–12–31). doi: 10.3399/bjgp22X718241.

27 | Honouring inspirational stories of medical co-leadership

If we do a quick search of our medical literature, we will find many examples of inspirational medical co-leadership over hundreds of years or more. We not only applaud our current and past medical leaders, but every doctor who makes a difference in the lives of their patients every day.

In our final chapter, we wish to honour a number of other doctors who are also driven by a passion to serve others as well as a fierce determination, a quiet humility and an inclusive approach to co-leadership:

- Professor Catherine Crock
- Dr Dinesh Palipana
- Dr Richard 'Harry' Harris
- Professor Helen Milroy

Professor Catherine Crock

If you've ever experienced self-doubt or fear of public speaking, you need to hear the exceptional Dr Catherine Crock's story. Throughout school and university, she was so shy she feared raising her hand in class or lectures to answer a question.

Cath reflects on her advocacy journey over a number of decades at the Royal Children's Hospital in Melbourne, Australia, like this:

> I'd look at distressed children having procedures without adequate pain management and I asked myself, 'what if this were one of my children?' And from that moment, I felt compelled to do something about this. I'm actually intrinsically very shy, but I started to speak with some of the mothers, and asked the parents how I can help them.
>
> After I spoke to dear, anaesthetist colleagues about options to improve pain management, they initiated pain interventions for oncology procedures such as bone marrows and lumbar punctures. Then people started talking about the benefits of pain management, and adopted it in other treatment and procedure rooms of the hospital. The momentum grew.

DOI: 10.1201/9781003296829-32

We sedated children and clustered different interventions under the one anaesthetic, including nasogastric tubes, IVs or access ports, immunisations, bone marrow, and lumbar puncture. This revolutionised our patients' experience of procedures because they were usually in recovery within fifteen minutes. When they recognised the positive results, parents also helped drive change and helped to raise some of the money to fund the first pain management nursing role at the Royal Children's Hospital in Melbourne.

In my early career, things were pretty challenging for me and at times a bit of a blur. My children were young and there was just wall-to-wall mashed banana and children and nappies and all that at home. Breast feeding and part-time work, children at crèche and primary school – a bit of a juggle but they've grown up to be quite independent and I think that's been good for them and good for us. I was very protective about my own kids – like a lioness keeping them from harm. This is also how I felt about children at the hospital and it helped me drive change despite resistance in some quarters.

From this experience, I quickly learnt what really mattered to my patients and their families, particularly when they were having a difficult healthcare journey. The families told me about times when the system did not feel kind to them, and aspects of the environment which raised their anxiety. They talked about bringing the arts, music and culture into a healthcare setting, to try and reduce stress in difficult situations.

From these discussions, the Hush Foundation was founded to bring composers, musicians and other creative people into hospital spaces. They identified the cacophony of noises that raised people's anxiety levels, and the sort of music that could improve people's emotional state in these environments. Over the past 20 years, 18 albums of specially composed music by famous Australian musicians and composers have been produced and used in hospital waiting rooms, treatment rooms, operating theatres, general areas and for the public.

The Hush Foundation has also worked with actors and playwrights in three plays to raise awareness of what goes on behind the scenes in healthcare for the patients, families and staff. These plays have been presented over two hundred times in Australia and internationally, with audiences of over 15,000 people. Frank feedback from every audience paints a picture of a healthcare culture in crisis – a system where we are continuing to lose good people because the system is not treating them with kindness and respect. Healthcare professionals also resonate with the plays, because they recognise the behaviours in their own workplace that lead to discord, an unsafe working environment and things going wrong for patients.

Out of this feedback, came the Gathering of Kindness, which is a growing movement of people committed to a kinder way of being in healthcare. Using the *arts including music, theatre, storytelling and listening, the Gathering of Kindness aims to inspire acts of kindness to influence culture and behaviours. The Hush Foundation through the Gathering of Kindness now provides many hospitals and health services with resources to help spark important conversations amongst staff about healthcare culture.*

In my own team, we encourage colleagues to connect, human to human, and to share their vulnerabilities. We now begin each working day checking in on each other, talking about how we are feeling, asking for some support and reaffirming that the team has each other's backs. I am proud to be part of a joyful team where people love coming to work together because they feel safe and are always treated with kindness and respect.

Embedding kindness in the healthcare system can be done. As with most major changes in healthcare, it helps if hospital boards are more proactive in assessing their role. It also helps if leaders have a vision of what can be achieved. But it starts with individuals – colleagues showing a level of kindness and care towards each other which will flow on to the patients and families. Let's talk about kindness performance indicators. Staff and patient perceptions of cultural and behavioural issues can be part of the performance assessment at all levels. It can be transformative to teams and make a big difference to the joy and meaning in our work and to the lives of the people in our care.

Professor Catherine Crock, AM, is a physician at the Royal Children's Hospital in Melbourne and chair of the Hush Foundation. For more information about her work refer to www.hush.org.au, www.gatheringofkindness.org.

Dr Dinesh Palipana

I was 25 years old. I was halfway to becoming a doctor, and I was living in the beautiful city of Gold Coast in Australia. Life was good.

One ordinary Sunday evening, I went to visit my parents, which was a two-hour drive that I did all the time. In a second, everything changed. I hit a water puddle on the road and my car began to slide all over the road. I lost control. I was terrified. The car went up an embankment, and when it came back down, the nose slammed into the tarmac, and then it began to fly through the air, nose to tail.

When the car finally stopped rolling and the destruction ended, I looked around. My things were scattered all over the road. My white t-shirt was red with blood. But then, I realised the worst thing. I tried to get out of the car and I couldn't move. I couldn't feel my legs and my fingers weren't obeying my command. The accident site became a hive of activity and blue and red lights flashed, and I was cut out of the car. When I was in the ambulance, I had so many emotions, but in amongst the pain and the confusion and the fear, I thought, 'Will I ever become a doctor now?' And this thought came in waves and it twisted away like a knife in my chest.

I spent seven months in hospital and four more years putting my life back together. Every single day I thought about going back to medical school and this was despite people telling me that it's just a pipe dream now, it's no longer an option. Fortunately, the educators and my university were great, and their belief in me made me believe that maybe this is possible.

So I took a giant leap of faith, a very scary one, and I started back. Before I officially began, I spent an intensive couple of weeks just re-learning how to hold a stethoscope, examine a patient, and how to get around in a hospital environment again. I had to find new and adaptive ways of doing things, like putting in sutures with a bit of help, or getting a needle in for a drip.

When I formally came back to medical school, I did the same rotations and activities as everyone else. There were a lot of eyes on me, but, this is how I wanted it. I wanted my degree to be as credible and robust as everyone else's.

When you look at me, you might see the obvious mobility issues, the physical paralysis. But, the physical problems in a spinal cord injury go a lot deeper. Everything from my cardiovascular system to my digestive system is affected. My lungs don't work as well as they used to. My skin doesn't respond to temperature changes anymore, so I am like a lizard. From a life-style perspective, everything takes a lot longer. If I have to be somewhere in the morning, I sometimes have to get up three to four hours before I need to be there.

Despite all the barriers, I took the opportunity to go to Boston, for a clerkship at the Harvard University, and I got a distinction with honours there. After two very long years of post-accident study, I finally graduated medical school with awards for excellence, and this was made possible with my mum, who was there every single day. After thinking at one point that I might never be able to become a doctor, it wasn't until I went across that stage that I realised that I had made it.

After I graduated, I was promptly registered as a doctor with my other colleagues. My friends got their job offers a couple of months later. My letter said that my application had been pulled because I have a spinal cord injury. The health authority told me that it would take a few weeks for them to figure out what to do with me. But the weeks turned into months and as the months went on, it quickly became apparent to me that every domes-tic doctor gets a job, unless they have a physical disability. I thought my *undergraduate law degree may come in handy at a time like this, but the law wasn't on my side.*

'Can you even type?' I was once asked by senior doctors. Well, I can, actually. Most likely faster than any of them, but they responded 'Well, considering your physical capacity, you probably do need to find a non-clinical specialty'. Fortunately, this view wasn't shared by everyone, and I had a great community behind me. I had friends, advocates, family, politicians and the media, who all rallied around me, and they fought. After they advocated for me publicly and privately, behind the scenes, I got a job offer two days before everyone started work.

Work has been amazing. I have loved every single minute of it. I have worked in emergency, surgery, internal medicine, obstetrics and gynaecology, and in my first year, along with some of my very talented colleagues, I got nominated for an intern of the year award. And that was really special for me, because at one point I didn't even know if I could make it.

Medicine is an intellectual activity. Not all doctors perform surgery. Not all doctors perform resuscitations. But every single doctor is required to exercise their intellect. I believe people with a disability have a role to play that is far beyond the patient in front of them in our healthcare system. I believe that the solutions to our most complex problems will come from having a diversity of perspectives, not more of the same.

I was talking about my experience with one of the emergency doctors, a very highly respected specialist. She told me, 'You've always loved emergency medicine, haven't you? Why don't you give that a try? We'd support you.' And true to their word, they have been one of the most supportive groups that I've come across.

A puddle of water on a highway caused an accident, and it changed my life forever. But it wasn't the accident that threatened to stop me from becoming a doctor. It isn't my physical capacity that threatens to halt my career. It's the attitude of people towards difference, and that is something we can choose to change today.

Dr Dinesh Palipana is a Senior Resident at Gold Coast University Hospital and Advisor to the Disability Royal Commission, which was established in April 2019. He has quadriplegia as a result of a motor vehicle accident that caused a cervical spinal cord injury halfway through medical school. Dr Palipana is a founding member of Doctors with Disability Australia (DWDA), a national advocacy organisation working to remove barriers, bias and stigma in the medical profession for students, doctors and health professionals. http://dwda.org.au/. He recently published his autobiography *Stronger* through Pan Macmillan (www.panmacmillan.com.au/9781761262845/).

Dr Richard (Harry) Harris

Dr Harry Harris has enjoyed an extraordinary career in medicine, which has enabled him to combine his expertise in diving, wilderness and remote area health. Now practising anaesthetics in Adelaide, he worked with AusAID in Vanuatu for two years providing anaesthesia and intensive care services in the setting of a developing medical system.

Harry's passion for cave diving goes back to the 1980s and has taken him to the corners of the globe in search of new adventures. As a member of a diving group called the Wetmules, he has explored some of the world's deepest caves, among them the Pearse Resurgence in New Zealand to 245m depth, Daxing Spring in China to 213m and Song Hong Cave in Thailand to 196m to name a few.

His love of underwater exploration has led him to work on National Geographic documentaries, feature films and with various teams worldwide in the role of diver, underwater cameraman and of course medical support. A member of the Explorers Club of New York, in 2015 he was recognised with an Australian award for Outstanding Contributions to Cave Exploration and in 2017, he was awarded The Australasian Technical Diver of the Year.

In July 2018, Harry made worldwide headlines when he joined an international team to rescue a group of 12 boys and their soccer coach from a flooded cave in Chiang Rai, Thailand. Under great pressure, he swam through the narrow cave system to assess the health of those trapped, giving the medical all-clear for each evacuee and administering an anaesthetic to each of them within the cave to facilitate their rescue.

Later in 2018, he received the Star of Courage, Australia's second highest civilian award for bravery, and the medal of the Order of Australia for his role in the cave rescue. Harry's efforts were also recognised when he was named South Australia's Australian of the Year and joint Australian of the Year 2019, with his dive partner Craig Challen.

Although Harry was key to the rescue's success, he credits the extraordinary teamwork of over 5,000 people at the cave site and around the world for the massive logistical exercise. Embarrassed to be labelled as a hero, he remains quick to point out that it was the boys who displayed courage, not him.

However, he acknowledges his difficult personal decision to sedate the boys with ketamine to enable them to be taken through 2.4 kilometres of tunnels filled with water to reach the cave entrance. Before Harry first entered the cave, he was warned by others the children and their coach were all likely to drown as weather forecasts suggested there were only about three days before further flooding in the cave. At the time, Harry was acutely aware that his decision about sedation could have catastrophic personal consequences if the mission failed. He had to weigh this risk against the greater risk that the boys would suffer terrible deaths if he did nothing.

On what should have been one of the happiest days of his life after the successful cave rescue, Harry's father, a retired doctor, passed away. In a tribute to his late father, Harry said: '*I was devastated as I was very close to my father. I was raised in a loving family, and when I was a child, I always wanted to be like my dad. He was very kind and everyone loved him.*'

In another moving tribute to the 12 brave boys and their coach, Harry described being reunited nine months after the cave rescue:

> *As we sat cross legged on the floor, each of the boys came over and knelt in front of us. Hands together, they bowed. Each rested his head for a moment on our knees and then gave us a hug. When I asked them what they remembered about the day they left the cave, they all started laughing; 'good boy good boy jab jab', as they mocked my pre-anaesthesia technique. Since being rescued from the cave, they appear to be remarkably unscathed, which many people find surprising. I had theories about this; because they grew up in a hard environment, they were ready for challenges, and courageous in adversity. This is a lesson for us all.*

With these reflections in mind, Harry continues to use his role as Australian of the Year to advocate for sensible risk-taking in young people, to build independence, resilience and improved mental health:

> *This has given us an amazing opportunity to travel around the country talking to schools, community groups, clubs, corporations and charities. Our messaging is pretty simple . . . push outside your comfort zone, do hard things, test yourself whenever possible and spend some more time outdoors away from devices. Build confidence and resilience through sensible risk-taking, especially for kids.*
>
> *The year has provided a great opportunity to give something back, and I have been working with three organisations in particular. The KIDS Foundation which does amazing work around child accident prevention and post-trauma support, Operation Flinders which takes at-risk youth into the remote South Australian bush to help get them back on track, and finally the Wilkins Foundation which aims to promote the adventurous ideals of the explorer Sir Hubert Wilkins, and help kids find their 'inner explorer'.*

Dr Richard 'Harry' Harris is co-author of the book *Against All Odds* with Craig Challen. He currently works in anaesthesia and aeromedical retrieval medicine in Adelaide, South Australia. He has expertise in diving, wilderness and remote area health. Dr Harris has a professional and voluntary interest in search and rescue operations, establishing the first sump rescue (deep, scary caves) training course in Australasia. The 2018 Thailand Cave Rescue was an opportunity to put this training to work.

Professor Helen Milroy

Nana Ninju, Helen Milroy. I'm a proud Palyku woman. My mob are from the Pilbara region in Western Australia. I grew up in Perth in the 60s in a time when there were very low expectations for Aboriginal kids, but not so in my family. My mother and grandmother always said to me, 'You could do anything you put your mind to.' And so, I did.

I have had a most interesting and challenging career, and never really thought it wasn't possible. In fact, I remember telling a guidance officer at school one day that I wanted to be a doctor. She laughed at me, straight in my face, and said it was a complete waste of time and that I would just get married and have children. She was partly right. I did get married and have kids, which I'm very proud of, but I also became a doctor. And in fact, the first Aboriginal doctor in Australia. I do, however, want to acknowledge that we had our own proud heritage of traditional healers in this country for a very long time that kept us in good stead and they still look after us today.

People have said I was ambitious, but I wasn't really. I was actually never ambitious; I was just determined and I was going to make a difference and no one was going to tell me otherwise. When I saw problems in health and mental health in particular for my mob, I was prepared to speak up and be part of the solution. When I spoke up a lot, I'm sure they gave me jobs to do just to keep me quiet, and I was given many opportunities, which I took on the challenges of wholeheartedly. That led to a career that varied from being a clinician to a Royal Commissioner. And many different roles in between. And I have absolutely loved all of them. I also paint, write and illustrate children's stories and I'm not sure what's coming next.

I do, however, owe all of my success to my mother, Gladys, and my grandmother, Daisy. Can you imagine what it was like growing up as an Aboriginal woman in the early 1900s? Their enduring support and encouragement were invaluable. These two incredible women endured many hardships, many traumas, but never wavered in their absolute commitment to me and my growing up and the family. They remain today the most amazing and inspiring women I have ever known. And I still hear those words: 'You can do anything you put your mind to.'

So, what I have I learnt from my own journey and what can I pass on to our new graduates? Well, you have to surround yourself with people who support you for who you are. I remember reading a quote once by Oscar Wilde that said, 'Be yourself because everyone else is already taken.' I thought that gave me a great sense of comfort. I thought, 'Wow, that's fantastic. I just have to be who I am.' You have to be able to drown out or ignore those people who put you down. Take courage and draw strength from those people who have the attributes of a good leader, and I believe those things include strength of character, personal integrity, kindness and compassion. You can only be a true leader by bringing everyone with you, not by standing on others. Also believe that you can make a difference. Everyone can in some way be passionate and committed. Keep an eye on the long game, which requires persistence and effort. Be courageous and be prepared to stand up for what you believe in. If you don't, who will?

It was only by speaking up that I was given the many opportunities to contribute in the way I have.

No one is born to be successful, but some people do have a better start to life and we of course do need to address the significant inequity and inequality, which means in society today and within human services. But, on an individual level, it is what we make of our own journey that counts. Each one of us can forge our own path, made that little bit easier by those who have gone before us. And collectively, we can achieve a great deal. Don't ever forget our shared humanity, and what you can achieve for others.

We all have a lot to offer in life, society, and in any professional industry we choose to work in over our careers. Who would have thought in 2021 we would find ourselves dealing with a global pandemic and having to adapt to rapidly changing circumstances and develop new and innovative ways to deliver services? We can do anything we put our mind to.

I would like to pass on the collective wisdom from my grandmother and mother. Firstly, you have to be good to people because you don't know if you might be related. So, it's worth putting in the effort. Treat people like family, and then you'll know that they'll get the best care that they possibly can. At the end of the day, we have a shared humanity and we all want the same thing. We want the best for our future generations. You have to be good to the country and walk lightly on the landscape, our ancestral homelands.

Mother Earth gives us life and takes whatever we throw into the earth and creates something beautiful. Places we want to come to, live in and play in with our children. Places to call home, places to build nations.

And finally, be good to yourself. So many of us look after everyone else, often at our own expense. Be kind to who you are. Sometimes you need to be more forgiving of yourself, particularly when you are often forgiving of others. Give yourself time to be creative, enjoy life and look forward to the opportunities that await. And make sure that there is always someone who is also looking after you. You never really know what is around the corner, or what your next adventure might be. So be ready to embrace what life has to offer. You can do anything you put your mind, heart and spirit to.

Professor Helen Milroy is a descendant of the Palyku people of the Pilbara region of Western Australia, and was born and educated in Perth. This is a copy of her graduation address at the University of Western Australia (https://www.youtube.com/watch?v=aNzshrBdhG4). Australia's first Indigenous doctor, she studied medicine at the University of Western Australia and is currently Professor of Child and Adolescent Psychiatry at UWA, Honorary Research Fellow at Telethon Kids Institute and a Commissioner with the National Mental Health Commission.

Professor Milroy was the WA 2021 Australian of the Year and was joint winner of the 2020 Australian Mental Health Prize. *Wombat, Mudlark and Other Stories* is her first book for children.

Summary

Medical co-leadership is about building relationships and trust with like-minded colleagues, working constructively together to make a difference in others' lives. It is a collective mindset which recognises that every challenge is an opportunity to learn, listen with empathy and respond to feedback.

Drs Catherine Crock, Dinesh Palipana, Harry Harris and Helen Milroy have displayed shining examples of co-leadership, by stepping outside their comfort zones to work with others to meet extraordinary challenges. In doing so, they have discovered that co-leadership really matters – it can transform and save lives.

28 In conclusion

Doctors in general, . . . suffer from poor mental health and are less likely to seek evidence-based treatment for it than the general population. Does this strike anyone as sadly ironic that dire health issues are presided over by a profoundly unhealthy physician population?

> Tim Baker, journalist, author of Patting the Shark
> and cancer survivor

Tim Baker's poignant reflections on his oncologist's burnout on p 99 are a powerful reminder to us to protect our psychological and physical health with priority. For too long, our chronically underfunded, fragmented and unsustainable health systems have relied on the good will and altruism of doctors and other health professionals, to 'process' more and more patients in less time with inadequate funding, and work longer hours in physically and mentally unsafe workplace conditions – at great personal cost. This is no longer tolerable. Acute on chronic occupational stress has worsened since recent public health crises, and is compromising patient care and resulting in critical health workforce shortages.

As noted by Dr Louise Stone on page 19:

> *Unfortunately, the one thing we know in our profession is that bleeding hearts eventually cease to beat. Doctors are burning out. This causes one of two outcomes; they become cold and sometimes unintentionally cruel foot soldiers in a dysfunctional system, or they become unwell themselves. . . . Sprinkling a little bit of light cognitive behavioural therapy on the surface of the problem gives an illusion of care, but little real support.*

The good news is this. Every doctor has more influence than realised to effect health system and workplace change through co-leadership and strong relationships with like-minded colleagues. World turmoil continues to impact people's lives across the globe, but ongoing crises can also become positive catalysts, galvanising the medical profession to advocate for transformation of health

DOI: 10.1201/9781003296829-33

systems. Many doctors have recently demonstrated how to become agents of change to make positive differences – together.

Across the world, doctors are a diverse group of professionals, and our shared traits have come to the fore as we continue to unite to respond to ongoing adversity – we are hard-working, dedicated, courageous – and deeply concerned. In the current challenging environment, extraordinary stories have emerged. In sometimes dire situations, doctors have banded together to drive healthcare innovation such as advances in digital technologies; expand telehealth provision; set up new services for isolated rural communities and war-torn countries; rapidly establish vaccination centres; roll out new education and training programs; and provide strong advocacy on planetary health. Our healthcare activism must continue.

Every Doctor is a clarion call to reimagine a health system where every doctor is encouraged and supported to:

1. Prioritise psychological and physical protection first
2. Promote healthy workplace cultures, fairness and safety
3. Build strong relationships by sharing challenges
4. Save lives through medical co-leadership

Written with empathy, but no holds barred, *Every Doctor* also challenges the medical profession to get its own house in order. It highlights ways to make our medical organisations work for us; to eliminate the stigma of mental illness in the medical profession and the community; to prevent, recognise and manage mental and physical workplace injuries; and to support and nurture every earlier career doctor. Together, we can address high levels of mental health problems and suicide in doctors, and Dr Grant Blashki sums this up beautifully in his piece on mental health on p 161: '*As a general practitioner, I can tell you, never underestimate the ability of the mind, and the capacity of human beings to recuperate and mend themselves*'.

Medicine can be deeply rewarding career. The contributions of our many esteemed colleagues to *Every Doctor* are cause for optimism (p x–xiii). Their stories send a deeply authentic message of love, hope and acknowledgement for all doctors, who are continuing to serve communities across the world with courage and dedication – you are not alone.

We hope *Every Doctor* will begin a new conversation about mending our health system, our workplaces, and ourselves. As ICU specialist Associate Neil

Orford highlights in his story on page 15, this conversation must begin with listening.

> *Over the last few years of COVID-19, when I have stopped and listened, I have heard a lot in this silence. I have heard what patients value, what they are afraid of losing, and what they have lost. . . . In the silence of our patient interactions, we learn what matters. Perhaps we should do this as a society. Damp the noise and listen.*

Summary

Every Doctor is brimming with poignant and hopeful quotes and stories from a diverse array of doctors like Drs Louise Stone, Grant Blashki and Neil Orford. Their wise words challenge us to reflect on what we can learn from the harsh realities of medicine and life.

To meet the inevitable challenges, every doctor can protect themselves psychologically, nurture a positive workplace culture, build strong relationships with each other and work together as co-leaders to effect change locally and globally. Most of all, we can rediscover joy in our lives and our work.

We are continuing to listen and learn. Your feedback matters.

Please contact us with your comments via www.everydoctor.org.

Index

Printed in the United States
by Baker & Taylor Publisher Services